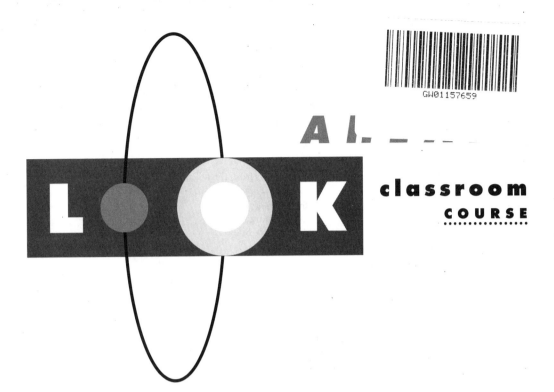

# LOOK classroom COURSE

## TEACHER'S BOOK 2

MADELEINE DU VIVIER

ANDY HOPKINS

JOCELYN POTTER

Look Ahead: a partnership between

 BBC English

 The British Council

 University of Cambridge Local Examinations Syndicate (UCLES)

 Longman ELT

 with the cooperation of the Council of Europe

**Longman**

**Look Ahead Consultants**

The authors and publishers would like to thank the following consultants who regularly commented on these classroom materials during their development:

Ron Banks, France
Gabriella Barbier, Italy
Anna Cerchietti, Italy
Norberto Cerezal, Spain

Cultura Inglesa Rio, Brazil
Hanna Komorowska, Poland
Ignacio Sola, Spain
Chris Tribble, Latvia

We are also grateful for additional comments from the following:

Gill Adams, Brazil
Ingrid Boczkowski, Germany
Gill Caldicott, UK
Dorothea Carvalho, UK

Cultura Inglesa São Paulo, Brazil
Chris Lynch, Japan
Susan Maingay, Latvia
Steve Owen, Spain

**Acknowledgements**

Acknowledgements of copyright material used as reference sources for the *Look Ahead* Classroom Course:

Council of Europe: for the use of its revised and expanded Waystage and Threshold level specifications (© Council of Europe 1990).

Simon Greenall and Judy Garton-Sprenger: for their Course Designs created for BBC English for the *Look Ahead* project (© BBC 1993).

Terry O'Neill, Peter Snow and Bob Marsden; for their television scripts (© BBC 1993) for *Look Ahead* programmes 16–30, drawn upon in this book.

**Cover photographs by** Robert Harding Picture Library for middle right. The Image Bank for top left. Pictor International for bottom. Telegraph Colour Library/L. Bray for top right, /Peter Scholley for middle left.

**Longman Group Limited,**
*Edinburgh Gate*
*Harlow*
*Essex*
*CM20 2JE, England*
*and Associated Companies throughout the world.*

© Longman Group Limited and The British Broadcasting Corporation 1994
*All rights reserved; no part of this publication*
*may be reproduced, stored in a retrieval system,*
*or transmitted in any form or by any means, electronic,*
*mechanical, photocopying, recording or otherwise,*
*without the prior written permission of the Publishers.*

First published 1994
Reprinted 1995
Third impression 1996

Set in Monotype Photina 10.25/11.5pt and Adobe Syntax 9.25/11.5pt
Produced through Longman Malaysia, CLP

ISBN 0 582 09839 4

# Contents

## Introduction — 5

**The course** — 5
Why is the *Look Ahead* course special? — 5
What levels does the Longman classroom course cover? — 5
What are the components of the Longman classroom course? — 5

**Underlying principles of the Longman classroom course** — 5

**Key features** — 6
What are the key features of Students' Book 2? — 6
What are the key features of Workbook 2? — 7
What are the key features of Teacher's Book 2? — 7
What is recorded on the Class Cassettes? — 8
What is recorded on the Workbook Cassette? — 8
What are the features of the Classroom Video? — 8

**Methodology and classroom practice** — 8
1. Presenting new language — 10
2. The Discovering Language boxes — 10
3. Handling guided practice activities — 10
4. Dealing with new vocabulary — 10
5. Managing freer communicative activities — 11
6. Handling reading activities — 11
7. Handling longer listening activities — 12
8. Handling writing activities — 12
9. Error correction — 13
10. Exploiting illustrations — 14
11. The importance of sounds, stress and intonation — 14
12. Using the video material — 15
13. Using the Summary section — 16
14. Use of the mother tongue — 16
15. Supplementing the course — 16

## Lesson Notes — 17

## Language Awareness Worksheets — 127

## Workbook Answer Key and Tapescript — 140

## Word Review — 153

## Wordlist — 156

# Introduction

## The course

### Why is the *Look Ahead* course special?

The Longman *Look Ahead* classroom materials have been produced as a result of a unique collaboration between BBC English, the British Council, the University of Cambridge Local Examinations Syndicate (UCLES) and Longman ELT, with the co-operation of the Council of Europe.

**SYLLABUS**
The core syllabus for the *Look Ahead* corpus is based on the Council of Europe's revised and extended Waystage and Threshold specifications (Council of Europe Press, 1991), the most comprehensive statement of language learning objectives yet available for the 1990s and the new millenium.

**ENGLISH LANGUAGE EXAMINATIONS**
New tests at Waystage level (the Key English Test – KET) and Threshold level (the revised Preliminary English Test – PET) have been devised by UCLES based on these latest specifications.

**BROADCAST TELEVISION SERIES**
BBC English has used the same Waystage and Threshold specifications to produce a series of sixty television programmes for English language learners. These programmes are accompanied by self-study materials, marketed directly to learners at home by the BBC.

**LONGMAN CLASSROOM COURSE**
Longman English Language Teaching has produced a four-level classroom course, which takes as its core the Waystage and Threshold specifications. Extracts from the BBC television programmes have been selected according to their appropriacy for classroom use and are available on an optional video cassette which accompanies the Longman classroom materials. These Longman materials form the complete *Look Ahead* course for the classroom.

### What levels does the Longman classroom course cover?

The course comprises four levels:

Level 1    Beginner/Elementary
Level 2    Post-elementary/Pre-intermediate
Level 3    Intermediate
Level 4    Upper-intermediate

*Look Ahead* Level 1 is for students with little or no knowledge of English. *Look Ahead* Level 2 takes students beyond the Council of Europe Waystage level. *Look Ahead* Levels 3 and 4 take students up to and comfortably beyond the Council of Europe Threshold level.

### What are the components of the Longman classroom course?

At each level, the course consists of:

– a Students' Book,
– a Workbook,
– a Teacher's Book,
– a set of classroom audio cassettes (Class Cassettes),
– a Workbook audio cassette (Workbook Cassette),
– an optional set of two video cassettes.

## Underlying principles of the Longman classroom course

The writing of the *Look Ahead* classroom course has been influenced by the following beliefs about English language learning:

- Learners are intelligent individuals, who are already proficient in at least one language.
- Learners want to know what they are learning and why. They also **need** this information in order to become more independent as learners as they progress.
- Learners need to develop at the same time a knowledge of grammar, vocabulary, functional language and communicative skills. Attention to the systems of the language is crucial, but the development of fluency and contextual

appropriacy are equally important goals.
- Learning takes place most effectively when learners are actively engaged in the learning process.
- Topics should be interesting, varied and relevant to students' lives.
- Learners need to be provided with every possible opportunity to use new language in contexts which are meaningful to them.
- Cross-cultural understanding is an important aspect of language learning.
- Learners want and need to be able to measure their own progress.
- Learners need resources to help them continue learning outside the classroom.
- Teachers want materials that take into account all of the above and are presented in a clear, principled manner, but that also allow for flexibility of use.

# Key features

## What are the key features of Students' Book 2?

### A MULTI-SYLLABUS APPROACH
Each unit provides presentation and practice of grammar, vocabulary, functional language, phonology and skills.

### FOCUS NOTES
Each double page, apart from the final Development section of each unit, includes Focus notes in the left-hand margin. These notes highlight the main areas of vocabulary, functional language and grammar presented or practised on that double page. This means that learners have a clear understanding at the beginning of each double page of what their learning objectives are.

### DISCOVERING LANGUAGE
The Discovering Language boxes in each unit encourage learners to reflect on a particular area of grammar and to deduce rules from clearly contextualised examples. Learners then have the opportunity to test these rules through guided and freer practice activities.

### A WIDE VARIETY OF TASK TYPES
Tasks encourage students' active involvement in the learning process through activities which involve discovery, problem-solving, language use and creative response. Information-gap activities are a regular feature.

### STIMULATING AND RELEVANT TOPICS
Each unit contains a number of related topics. These topics have been chosen for their general interest and for the useful vocabulary and functional language which they generate. Their exploitation encourages personal involvement, as learners are asked to relate the topics to their own experiences and interests.

### COMPARING CULTURES
Regular Comparing Cultures sections allow learners to reflect on the similarities and differences between their own and other cultures. The intention is not to promote the value of particular cultural conventions in one part of the world over any other, but to raise awareness of cultural variety.

### DEVELOPMENT
Each unit ends with a double-page Development section. Most Development sections feature aspects of the lives of real people in Britain or the USA. The sections offer freer, contextualised practice of key language areas and encourage fluency development. At the same time, they provide further training and practice in the four skills (speaking, listening, reading and writing). Some of these activities can also be used to prepare students for viewing the real-life interviews on the optional classroom video cassettes.

### SUMMARIES
The Development spread includes a two-part Summary of the key language presented in the unit. In the first part, new language functions are listed with examples. In the second part, new grammar areas are set out in more detail than in the brief Focus notes. For further information, learners are directed to the Grammar Reference section at the back of the Students' Book (see below).

### PROGRESS CHECKS
There are five two-page Progress Checks, one after every third unit. These are informal tests of the grammatical, functional and vocabulary areas presented in the previous three units. They can be done in class or as homework assignments. They give students and teachers an opportunity to monitor progress and to decide whether remedial work is appropriate before errors become too firmly established. A feature of each Progress Check is a section on Common Errors. This section highlights

the mistakes which are often made by students of English at particular stages in their language learning, and encourages students to correct them.

### GRAMMAR REFERENCE
There is a Grammar Reference section at the back of the Students' Book containing clear and straightforward explanations of the grammar presented in the Students' Book.

## What are the key features of Workbook 2?

### LANGUAGE FOCUS
A wide range of activities provides further controlled practice of the main grammatical, functional and vocabulary areas presented in the corresponding unit of the Students' Book.

### SKILLS FOCUS
Integrated skills tasks require learners to work with a listening or reading text and then to produce a piece of related written work.

### HELP YOURSELF
Regular Help Yourself sections provide learner-development activities, such as *Talking about grammar* and *Explaining what you mean*, which encourage students to reflect on language and the language learning process. Their purpose is to help students make the most of their own learning potential.

### SOUND/SPELLING LINKS
Regular Sound/Spelling Links sections draw attention to common links between sound and spelling in English. The sections are designed both to develop an awareness of spelling patterns and to help learners with their pronunciation.

### SOUND CHECK
In Sound Check sections, consonant sounds that commonly cause problems are presented and contrasted.

### WORD REVIEW
A review list of key vocabulary from the Students' Book is contained at the back of the Workbook. Words are listed in alphabetical order by unit, for ease of reference when students are revising. The Word Review is also recorded on the Workbook Cassette so that learners can practise their pronunciation as they revise key vocabulary.

### FLEXIBILITY OF USE
Workbook activities can be used in several different ways, depending on the needs of a particular class:

- as follow-up homework,
- as additional individual study activities, either in class or in a self-access centre,
- as additional class activities with students working together.

A full Answer Key to the Workbook and the Workbook Tapescript is provided at the back of this Teacher's Book.

## What are the key features of Teacher's Book 2?

This Teacher's Book contains the following information and activities:

### INTRODUCTION
The Introduction describes the principles which underlie the Longman classroom course and contains extensive notes on suggested methodology and classroom practice.

### DETAILED LESSON NOTES
There are detailed teaching notes for each Students' Book unit to help teachers in their lesson preparation. These are organised under a number of clear headings. Focus notes provide a summary of the main teaching points in each lesson. Like the Focus notes in the Students' Book, they highlight key vocabulary areas, functional language and grammar. These notes are followed by a suggested procedure for each Students' Book exercise. Background notes give additional cultural information to help teachers from different backgrounds respond to their students' questions. Extra practice sections suggest further, optional activities to supplement those in the Students' Book. Tapescripts and keys to the Students' Book exercises are also provided within the Lesson Notes.

### LANGUAGE AWARENESS TASKS
Towards the back of this book is a unique Language Awareness section for teachers. This consists of six photocopiable worksheets, complete with answer keys. These worksheets draw attention to the complexities of certain key language areas which are presented in the Students' Book (e.g. modal verbs, stative verbs). The worksheets ask teachers to reconsider the

rules of form and usage that are taught to pre-intermediate students and to explore patterns and contexts of use in greater depth. We have provided these worksheets for teachers because although pre-intermediate *students* need a straightforward set of rules governing form and usage, *teachers* generally feel the need for a more thorough knowledge of the rules (and their exceptions), which will enable them to deal with students' questions and problems as they arise.

The worksheets can be used in a variety of ways. They can be used by individual new teachers or as an aid to structured teacher development sessions.

## What is recorded on the Class Cassettes?

The set of Class Cassettes contains all the dialogues, listening comprehension materials and pronunciation, stress and intonation activities in the Students' Book. The tapescripts for each unit appear in the Lesson Notes in this Teacher's Book.

## What is recorded on the Workbook Cassette?

The Workbook listening comprehension materials and the Sound/Spelling Links and Sound Check exercises are recorded on the Workbook Cassette. The Word Review is also recorded, to enable students to review and practise their pronunciation by listening to the words and repeating them. The complete Workbook tapescript is included at the back of this Teacher's Book.

## What are the features of the Classroom Video?

The classroom video material is an optional component of the course. We do not assume that every teacher in every institution will have access to a video recorder, and the audio Class Cassettes provide all the necessary listening input to the classroom materials.

For those who do have access to a video recorder, the classroom videos are a valuable source of enrichment and extension material. The video material consists of fifteen units, each of which corresponds to a unit in the Students' Book. Each unit is about six minutes in length and includes the following:

- A short presenter's introduction to the general topic of the unit.
- Scenes from an ongoing story about the personal and professional lives of a group of people working for a company called MAP Advertising. Many of these conversations are also recorded on the audio Class Cassettes and relate to tasks in the main body of each Students' Book unit. It is recommended that the video conversations are used to consolidate new language already presented through the Students' Book.
- A short cartoon which exemplifies key language points. This does not occur in every unit.
- A real-life interview with someone from Britain or the USA, showing scenes from their everyday lives. Extracts from most of these interviews are also recorded on the Class Cassettes and relate to tasks in the Development section of most units in the Students' Book. Through these interviews, students are exposed to natural speech. Comprehension therefore involves drawing on all their previous experience of English, and on their ability to use visual clues to make informed guesses about new language. We recommend that this part of the video is used for review and consolidation purposes after completing the Students' Book unit. This will require access to a video recorder for a maximum of one lesson a week.

A full video tapescript and detailed suggestions on how to exploit the video material are contained in each video cassette box. General suggestions for video exploitation are included in part 12 of the Methodology and Classroom Practice section below.

# Methodology and classroom practice

Variety and flexibility of approach are crucial if we wish to hold the attention of a class over time, and an overview of all the possible teaching techniques is obviously beyond the scope of this short introduction. However, we feel that some explanation of the approaches implicit in the Students' Book, and some standard procedures for particular activity types, may be helpful.

# 1 Presenting new language (grammar and functional language)

## DIALOGUES

New language is often presented in *Look Ahead* through dialogues which are both recorded on the Class Cassettes and printed on the Students' Book page. Presentation of language through dialogue is obviously useful since it provides a meaningful context for the new language. The Lesson Notes in this Teacher's Book provide specific suggestions for exploiting particular dialogues and many teachers will want to work with the dialogues in their own way, perhaps even using them for reinforcement after a different kind of language presentation. However, we provide here one possible way of working with them.

1. Before students listen, ask them to look at the accompanying picture and to think about the situation and context. Pre-teach any necessary vocabulary. Ask students questions which they can try to answer and which they can then keep in mind as they listen, e.g. *Who are these people? Where are they? What are they doing? What are they talking about?*

2. Ask students to listen to the cassette while they read the written dialogue. Check their understanding of the situation and do any accompanying comprehension tasks in the Students' Book.

3. Focus on the language content. Read or play key lines from the dialogue, especially where stress and intonation patterns are important, and ask students to repeat what they hear in chorus and individually.

4. Ask students to read the dialogue in pairs and then to change roles.

5. With their books closed, pairs of students act out the dialogue, using their own words to supplement the lines that they remember.

6. Move on to the Discovering Language box or practice activities in the book.

## TEXTS

New language is also presented through texts which are intended to be read rather than heard. Some of the language that is presented in this way is commonly used in both spoken and written English (many verb structures, for example). In other cases, the language may be important to the understanding and production of a particular type of text (such as linguistic conventions in letter-writing). A possible procedure for handling reading texts is given in Section 6 below, but when the main aim is the presentation of new language, one approach is as follows:

1. Before students read the text, draw their attention to any accompanying illustrations and the title or heading of the text. Elicit useful vocabulary and ask general ('gist') questions to direct their attention to the overall purpose and/or meaning of the text, e.g. *Where is this from? Who is it for? Who is X?*

2. Ask students to read the text silently.

3. Check the answers to the gist questions, and ask more detailed comprehension questions.

4. Ask questions that focus on the use of the new language, e.g. *Does X do these things every day? So how often does she ...?*

5. Students work together to identify examples of the new language in the text, e.g. past tense verbs.

6. Move on to the Discovering Language box or practice activities in the book.

## ALTERNATIVES

Some teachers will wish to present new language in their own way and then to use the dialogues or texts in the book for consolidation. Types of presentation may be:

- Closely linked to the presentation material in the book, e.g. with books closed, provide verbal or visual prompts and elicit as much of the Students' Book presentation dialogue as possible, feeding in new language as it is needed.

- Loosely linked to the presentation material in the book, e.g. choose a photograph from a previous unit and ask students to remind you of the situation. Extend the context, asking questions so that students perceive the need for language that they do not yet have, and then give them the language to answer your questions.

- Separate from the presentation material in the book, e.g. set up your own situation through a blackboard picture story, mime, etc. and ask students to tell you what is happening or being said. Help them with the language that they need to complete the task. (There are often suggestions for different presentations, or consolidation of a structure, in this book.)

- Linked to the reference material in the book (grammar only), e.g. ask students to read the relevant part of the Grammar Reference section and then to 'teach' you the forms and uses of a new structure.

## 2 The Discovering Language boxes

The Discovering Language boxes draw students' attention to contextualised examples of certain new language structures. They are designed to assist an inductive ('discovery') approach to grammar teaching, encouraging students to reflect on language patterns and to formulate possible rules. Students may find this easier if they work in pairs or small groups, and you may want to allow the use of the mother tongue in monolingual classes until students become more confident in English. Get students to read the relevant examples of the language and then ask them for rules, formulated in English if possible. Write the best rule or rules on the board, eliciting improvements where necessary. In the early stages of the course you may need to provide a clear rule at the end of the discussion, but as the course progresses students can be referred to the Grammar Reference section for more help with form and usage. The Summary section at the end of each unit highlights the formal characteristics of the main grammar points, and students will find this helpful for a quick reminder (of a verb form, for example) and for revision purposes.

## 3 Handling guided practice activities

Practice activities in the book follow the presentation of new language. Task types vary, but the aim at this stage is normally accuracy – the correct manipulation of language patterns. You may wish to supplement these activities in class with further tasks from the Workbook, or to add more of your own. It may be beneficial for students to work together so that they can learn from each other, since the practice activities are designed as teaching and not testing tools. You may wish to inject an element of competition into, for example, a gap-filling exercise, so that students with correct answers score points for their team.

Here is one simple approach to a guided practice activity:

1 Remind students of the new language (if the presentation of that language took place in a previous lesson), e.g. by asking a pair of students to act out an approximation of the presentation dialogue from memory.

2 Ask students to read the instructions. Check that they have understood by giving them a minute or two to think about the first question and then eliciting the answer, accepting corrections from other students if necessary.

3 Students work through the activity in pairs and then turn to a different partner to compare and, if necessary, amend their answers.

4 Ask individuals for answers in an appropriate form for that activity. If the task was the completion of a chart, for example, you may want to draw the chart on the board (or an overhead transparency) and ask individual students to come to the front and complete different boxes.

5 Identify any problems that some students still have. Highlight them and draw attention to relevant sections of the Summary at the end of the unit. Make a note to do a further check when the language is recycled later in the unit. Alternatively, ask students to do a related Workbook exercise.

## 4 Dealing with new vocabulary

New vocabulary is often presented in *Look Ahead* in topic sets. A variety of tasks in the Students' Book – labelling pictures, matching or grouping words, and so on – helps students to understand new words. Many teachers like to present vocabulary in such a way that students' attention is focused on the front of the classroom rather than the book. You can use aids like wallcharts, magazine pictures, drawings or real objects, and techniques like drama (including mime) to convey the sense of new words before moving into the Students' Book. A quick, lively vocabulary drill (repetition in chorus and then individually) is helpful to establish sound and stress patterns before the words are used more freely. Note that the important new words in each unit are recorded on the Workbook Cassette, so students can listen to them at home.

Consider allowing students to do vocabulary practice activities in groups, and ensure that each group has access to a good dictionary, e.g. the *Longman Active Study Dictionary of English*, so that it becomes an automatic and valued resource. Encourage students to write down new words in a way that is both meaningful and accessible to them so that they can refer to and build on their lists later.

Vocabulary is recycled throughout the book, but there are many well-established ways of keeping new words in students' minds as the course progresses. Hold quick quizzes; draw up simple crosswords and word boxes, or play popular word games. Finally, encourage students to experiment freely and without inhibition in activities where the main aims are fluency and successful communication rather than total grammatical accuracy. This will help them use new language with confidence.

## 5 Managing freer communicative activities

Every classroom activity is of course communicative in some sense, but certain exercise types in the Students' Book are designed to encourage spoken fluency and successful communication rather than complete accuracy. The two main types of task used in *Look Ahead* for these purposes are information-gap activities and discussion.

### INFORMATION-GAP EXERCISES

Pairs of students (A and B) look at different pieces of information in the Students' Book. Student A's information is given in the main body of the unit, and Student B's information is supplied in a separate section towards the back of the book. Students then exchange information in English without looking at each other's books.

A possible procedure for this kind of information-gap activity is as follows:

1 Organise students into pairs and ask A and then B students to identify themselves. Check that students know what to do and are each looking at the correct Students' Book page.

2 Ask a couple of good students to demonstrate the activity to the class, or demonstrate it yourself with one student.

3 Walk around the class and monitor what is going on while students are doing the activity in pairs. It is better not to interrupt unless they are having real difficulty or they ask for help. Note down any common errors relating to the language patterns being practised.

4 Stop the activity when most students have finished, ask for feedback, and discuss any problems or mistakes that you or the students themselves have identified.

### DISCUSSION

*Look Ahead* encourages students to give their own opinions and to talk about their own lives through discussion of cultural differences, personal experiences, and the content of photographs, etc. Once again, the emphasis is intended to be on fluent communication. This is particularly important in the Development sections on the last two pages of each Students' Book unit. Each pair or group discussion is an opportunity for students to develop communication strategies and to say what they mean, even if they do not have the right words or complete control over appropriate structures.

One approach is as follows:

1 Arrange students into pairs or groups, and make sure that they understand the task.

2 Start the discussion by asking a question which focuses attention on one aspect of the topic, and then encourage students to continue the discussion in their groups.

3 Monitor students while they are talking, intervening if requested but otherwise simply noting any important problems.

4 Stop the discussion when a number of groups have stopped talking.

5 Ask a student from one group to tell the class about his/her group's feelings or experiences and encourage other students to say if they have different feelings or experiences.

6 Ask if students had any language problems during the discussion, and then point out problems that you noticed. Ask the class if they can solve the problems before you provide solutions for them. You might also need to draw attention to the fact that some students participated more than others and ask why that was.

7 Finally, encourage students to ask you about your feelings and experiences, particularly if you have a different perspective that they might find interesting.

## 6 Handling reading activities

In *Look Ahead* students are asked to read a variety of texts, from posters and leaflets to longer passages such as extracts from newspapers and magazine articles. Longer texts often contain vocabulary which students have not seen before. Students should be encouraged to adopt strategies such as reading for gist first, in order to understand the main ideas and to guess the meaning of new words from context. Most longer reading texts have a title and an illustration; these can help students to speculate about content before they start to read. There are clear tasks in the Students' Book, and in the Lesson Notes in this Teacher's Book, but one possible way of approaching reading texts is as follows:

1 Ask students to think about the title and picture, and what these tell them about the text. Ask general questions, e.g. *Why is this person famous? What kind of text is it?* but do not supply answers, since it is important that students themselves are eventually able to answer the questions correctly.

2 Students read silently, looking for answers to the general questions and checking their own predictions. They now have a purpose for reading and for looking for particular information. If they can find that information, they should not worry about what they do not understand.

3 Students work alone or together to answer the comprehension questions in the Students' Book. If they work together, an additional benefit will be the need to justify answers to a partner.

4 After a quick comprehension check, direct students to any follow-up activities in the book.

5 You may then want to analyse the text more closely with your students. Encourage students to guess the meaning of new words.

## 7 Handling longer listening activities

As with reading activities, it is important that students recognise a clear purpose for listening. This may, for example, be to confirm predictions about content or relationships between speakers.

1 Ask students to use illustrations and other clues to make hypotheses about the context and therefore the content of the listening text. If you wish, provide them with general 'gist' questions.

2 Play the tape once so that students get the general idea and have the opportunity to confirm or revise their predictions.

3 Direct students' attention to the listening comprehension exercises in the Students' Book, giving them time to read and think about them.

4 Play the tape again and get students to discuss their answers in pairs.

5 Elicit the answers, playing key passages a third time if necessary.

6 You may wish to play the whole tape once more so that students have the satisfaction of listening to something that they now understand.

## 8 Handling writing activities

Writing tasks at this level tend to be straightforward and highly structured. The emphasis is on constructing relatively simple texts, using the vocabulary and grammatical forms covered in the unit. However, within these limitations, students are introduced to a variety of written text types in *Look Ahead 2*, such as letters and forms, narrative and description. Writing tasks are often difficult to manage in the classroom because some students work much faster than others or produce much shorter texts, but it is often better for writing to be done, or at least started, in class rather than at home, so that you can monitor the work and provide encouragement. Possible modes for classroom writing are as follows:

– students write alone,
– students work in pairs, with one student writing,
– students work in small groups, with one student writing.

One approach to the task is as follows:

1 Check that students understand the instructions in the Students' Book. (*What kind of text is it? How many paragraphs? Which tenses?* etc.)

2 Elicit an example text orally from the students, writing it on the board one sentence at a time and asking for improvements.

3 Set a time limit for individuals or groups to write their own text.

4 When students have finished, ask them to look again at their own work or to read another student's piece of work and to check the following: the structure of the text (have they followed the guidelines?), the vocabulary (have they chosen the best words, and are those words spelt correctly?), the grammar and the punctuation.

5 Collect neat pieces of writing for marking. Ask for heavily edited or untidy scripts to be rewritten and submitted in the next lesson.

# 9 Error correction

Many teachers nowadays subscribe to the following general principles of error correction:

- All students make mistakes as they experiment with new language. A cautious student is unlikely to learn as quickly as one who takes more risks while exploring the parameters of what has been taught.
- The correction of these mistakes, properly handled, is an important stage in the learning process of each individual student. The way in which errors are corrected can also have an important positive or negative effect on student morale and confidence.
- If a student is given the opportunity to identify and correct his/her own errors, the correction will be more memorable.
- Outside the English Language Teaching environment of lessons and examinations, successful communication, however flawed, is generally more important than the ability to use a limited linguistic repertoire correctly. This is another reason why errors should not be made to seem disproportionately important in class.

## CORRECTING SPOKEN ENGLISH

The extent to which correction is appropriate depends, of course, on the aim of each activity. When new language is being presented and practised, accuracy of form is fundamental and students must also be able to produce the correct sound, stress and intonation patterns associated with the language in context. If you are presenting and checking language orally, you will be aware of any problems immediately and can correct mistakes as they occur. During controlled practice of specific language items, students should be able to correct themselves or each other; if they are unable to do this, the language may need further presentation. When, on the other hand, your main objective is to encourage an exchange of information and ideas, accuracy will be less important than the fluent and successful communication needed to complete the task. You will, however, probably not wish to ignore errors completely, particularly if they relate to language that has been taught. Some possible ways of dealing with these errors are as follows:

- Encourage students to ask each other or you about mistakes that they think they have made.
- While you are monitoring a speaking task, make notes on common or important errors that you hear. After the activity, draw attention to the problems orally or on the board and ask students if they can correct them.
- Record one pair or group of students doing the task. Then play the tape back to the class. Pause it from time to time to highlight examples of particularly successful communication but also to demonstrate significant problems. Allow the original speakers the first attempts at correction; then, if necessary, encourage supportive contributions from other students or correct the mistake yourself.

## MARKING STUDENTS' WRITING

At this level we tend to be concerned with layout, vocabulary, grammar and punctuation. We do not expect sophistication of style, argumentation, development, etc. Since students need to develop confidence in second language writing, it is important to be positive and to give encouragement when marking written work as well as to point out problems. This might mean indicating only errors which relate to language that has been taught, and ignoring problems that will be dealt with later. Many teachers find it useful to show errors without correcting them, so that students themselves can have the satisfaction of improving their work. This requires use of a marking scheme that everyone understands. You can, for example, underline important errors and write a code in the margin to show the type of error: G for grammar, V for vocabulary, Sp for spelling, P for punctuation, etc. This system of correction also means that you will need to take the work in again, to check that corrections have been made.

Some teachers supply marks for written work at the end of term. You may decide to use the Students' Book writing tasks to teach writing skills, and the Workbook tasks for formal grading. Alternatively, you may feel that it benefits students to be given a formal mark for each piece of writing. In either case, it should be clear to students how you arrive at this mark and what they need to work on.

One way is to adopt a standard system like the one below, to which other criteria can be added for higher-level writing tasks.

| | | | | | | | |
|---|---|---|---|---|---|---|---|
| Organisation (layout, paragraphing, etc.) | 0 | 1 | ②  | 3 | | | 2 |
| Vocabulary | 0 | 1 | 2 | ③ | 4 | 5 | 3 |
| Grammar | 0 | 1 | 2 | 3 | ④ | 5 | 4 |
| Spelling | 0 | 1 | ② | 3 | 4 | | 2 |
| Punctuation | 0 | ① | 2 | 3 | | | 1 |
| | | | | | | Total /20 | 12 |

The advantage of a system like this is that students can see not only where improvement is needed but also what they have done well.

## 10 Exploiting illustrations

The photographs and illustrations in the Students' Book serve a number of purposes. They make the material livelier and more visually attractive, and there are clear pedagogic reasons for drawing attention to them. Tasks relating to the illustrations are usually part of the given cycle of work, but ideas for exploiting each picture in different ways include the following:

- prediction (before a reading, listening or writing task),
- setting the scene or situation,
- providing cultural information (about buildings, rooms, dress, body language, etc.),
- revision of vocabulary, grammar or functional language, whether or not it is related to the accompanying task, e.g. functional language through the creation of new dialogues,
- reminding students about the roles, relationships and personal details of characters who reappear through the book.

The English Around You cartoons in the Students' Book are a special case. Each one contextualises a new and useful piece of language in a style which is intended to be memorable. These pieces of language are not normally related directly to the main teaching points of the lesson and it is not intended that too much time be spent on them. When drawing attention to them, it would be appropriate in the early stages of the course to ask a monolingual class for a translation. At later stages, students can answer simple questions about the cartoons to show their understanding. If you wish, students can also create a larger context for the language. They expand the cartoon situation and act out a longer conversation which includes the target language, using suitable actions and props. Another possible task is for students to imagine a completely different situation and to role play that situation but including the target language.

## 11 The importance of sounds, stress and intonation

Students should be intelligible when they speak English both to a native speaker of English and to a non-native speaker with whom there is no other language in common. Inappropriate sounds, stress and intonation can lead to misunderstanding. For this reason, pronunciation is an important thread in the *Look Ahead* multi-syllabus. The different sounds of English, which students should be able to recognise and produce, are presented methodically through the first two Students' Books and Workbooks.

Students need to know the basic stress pattern of each new word, and how words are stressed or unstressed in sentences and longer stretches of spoken English to convey different emphases and meanings. They also need appropriate intonation to convey attitude, e.g. to sound interested or sympathetic, and intonation patterns which express the intended meaning. The Students' Book activities focus on these elements of language, and every listening text – particularly every dialogue – is an opportunity for recognition and imitation. Ask questions about people's moods (e.g. *Is she happy?*) and about the functions of language (e.g. *Is that a question or a statement? Is that a command or an invitation?*), and drill lines of the dialogue so that stress and intonation patterns begin to feel natural to students.

### DRILLING

Drilling, or mechanical repetition, helps to make sound, stress and intonation patterns intuitive and is particularly useful when new language or new uses of language are being presented. It also provides a change of pace and focus in the lesson. Most teachers use a few key words to introduce the stages of a drill:

1 *Listen!* before giving the model.

2 Write the model on the board and indicate any special features, e.g. a rising tone at the end.

3 *Listen!* before giving the model again.

4 *Everyone!* to invite the class to repeat in chorus.

5 *Again!* for further repetition in chorus.

6 Call the names, at random, of particular students for individual repetition.

If the drill is part of a dialogue (e.g. two lines), the stages might be as follows:

1 Drill each line chorally and individually.

2 Draw attention to special features.

3 Choose a student to demonstrate the exchange with you.

4 Choose a different student and demonstrate again while you take the other part.

5 Ask students to practise in pairs and to change roles.

These exchanges will then become 'routines' in the students' linguistic repertoire and are likely to be remembered as a chunk of interaction.

## 12 Using the video material

The *Look Ahead* classroom videos are intended to reinforce and extend the Students' Book material rather than act as a presentation vehicle. For this reason, use of the videos is optional. At the end of each unit a lesson can be dedicated to video-based activities as a means of consolidating and expanding what has been taught.

There are many ways of working with the video material, but possible approaches to the three main components are outlined below. A full video tapescript and more detailed suggestions on how to exploit the video material are contained in each video cassette box.

### THE MAP ADVERTISING STORYLINE

These drama episodes can be used to reinforce and practise selected functional and structural language from the related Students' Book unit in a controlled way. Since the episodes contribute to an ongoing story, students will soon become familiar with the characters and this can be exploited. Students will already have heard many of the sequences on the Class Cassettes before they see the video.

1 Turn the volume off and start the sequence, then press the pause button on the video recorder. Ask students to tell you about the characters and the situation.

2 Keep the volume off and play the whole sequence while students, with their books closed, try to remember (or to imagine) what the characters are saying at each stage in the conversation.

3 Play the sequence again a little at a time, still with the sound off, and ask individual students to supply each character's line.

4 Play it once more with the sound on, so that students can check how close they were to the original dialogue and notice the facial expressions, gestures and other body language used by the characters.

5 Ask students to act out the conversation in pairs, with the same actions and body language.

### THE CARTOONS

Cartoons are also used to consolidate knowledge of functional language and grammar; the language is re-presented in humorous and therefore memorable contexts. The cartoons are very short and do not occur in every video unit. They are not included in the Students' Book, so they will be new to students.

1 Pre-teach any key vocabulary through quick blackboard drawings – if, for example, the cartoon characters are animals, students are unlikely to know the words for those animals in English.

2 Play the cartoon once and then ask about the situation.

3 Play it again without the sound and ask students to write down what they think or remember is being said.

4 Ask pairs or groups of students to write the script for the cartoon and then to read it while you play the sequence again silently.

5 Play it one more time with the sound so that students can compare the original with their own script.

### THE REAL-LIFE INTERVIEWS

The interviews provide review and extension material for each unit in a specific cultural context. One or two of these documentary interview segments will be new to the class, but most relate to the Development pages in the Students' Book so some of the content will already be familiar to students through the Students' Book and the Class Cassettes. Since the language of these interviews is natural speech, students are expected to draw on all their previous knowledge of English and to use visual clues to make informed guesses about new language. They should not expect to understand every word, but will be able to follow the gist of what is said. One possible procedure is as follows:

1 Write on the board general questions which exploit the documentary/cultural element for students to consider while they watch, e.g. *What is the same in your country? What is different? What is interesting? What is surprising?*

2 Play the whole sequence, and then ask for feedback.

3 If you have time, use parts of the sequence to do further teaching. Teach new vocabulary by building up a description of a scene with the

students and supplying the words that are needed. Focus on body language or accent. Revise grammar and vocabulary through the writing of a soundtrack for the documentary.

## 13 Using the Summary section

The Summary section at the end of each unit can be used in several ways. Here are some possibilities:

- It can be used as a quick check at the end of every unit. Students read through it and ask you if they have any questions on the language covered.
- It can be used for extra practice. Ask students to think of other examples of the functional language, preferably related to their own lives, and to provide contexts.
- It can be used for revision at the end of the course. Students can read through the Summaries to identify any problems they have; these can then be researched in more detail in the Grammar Reference section.

## 14 Use of the mother tongue

In multilingual classes all teaching and learning must obviously be done through the medium of English. When students share the same first language, however, teachers can have difficult decisions to make. On the one hand, you may believe that if students study English for only a few hours a week, they should make the most of the opportunity to work entirely in English. This will help students to learn to think in English and to develop strategies for overcoming language problems, as they would have to do in an English-speaking environment. On the other hand, you may feel that it is unrealistic and artificial to ignore students' competence in their first language and to deny them the opportunity to ask questions and discuss problems which they cannot hope to express in English. You may also feel that it is not possible to ensure that every student in a large class speaks English all the time.

One solution is to set guidelines (or rules!) for times when the first language may or may not be spoken and to make these very clear. They can be enforced by a fine-box, for example, the proceeds of which fund an end-of-course party or a local charity. Any of the following might be times when use of the first language is allowed:

- A quick translation of a word or phrase to show understanding.
- The last five minutes of each class, when students can ask questions or raise problems.
- Pair or group work when there will be a product in English that can be displayed. If, for example, students are working together to produce a written text, they will have something in English to show for their work even if discussion of what to write has been in the first language.
- The formulation of grammar rules, especially if students do not have all the necessary metalanguage (clause, tense, etc.).
- Discussion of cultural similarities and differences, which students might want to explore more deeply than their English allows.

In the last three cases, the teacher can still insist that all feedback to the teacher and to the class as a whole should be in English.

## 15 Supplementing the course

This course, with its different components, is complete and needs no specific supplementation. However, each teacher has an individual style of teaching and each class has its own needs. The progression of tasks through the Students' Book does not in any way rule out additional activities which you might want to introduce. Some are suggested in the Teacher's Book Lesson Notes. Others might include:

- Games and puzzles.
- Revision of vocabulary using pictures of famous people and places e.g. revision of relationships using local soap opera characters.
- Vocabulary extension using local signs, posters, etc. written in English.
- Further practice in reading skills using locally available texts in English that relate to a unit topic e.g. tourist leaflets or graded readers.
- Further practice in listening and communication skills, by inviting English-speaking friends into your classroom.
- Creative writing activities that need little input from you e.g. writing sentences that include three apparently unrelated words.
- Project work suggested by topics in the book and involving team work inside and outside class.
- Additional drama and role-play activities based on characters in the book or imaginary characters that students can identify with.

Specific ideas for these and many other activity types can be borrowed from teachers' resource books – or from friends and colleagues.

# Lesson notes

## Welcome!

### Getting to know *Look Ahead 2*

The aims of these two pages are to familiarise students with some of the topics presented in the book and to stimulate their interest in the book, and about the subjects they are going to study.

**EXERCISE 1**
In pairs or small groups the students look at all the pictures and guess what topics they might be illustrating. Discuss the topics as a class, but do not confirm the students' guesses. Encourage them to say something, however simple, about the topics in English. Discuss the topics further in L1 if you wish.

**EXERCISE 2**
Divide the class into As and Bs. The As describe the pictures to the Bs, who match the descriptions to the unit titles in the contents chart.

**EXERCISE 3**
Students discuss their answers with another pair. Finally, check as a class.

**KEY**

Unit 1  C    Unit 2  E    Unit 3  B    Unit 4  G    Unit 5  M
Unit 6  J    Unit 7  N    Unit 8  I    Unit 9  O    Unit 10 L
Unit 11 F    Unit 12 D    Unit 13 K    Unit 14 H
Unit 15 A

## 1 At the weekend

### Special interests

> **Focus**
> - Interests
> - Giving opinions
> - Giving reasons
> - Present simple/present progressive contrast
> - *I'd like* + infinitive with *to*
> - Conjunction: *because*

**EXERCISE 1**
To introduce the lesson, revise the present continuous by asking a student *What are you doing now?* Elicit *I'm + ing*. Then get a student to ask you the question. Practise this exchange chorally and individually. If the students need more practice of the language, display a few pictures of people doing things, e.g. swimming, gardening, reading. Students work in pairs to ask and answer about the pictures, e.g. *What's he doing? He's reading a paper.*

Next, refer the students to the pictures and the texts. Establish that they need to read the texts only to find out what the people are doing and not to worry if they don't understand all the vocabulary. They then do the exercise with their partner. Check answers as a class.

**KEY**

1  He's bungee jumping./He's jumping off a bridge.
2  He's looking at one of his rocks.
3  She's juggling.
4  They're preparing to ski.

**Extra practice**
To revise free-time activities from *Look Ahead 1*, write the names of hobbies on the board with the letters mixed up, e.g. *rgiadnneg* (gardening). The students work in groups and decipher them.

**EXERCISE 2**
Copy the chart onto the board. Ask the students to read the first text and then complete the chart together. Next, the students work in pairs to complete the chart with the information from the other articles. Check as a class.

**KEY**

| NAME | COUNTRY OF BIRTH | HOBBY | REASONS FOR INTEREST |
|---|---|---|---|
| 1 Mark Coleman | New Zealand | bungee jumping | good fun |
| 2 Robert Haag | the United States | rock collecting | adventures a challenge |
| 3 Alison Peterson | Britain | juggling | very relaxing |
| 4 Mary Grove | Canada | heli-skiing | exciting |

## UNIT ONE

### 📼 EXERCISE 3

You may need to revise the adjectives with your students before they listen to them on tape. If this is so, write them on the board and draw this grid:

| POSITIVE | NEGATIVE | CAN BE POSITIVE OR NEGATIVE |
|---|---|---|
| | | |

The students work in pairs/groups of three to categorise the adjectives. Check as a class. You may need to check their understanding of the adjectives, e.g. *Is skiing cheap?* (No, it's expensive.) Next, play the tape, stopping after each phrase for the students to repeat. Then direct the students back to the four hobbies (and any others you have introduced). In their pairs/groups, they describe the hobbies using the adjectives.

#### TAPESCRIPT

1 It's dangerous.  2 It's boring.  3 It's frightening.
4 It's expensive.  5 It's fun.  6 It's exciting.
7 It's easy.  8 It's crazy.  9 It's relaxing.  10 It's cheap.
11 It's difficult.  12 It's challenging.

#### Extra practice

1 If your students don't know each other very well, they can use the chart in Exercise 2 to interview each other about their hobbies.

2 The students work in pairs. One thinks of a hobby, the other must guess what it is by asking questions, e.g. *Do you do this in winter? Is it dangerous?* They can ask a maximum of eight questions to guess the hobby.

### 📼 WORD STRESS EXERCISE 4

Copy the stress patterns onto the board and direct the students to the adjectives from Exercise 3. To demonstrate the task, write the four stress patterns on the board, say *Fun, which pattern?* and write *fun* on the board under O. They then do the exercise in pairs. Play the tape again for students to check. If necessary, drill the adjectives under each pattern.

#### KEY

O o o   dangerous, difficult, challenging
o O o   expensive, exciting, relaxing
O o   boring, frightening, easy, crazy
O   cheap, fun

#### Extra practice

If you have a class of new students, write the stress patterns for their names on the board. They work in groups of four and write the names of the students under the correct patterns.

### DISCOVERING LANGUAGE EXERCISE 5

To introduce the comparison of the two tenses, draw pictures to elicit the daily routine of a person, e.g. *He gets up at 7.00. He goes to work at 8.00. He has lunch in the canteen.* Use the pictures to elicit question and answer exchanges, e.g. *What does he do at 7.00? He gets up.* Then show the students another picture of the same person and explain that he's on holiday at the moment. Ask *Is he working now?* Elicit *No, he isn't.* Prepare some holiday activity pictures (e.g. sleeping, swimming, eating in a restaurant). Display each picture and ask *What's he doing now?* and elicit *He's + ing.* Check the concept by asking *Is he doing this now?* (Yes) *Does he do this every day?* (No) Drill each exchange chorally and individually. Finally do a half-and-half drill combining both tenses: using the everyday pictures, half the class says *He usually gets up at 7.00* and the other half responds *But today, he's sleeping.* Then they change 'halves'.

Next, copy the four sentences in the exercise onto the board and students copy them into their notebooks. In pairs, they underline the verbs and decide if they are present simple or present progressive. Check as a class. If necessary, revise how the two tenses are formed. Then point out the four explanations of their uses. In pairs, students match the sentences and the uses. Check as a class. As a further check, ask students to find 'contrasts' in the texts, e.g. *Mark is living in Britain./In his free time he jumps off bridges.*

#### KEY

1 c   2 d   3 a   4 b

#### Extra practice

1 To revise the present progressive, show a short piece of a film or TV programme on video (it doesn't matter if it is not in English) with the sound turned down. Students write or record a 'running commentary'.

2 Find some 'activity' pictures, e.g. of a street scene, a scene in a restaurant, etc. Cut each one up into about five pieces. The students mingle and describe to each other what is happening in their piece in order to find the other parts of their pictures. This practises the present progressive.

3 To revise the present simple, the students work in groups to write a routine for a job or for a famous person. They read it out to the class, sentence by sentence, and the others must guess what job it is or who the person is. The first group to guess correctly then describes their routine.

## EXERCISE 6

Use the pictures to check understanding of the verbs and nouns in the exercise. Then divide the class into pairs. Direct Student A to the instructions on page 9 and Student B to those on page 116. To demonstrate the task, ask *What's the woman doing in your first picture?* and elicit the answer. Establish that the students must decide the correct order of the four pictures. They then do the exercise in pairs. Monitor and make a note of any errors. For feedback, first elicit what they think the correct order is and write the numbers of the pictures on the board. Then ask volunteer students to describe the pictures in this order and decide as a class if the order is correct. Use the board to correct any errors.

### KEY

4, 1, 3, 2

## EXERCISE 7

To introduce the exercise refer the students back to the picture in Exercise 6. Write *She wears ...* on the board and complete the sentence as a class. Point out the use of the present simple. Each student writes at least four sentences about the picture. Encourage them to compare their sentences. Then the students dictate their sentences to you. Write them on the board, including any errors and correct them as a class.

### KEY

Suggested answers: She wears a harness and a friend ties an elastic rope around her ankles. She jumps off the bridge. She falls and hangs under the bridge. Another person helps her into a boat.

## EXERCISE 8

Display one of your own activity or hobby pictures and say *I would/wouldn't like to try* (hobby) *because it's* (adjective). *What about you?* Elicit an answer and then get a student to ask you. Next, refer the students back to the pictures in Exercise 1 and they do the same in pairs. Then they write down four of their sentences. Make sure they check each other's work. For feedback, write the names of the hobbies on the board and ask the students to read out their sentences relating to each hobby. Encourage discussion of their opinions and correct any errors.

## ENGLISH AROUND YOU

Direct students' attention to the cartoon. Ask if anyone knows French (unless your students are French!) and ask for a translation into L1 of 'au secours'. Give the English equivalent (*Help!*) if necessary, but try to elicit it first. Make sure students understand the joke (it's a bit too late for her to ask for the translation).

# Frequency

### Focus

- Leisure activities
- Housework
- Percentages

- Talking about routines
- Talking about frequency
- Expressing percentages

- Expressions of frequency: *once/twice/three times a year*
- Question: *How often?*
- Adverbs of frequency
- Verb/noun collocations
- Further practice: present simple

## EXERCISE 1

Direct the class to the picture and elicit what Rachel is doing (interviewing a man). Then refer the students to the instructions and make sure they understand *research assistant*. Write *Who is the magazine for?* on the board and play the conversation. Students check their answers in pairs and then as a class.

### KEY

The magazine is for people between eighteen and twenty-five years old.

### TAPESCRIPT

RACHEL: Er ... excuse me.
MAN: Yes?
R: Could I ask you some questions?
M: Of course. Sit down.
R: It's nice here.
M: Yes, it is. Er, what do you want to know?
R: I work for an advertising agency, and I'm doing some research. It's for a new magazine for people like you.
M: People like me. What do you mean?
R: People between eighteen and twenty-five years old.
M: OK.

## EXERCISE 2

Copy the chart onto the board. Divide the class into As and Bs. The As make notes about the man and the Bs make notes about his wife, using the vocabulary to help them. Play the tape up to 'watch television' and check that they have written down the information for the correct person. Play the complete conversation, twice if necessary. Do not check the answers yet.

**TAPESCRIPT**

RACHEL: Er ... excuse me.
MAN: Yes?
R: Could I ask you some questions?
M: Of course. Sit down.
R: It's nice here.
M: Yes, it is. Er, what do you want to know?
R: I work for an advertising agency, and I'm doing some research. It's for a new magazine for people like you.
M: People like me. What do you mean?
R: People between eighteen and twenty-five years old.
M: OK.
R: Right. Um, what do you do at the weekend?
M: Well, on Fridays, my wife always goes to her exercise class. Then she visits friends.
R: Don't you go out?
M: Not on Fridays. I never go out on Fridays. I stay at home and watch television.
R: And on Saturdays?
M: On Saturdays my wife and I always go sailing together.
R: Really?
M: Mm. We love it. We never miss it. And then in the evening we go out.
R: Where to?
M: Different places. We sometimes go and see friends. We sometimes go to the cinema or a restaurant. But we always go out on Saturday evenings.
R: I see. And now Sunday. What happens on Sundays?
M: Nothing special. We often go for a walk. And I always cook a big Sunday lunch.
R: Oh. How often do you do the cooking?
M: Um, twice a week, three times a week.
R: Thank you very much. All I need now are your personal details – your name, job and so on. What's your surname?
M: Robinson.

## EXERCISE 3

Demonstrate the task by asking a B student *What does the woman do on Fridays?* and elicit *She goes to an exercise class.* Then ask an A student *Does the man go to an exercise class?* and elicit *No, he doesn't. He watches television.* Then say *On Fridays, the woman goes to an exercise class alone* and check that the students understand *alone*. Teach *together* also. Direct the students to the example sentences in the exercise and tell them to make similar exchanges. Monitor and correct where necessary. Finally, complete the chart on the board with the students' help, for a final check of their answers.

**KEY**

|  | FRIDAY | SATURDAY | SUNDAY |
|---|---|---|---|
| The man | watches television | goes sailing goes out: friends, cinema, restaurant | goes for a walk cooks lunch |
| His wife | goes to an exercise class visits friends | goes sailing goes out: friends, cinema, restaurant | goes for a walk |

**Extra practice**
If your students live with other people, they can interview each other about what these people do in their free time.

## EXERCISE 4

If you think this may be new language for your students, copy this grid onto the board:

| have breakfast | MON | TUES | WED | THURS | FRI | SAT | SUN |
|---|---|---|---|---|---|---|---|
| Sally | ✓ | ✓ | ✓ | ✓ | ✓ | ✓ | ✓ |
| Peter | ✓ | ✓ | ✓ | ✓ | ✓ | ✗ | ✗ |
| Roger | ✗ | ✓ | ✓ | ✓ | ✓ | ✗ | ✓ |
| Valerie | ✓ | ✗ | ✓ | ✗ | ✓ | ✗ | ✗ |
| Peter | ✗ | ✗ | ✓ | ✗ | ✗ | ✓ | ✗ |
| Stuart | ✗ | ✗ | ✗ | ✗ | ✗ | ✗ | ✗ |

Elicit (or give) sentences using the adverbs of frequency, e.g. *Sally always has breakfast. Peter usually has breakfast.* Drill each sentence chorally and individually. Highlight the position of the adverb. Then copy the adverbs onto the board and draw a scale, like this:

always ————————————————→

The students work in pairs and place the adverbs on the scale in order of frequency and discuss the difference between *rarely* and *occasionally*. Check their answers as a class and drill each adverb.

**KEY**

always, usually, often, sometimes, occasionally/rarely, never. (*Occasionally* has a more positive meaning than *rarely*.)

## EXERCISE 5

Focus students' attention on the sentences and do

the example sentence with the class. Then encourage them to do the exercise in pairs. To check their answers, write the correct sentences on the board with their help.

**KEY**

1. We often play tennis.
2. I rarely go out. (*only* gives it a negative meaning)
3. They never eat in restaurants.
4. She occasionally/rarely visits her grandparents.
5. He usually goes to the gym after work.
6. We sometimes go for a long walk.

## DISCOVERING LANGUAGE EXERCISE 6

Refer the students back to the sentences from Exercise 5. Direct them to the first two sentences: *He goes swimming **every morning** before school* and *He **always** goes swimming before school*. Ask *Which is a frequency adverb?* and elicit *always*. Do the same with 'an adverbial phrase'. Then discuss their different positions in the sentences and ask students to say which would be 1 and which would be 2 in the example sentence.

**KEY**

a) 2 An adverbial phrase usually goes at the end of the sentence or main clause.
b) 1 A frequency adverb usually goes before the main verb (except with the verb *to be* when it goes after the verb, e.g. *He is always happy*).

## EXERCISE 7

Direct students to the five sentences. They rewrite them, using the word or phrase given. They compare answers in pairs. Check as a class.

**KEY**

1. We watch a video every evening.
2. They never go sailing.
3. She rarely plays badminton.
4. He goes to the opera five or six times a year.
5. I always cook Sunday lunch!

### Extra practice

Prepare about five sentences/questions with mixed-up word order, e.g. *the/never/I/go/on/cinema/to/Sundays*, and write them on the board. The students write them with the correct word order.

## EXERCISE 8

**Note**: /s/ and /z/ are made with the teeth closed, the lips in an open 'smiling' position and the tongue flat in the middle of the mouth, not touching the front teeth. The difference between them is that /s/ is unvoiced and /z/ is voiced. To help the students hear the difference, ask them to put their fingers in their ears or their fingers on their throats as they make the two sounds. They should hear or feel the vibration of the voice as they say /z/. The sound /ə/ is called the schwa and is the common weak form sound. To practise this sound, ask the students to make a long *er* /ɜː/ and cut it short.

Copy the five expressions onto the board and play the tape once. Elicit the two different sounds. Then play the tape again, stopping to drill each expression chorally and individually. Establish that the students understand how the sounds are made.

**TAPESCRIPT**

/sə/ Once a year. Twice a month.
/zə/ Three times a week. Four days a week. Five times a day.

## EXERCISE 9

Direct the students to the phrases and pictures. Ask *Which picture is 'do the shopping'?* and elicit the answer (E). The students then do the exercise in pairs. Check the answers as a group. Drill the phrases if necessary.

**KEY**

1 E   2 A   3 F   4 C   5 D   6 B

## EXERCISE 10

Ask two students to read out the example exchange. The students then work in pairs and interview each other about themselves and their families. Make sure they make notes for Exercise 11. Make a note of any errors and use the board to correct them.

## EXERCISE 11

The students write sentences about their partner and their families using their notes from Exercise 10. Monitor and help. They can then exchange sentences and check for factual or grammatical errors. Alternatively, if you have a small class, they can read their sentences out to the whole class.

### Extra practice

Each student writes three sentences about their own personal routines, e.g. *I never go to the cinema*. Then they work in pairs and tell each other about their routines. They must try to remember the routines but they cannot make notes. They then exchange personalities and 'become' their partner. They work with another student and tell this partner about their 'new' routine, e.g. *I'm Sophie and I never go to the cinema*. They can do this two or three times. Finally, they work with the real person again and relate their routine back to them. The routines are often quite different!

## EXERCISE 12
Write the verbs on the board in a list and refer the class to the expressions in the Students' Book. Ask *Which verb do we use with: for a walk/a swim/a drink?* and write the verb next to the expression. The students then do the same with the other expressions. Write their answers on the board.

**KEY**

| | | |
|---|---|---|
| 1 go | 5 play | 8 have |
| 2 watch | 6 do | 9 make |
| 3 play | 7 go | 10 do |
| 4 go | | |

**Extra practice**

1 To revise the verb + noun collocations, write the verbs and expressions on separate cue cards. Hand out the cards at random, then the students mingle and find their 'partner'.

2 Using the same cue cards, the students can play *Snap!* Divide the class into groups of four, two students with the verbs and two with the expressions. They turn over the cards at the same time and shout *Snap!* when they see a correct pair of cards. The winning two students then take the pile of cards and the game continues.

## EXERCISE 13
In small groups, the students copy the chart into their notebooks. First they choose ten activities, which they enter into their chart, and write a questionnaire. They mingle and interview other students to complete the questionnaire. Monitor and make a note of any errors. Then they regroup to collate their information and write down their findings in the chart. Either they can report on their findings to the whole class or in groups, or they can make a wall poster for the others to read.

## COMPARING CULTURES EXERCISE 14
Direct the students to the chart. Ask *What does the chart show?* (The leisure activities of young British people) Check that the students understand *youth clubs* and *amusement arcades*. Next, ask *What does it tell you about young people and youth clubs?* and elicit three sentences. Drill each one chorally and individually. The students then work in groups of three and make sentences orally about the other activities. Monitor and note down any errors. Then ask different groups to give feedback on each activity. Finally, use the board to correct any errors.

**KEY**

Nearly 70% of young people in Britain never go to youth clubs.
20% rarely go to youth clubs. 11% often go to youth clubs.
26% per cent never do any sport. 38% rarely do any sport. 45% often do some sport.
8% never go to parties or discos. 22% rarely go to parties or discos. 70% often go to parties.
19% never go to the cinema. 79% rarely go to the cinema. 3% often go to the cinema.
62% never go to amusement arcades. 33% rarely go to amusement arcades. 5% often go to amusement arcades.

## EXERCISE 15
Ask *Do young people in your country do these things? What other things do they do?* and write any different activities on the board. If you have a multilingual class, the students can first discuss the exercise in nationality groups and then regroup to compare what happens in each other's countries. Monitor and make a note of any errors and use the board to correct them at the end of the activity.

## Around town

> **Focus**
> - Further practice: leisure activities
> - Justifying opinions
> - Stative verbs
> - *Would like* + infinitive with *to*

## EXERCISE 1
Write the numbers 1-6 in a list on the board. Check that the class understands the different types of people. Use the class to check understanding, e.g. *Are any of you animal-lovers? Are you young teenagers?* Next, direct the class to the advertisements. Establish that they do not need to understand all the vocabulary to do this exercise. Direct them to the first advertisement and ask *Is this to make money for developing countries?* (No) They work in pairs to do the exercise. Then encourage them to check their answers with another pair of students. Finally, check as a class.

**KEY**
1 D  2 C  3 F  4 A  5 E  6 B

## EXERCISE 2

Copy the synonyms/definitions onto the board. Point to *you don't pay to go in* and say *Find a word or phrase in the advertisements that means this.* (Free admission) The students then do the exercise in pairs. Encourage them to ask other students for help if they cannot find the answers. Then elicit the words/phrases from the class and write them on the board next to the synonyms/definitions.

**KEY**

1 free admission (B)  2 further details (C/D)
3 call (A/C)  4 kids (E)  5 in advance (E)
6 barefoot (E)  7 crafts (B)  8 gifts (B)

## EXERCISE 3

Direct the students to the advertisements again and draw the outline of the grid below on the board. Ask two students to read out the information about John. Complete the grid with the information. The students then work in pairs or groups to discuss the other people and make notes. Monitor and make a note of any errors. Encourage the pairs to exchange answers in groups of six and then discuss as a class, with students giving complete sentences. Finally, use the board to correct any errors.

**KEY**

|   |   | ACTIVITIES | REASONS |
|---|---|---|---|
|   | John | Third World Craft Fair (D) | He collects books and likes markets. |
| 1 | Tina | Single scene (B) | She's single and she wants to meet new people. |
| 2 | Liz and Steve | Barefoot boogie (C) | They like music, they are interested in other cultures and they can take their children. |
| 3 | Anne | Deeside Animal Park (F) | The park has lots of entertainment for young children. |
| 4 | George and Tony | Youth club (E) | They want to do things with people of their own age. |
| 5 | Kate and Andy | Ramblers' Club (A) | They like the countryside; they want to find new things. |

## EXERCISE 4

Organise the students into groups of four. Make sure they discuss all six activities. Monitor and make a note of any errors. If you wish to extend the activity, they can conduct a class survey into all the activities and find out which are the most and least popular. If you have a large class, divide them into large groups to do the survey. Alternatively, discuss as a class which are the most and least popular of the activities. Use the board to correct any errors.

## DISCOVERING LANGUAGE EXERCISE 5

**Note**: **Stative verbs** are those which are not usually used in progressive tenses with their basic meaning, e.g. *know, want, hate*. **Dynamic verbs** are those which are used in progressive tenses. Stative verbs when used in progressive tenses often change meaning, e.g. *I **feel** it's a good idea* (= I have the opinion) and *I'm **feeling** hot* (= I have the sensation).

Ask the students to read the five sentences and to name the tense of the verbs in italics. Then discuss why they are all in the present simple. Highlight the fact that the first verb in each sentence is in the present progressive, therefore we would normally expect other verbs to be in the same tense. Explain that the verbs in italics are not usually used in the progressive form.

## EXERCISE 6

Write the numbers 1–10 on the board and ask the students to copy them into their notebooks. Direct the students to the other verbs and the picture of Pam. Complete the first line together. Students do the exercise individually and then check their answers with their partners. Monitor and help. Elicit the answers and write them on the board.

**KEY**

1 don't believe   2 are you doing   3 want   4 know
5 is doing   6 is having   7 loves
8 Does he/understand   9 don't know   10 like

### Extra practice

Prepare ten to fifteen sentences/questions which use the verbs both correctly and incorrectly, e.g. *I'm believing you. He loves his job.* Divide the class into teams. Each team takes two pieces of paper and writes a large **C** (for correct) on one and a large **W** (for wrong) on the other. Read out your first sentence. Each team quickly confers and then holds up the appropriate card, depending on whether they think the sentence is correct or wrong. Give each team a point if they have the correct answer. You can give another point to one team if they correct the sentence and explain why it is wrong.

# Development

## SPEAKING EXERCISE 1

Direct the students to the pictures. They discuss the four questions in groups of three. Make sure they make brief notes. Then quickly check their answers to questions 1 and 2. Then write all their answers to questions 3 and 4 on the board but do not confirm yet which ones are correct

**KEY**

1 the United States – there's an American flag in picture A
2 Back row: mother, father, eldest son, middle son
  Front row: youngest son, daughter
3 B – having a barbecue, C – playing baseball,
  D – playing basketball

## LISTENING EXERCISE 2
**Background notes**
A **breakfast nook** is a small space, probably in or near the kitchen, where the family eats breakfast. In the context of the listening, it is a small room. You can also have a **chimney nook**, which is the small space beside/inside the chimney where you can sit.

**Movies** is the American English term for **the cinema**. To **crank up** the barbecue means to start it. It is informal American English.

**Fall** is American English for **autumn**.

Explain that students are going to check their answers to questions 3 and 4 in Exercise 1. Establish that the people on the tape sometimes use American expressions but that students will be able to understand their meaning from the context. Play the tape and then check their answers as a class. Erase the incorrect answers from the board.

**KEY**

3 They're having a barbecue and playing baseball and playing basketball.
4 Their house is fairly large. It's got four bedrooms, an office, four bathrooms, a front room, a dining room and a breakfast nook. It is safe to assume that it has also got a kitchen, so it has got at least thirteen rooms.

**TAPESCRIPT**

MAN: Our home here is – fairly large. We have four bedrooms, an office, a bunch of bathrooms, I think four bathrooms. Um, in England you'd say it was three reception rooms but it's a front room, a dining room and a breakfast nook. We do a lot of things around the house on the weekend. We garden quite a bit, working in our garden, and we play basketball on the basketball court we've got out the back.

BOY: Um, at the weekends here I go out a lot with my friends on Friday or Saturday night. Sometimes we go to the movies or just go to other people's houses and watch videos.

MAN: Usually Saturday afternoon we crank up the barbecue and that's our meal because during the summer it gets pretty hot here and sometimes you just want to be outside rather than be inside. In California you really have two seasons from our entertainment point of view – spring, summer and fall are very much the same type of activities and then winter is very different on the activities that we do on the weekend. Summertime activities are usually involved around the children's sports. My youngest son plays Little League – er, that's baseball.

## EXERCISE 3
Copy the activities and the members of the family onto the board in two columns. Check that the students understand the activities. Play the tape once and ask students to tick each activity they hear, then play the tape again, stopping after 'working in our garden' and elicit who does this (the whole family). Draw a line from the *whole family* to *gardening* on the board. Then play the complete tape. Encourage students to check their answers in pairs and then as a class on the board.

**KEY**

1 the older boy (the middle son): goes to the cinema (movies), watches videos
2 the little boy: plays baseball
3 the whole family: gardening, play basketball, have barbecues

## COMPARING CULTURES EXERCISE 4
Refer the students back to the activities in Exercise 3 and write *common* and *not common* on the board. Establish that the students must discuss which activities are common or not common in their countries. If you have a multilingual class, organise them into mixed nationality groups to compare their countries. Monitor and make a note of any errors. Discuss as a class and correct any errors.

## READING EXERCISE 5
Direct students to the picture of the telephone cards and ask *Do you use telephone cards? Why?* (To make a call, because you don't need cash) Write 1–6 on the board and refer students to the statements. Check that they understand *collect*. Then ask them to read the article and decide if the statements are true or false. They should correct the false ones. Encourage

them to check their answers with their partners and then as a class on the board. You may wish to check this extra vocabulary from the article: *a wide variety, blanks, to change hands, banknotes.*

**KEY**

1 True.   2 False. The first card was Italian.
3 False. There are different designs in each country.
4 True.   5 False. It is a cheap hobby to start.
6 True.

## SPEAKING EXERCISE 6

Refer the students to the three questions and the text. They discuss the questions in pairs and then as a class. If you have a multinational class, encourage the students to show their phone cards if they have them with them. Finally, decide as a class who has the most interesting hobby.

## WRITING EXERCISE 7

The students can write their paragraph in class or for homework. Then they work in groups of four and read out their texts without saying the name of the hobby. The others listen and guess what the hobby is. They can then swap texts with a partner and correct each other's text.

# 2 Doing new things

## Learning languages

**Focus**
- Languages
- Countries

- Talking about intentions
- Further practice: giving reasons
- Talking about ability

- *Going to* + infinitive
- *Want* + infinitive with *to*
- *Can/can't* + infinitive
- Adverbs of degree: *(very) well, a little, not at all*

## EXERCISE 1

To introduce the lesson, brainstorm all the words the students know for *hello* in foreign languages. Then direct the class to the chart. In groups of four, the students match the words with the languages. Check the answers as a class and add their own language(s), if necessary.

**KEY**

| 1 English | 6 German |
| 2 Chinese | 7 Russian |
| 3 Portuguese | 8 Japanese |
| 4 Bengali | 9 Spanish |
| 5 Arabic | 10 Hindi |

**Extra practice**

1 To revise countries and languages, write the names of several countries on the board, e.g. *France, Ireland, Italy, Eygpt, Spain, Portugal, the USA, Germany, Turkey, Britain, Greece, India, Japan, Brazil, Poland, Holland, Argentina*, etc. Then draw this grid on the board:

| ISH | IAN/AN | ESE | I | OTHER |
|---|---|---|---|---|
| English | German | Portuguese | Hindi | French |

The students place the languages in the columns according to their endings. They can also add other ones they know and the languages from the exercise.

2 Write the countries on the board. The students work in groups to name one thing that each country is famous for, e.g. *Spain – holidays; Italy – spaghetti.* They read out their item and the others guess the nationality. They won't always agree!

## 🔊 EXERCISE 2

**Note: Hundred, thousand, million** are used in the singular whether it is **one hundred** or **three hundred. And** is used before the number expressed by the last two figures, e.g. **456** is **four hundred and fifty-six, 15,689** is **fifteen thousand, six hundred and eighty-nine.**

Copy the numbers onto the board. Encourage the students to practise saying them in pairs and then practise each one as a class. To help the students make the /θ/ sound, ask them to put their tongue behind their teeth and blow hard. It may also help if they bite their tongue as they make the sound. If they confuse /θ/ and /ð/, establish that the two sounds are made in exactly the same way, the only difference is that /ð/ is voiced and /θ/ is unvoiced. Next, play the tape, stopping after each number for the students to repeat.

**TAPESCRIPT**

a thousand, ten thousand, a hundred thousand, a hundred and fifty thousand, nine hundred and ninety-nine thousand, a million

**Extra practice**
1 Divide the students into As and Bs and give each one a list of six large numbers. Each student dictates the numbers to their partner, who writes them down. To check their answers, they dictate the numbers to you and you write them on the board if they say them correctly.

2 To revise telephone numbers, the students mingle and find out the telephone numbers of all the people in the class. They then work in pairs and add all the digits in each one to find who has the biggest sum, e.g. *761032 = 19*.

## EXERCISE 3
To introduce the exercise, write the languages on the board and check they understand the meaning of *mother tongue speakers*. Then ask the class to close their books and to guess how many people speak each language. Write their estimates on the board.

Next, divide the class into pairs. Direct the As to the chart on page 16 and the Bs to page 116. Make sure they copy their charts into their notebooks. Ask the As *How many people speak Spanish?* and elicit the reply. (250 million) Make sure the Bs write the answer in their chart. If necessary, do the same with the Bs. They then do the exercise in pairs. Monitor and correct any errors you hear.

Next, draw a scale on the board, like this:

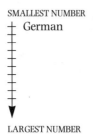

Elicit which language has the smallest number of mother tongue speakers and write *German* on the scale. The students then work in pairs and place the other languages in order on the scale. To check their answers, ask them to tell you the order of the languages and the number of speakers and write both on the board. Drill each number. Finally, compare numbers with their original guesses on the board.

**KEY**

| MOTHER TONGUE SPEAKERS (IN MILLIONS) | | | |
|---|---|---|---|
| English | 350 | Chinese | 1,000 |
| Japanese | 120 | German | 100 |
| Arabic | 150 | Portuguese | 135 |
| Russian | 150 | Spanish | 250 |
| Hindi | 200 | Bengali | 150 |

## COMPARING CULTURES EXERCISE 4
Write the languages on the board with the required number of blanks (countries) next to each one, e.g. *Hindi – 1 _____ ; German – 1 _____ , 2 _____* . Divide the students into groups of four and monitor and help as they do the exercise. Then elicit their answers and write them in the blanks on the board. If they are having problems with the pronunciation of the countries, drill them chorally and individually.

**KEY**

Possible answers:
1 Hindi – India
2 German – Germany, Austria, Switzerland
3 Arabic – countries of North Africa, e.g. Morocco, Tunisia, Egypt and countries in the Middle East, e.g. Iraq, Yemen, Kuwait, Saudi Arabia, United Arab Emirates, Jordan.
4 Spanish – Spain and Central and South American countries, e.g. Argentina, Mexico, Cuba, Uruguay, Venezuela, Ecuador (not Brazil, where they speak Portuguese).
5 English – Britain, the USA, Australia, New Zealand, Ireland, Canada, South Africa, and in some countries which used to be colonies, e.g. Nigeria, Zimbabwe, India (though the speakers in the last three are mostly second language speakers of English, not mother tongue speakers).

## EXERCISE 5
Direct the students to the text and ask *How many countries and languages does Alan mention?* Check their answers as a class. (Six countries and seven languages) Then, using this text as a model, the students write about their first language. They can do this individually or, in a multilingual class, in nationality groups. Monitor and help. If you have a mixed nationality group, they can swap texts and correct any errors. With a monolingual group, the students can read out their texts and you write one model text on the board.

## 📼 EXERCISE 6

Direct the students to the picture and establish who the people are (Rita and Julia) and where they are (MAP Advertising). Ask students if they can remember what their jobs are (account manager and secretary). Students can read the instructions to check the jobs. Next, write the two comprehension questions on the board and play the tape. Students close their books and listen. They check their answers in pairs and as a class.

Ask *Is Rita learning Japanese now?* (No) *Does she plan to study Japanese in the future?* (Yes) *How do you say this in English?* (She's going to learn Japanese) Drill the sentence chorally and individually. Then ask the class *What's she going to do?* and elicit the answer. Get them to ask you the question and drill the exchange chorally and in open pairs. Finally, play the tape again and the students shadow the conversation.

### KEY

1 She wants to study Japanese because she likes Japan and she wants to do something new.
2 She has time to study in the evening.

## DISCOVERING LANGUAGE EXERCISE 7

**Note**: The students have already met the present progressive for future use in *Look Ahead 1*. Both the present progressive and *going to* can be used to talk about plans/arrangements in the future that have already been decided, e.g. *I'm **seeing** him tomorrow* and *I'm **going to see** him tomorrow*. However, to talk about an intention which is not a specific arrangement or 'in your diary', you use *going to*, e.g. ***She's going to learn Japanese.*** It is an intention for the future but not a specific arrangement. You can use *going to* to talk about events that are in the near future, such as tomorrow, or further in the future, such as next year. It is quite common to 'drop' the infinitive when it is *go* or *come*, e.g. *I'm going to (go to) Spain next year.*

Write *going to + infinitive* on the board and remind students of the sentence *She's going to learn Japanese*. Then they write down all the sentences in the conversation in Exercise 6 that contain *going to*. Next, copy this grid onto the board:

|  | AFFIRMATIVE | NEGATIVE | QUESTION |
|---|---|---|---|
| I | am going to | am not going to | Am I going to? |
| He/she/it |  |  |  |
| You/we/they |  |  |  |

They discuss the exercise in pairs and complete the grid. Finally, check all the answers as a class.

### KEY

1 They refer to the future.
2 b) an intention
3

|  | AFFIRMATIVE | NEGATIVE | QUESTION |
|---|---|---|---|
| I | am going to | am not going to | Am I going to? |
| He/she/it | is going to | isn't going to | Is she going to? |
| You/we/they | are going to | aren't going to | Are you going to? |

## EXERCISE 8

Direct the students to the chart and ask *What's James going to do next week?* Elicit *He's going to paint his flat*. Drill the exercise if necessary. The students then work in pairs and ask and answer about the people in the same way. Monitor and correct any errors you hear. Then ask volunteer pairs to make sentences about the people and write them on the board exactly as they say them. Correct any errors as a class and then the students copy the sentences.

### KEY

James is going to paint his flat next week. He's going to go to Edinburgh next month. He's not going to visit Ireland next year.

Julia is going to begin a German course next week. She isn't going to play at the jazz club next month. She is going to change jobs next year.

Rachel and John are going to find a house next week. They are going to get married next month. They are not going to take a holiday next year.

## EXERCISE 9

To demonstrate the activity, write five things on the board that you want to do in your life and *Why?* next to them. (Make them as interesting as you can.) Then tell the class the first one, e.g. *I'm going to buy a house* and point to *Why?* Elicit *Why are you going to buy a house?* Give a reply and then do the same with the next thing on your list. Continue until you are sure that the students understand the activity. Next, ask the students to write down five things that they want to do in their lives. Divide them into pairs and they read the example exchange together. Then they do the same using their lists. Monitor and make a note of any errors. Get quick feedback of some of the things they want to do and then use the board to correct any errors.

27

UNIT TWO

**Extra practice**
(Both of these activities practise *going to*.)

1 Write these prompts on the board: *where/go? when/go? how long/stay? how/travel? where/stay? what/do? what/eat? what/drink? what/buy?* Explain that students are going to plan a holiday together. Elicit the question forms and tell them about the holiday you have planned. The students work in groups and plan their holidays. Then they regroup and interview each other about their holidays, using the questions.

2 Bring in pictures of objects, e.g. a glass of water, a ladder, a paintbrush. Display them and the students work in groups and decide what they are going to do with them, e.g. *I'm going to drink the water. We're going to wash the windows.* Alternatively, this can be done as a chain drill with the pictures.

### EXERCISE 10
Copy the two questions onto the board. Play the tape once. Students check their answers in pairs and then as a class.

**KEY**

1 She can speak English, Hindi, French.
2 She can write English and Hindi.

**TAPESCRIPT**

CLERK: Right. How many languages do you speak? Apart from English, of course.
RITA: I speak Hindi.
CLERK: Ah. How well do you speak it?
RITA: Very well. I can write it too.
CLERK: Any other languages?
RITA: I can speak a little French. But I can't write it at all.
CLERK: A little French. Can't write it. That's it?
RITA: Yes.
CLERK: And you want to join our beginners' class in Japanese?
RITA: Yes, please.
CLERK: Well, it's not going to be easy, you know. It's very different from English, Hindi or French.
RITA: I know. But I want to do it.

### EXERCISE 11
Refer the students to the four statements. Play the tape a second time. Students decide whether they are true or false, and correct the false ones. They check their answers in pairs and then as a class.

**KEY**

1 False. She can speak a little French.
2 False. She can write Hindi very well.
3 False. She can't write French at all.
4 True.

### EXERCISE 12
Ask the students to copy the chart into their notebooks and direct them to the questions. To demonstrate the task, choose a student to ask you the questions. Make notes on the board about yourself as you answer them. They then do the exercise in pairs. Make sure they complete the chart. Monitor and make a note of any errors and correct them at the end of the activity.

### EXERCISE 13
Using your notes on the board from Exercise 12, elicit complete sentences and write them on the board, e.g. *She speaks English very well.* Students then write about their partner using their notes in the chart. Finally, they swap texts and correct any factual or grammatical mistakes.

**Extra practice**
1 Prepare visuals of activities, e.g. *drive, speak Italian, cook, iron, sing*, etc. The students work in pairs and interview their partner about how well they can do these things. They make notes. Then they work in groups of four and tell the other students about their partner.

## After school

**Focus**
- Times, dates, days, months
- Money
- Further practice: leisure activities
- *Like* + *ing*
- *Enjoy* + *ing*
- Further practice: *would like* + infinitive with *to*
- *Want* + infinitive with *to*

### EXERCISE 1
Direct the class to the programme of courses and ask *How many courses are there?* They read the programme quickly. Elicit the answer. (Ten) Then they read it again, find one course that they like and discuss their choices with their partners. Finally, encourage class discussion about which courses they would like and wouldn't like to do, giving reasons with *because ....*

### EXERCISE 2
Refer the students to the exercise and check they understand *dishes* and *in good shape*. To demonstrate the task, ask *Which course is about writing good*

the task, ask *Which course is about writing good English?* and elicit *Problems with writing?* They then do the exercise in pairs. Check as a class by reading out the prompts and the students give the names of the courses.

**KEY**

1 Problems with writing?   2 Intermediate Italian
3 Photography   4 Cinema Studies   5 Foreign Cookery
6 Painting in Watercolours   7 Rock guitar club
8 Jazz Exercise for Women   9 Return to Learn
10 Family History

## EXERCISE 3

Divide the class into pairs. Direct the As to page 18 and the Bs to page 116. Ask a pair to read out the example exchanges. Drill the questions and write them on the board if necessary. Then the students ask and answer about the courses in pairs. Once the Bs have asked about two courses, they can change roles. Monitor and make a note of any errors. For feedback, volunteer pairs roleplay conversations for each course. Finally, use the board to correct any errors you heard.

## DISCOVERING LANGUAGE EXERCISE 4

**Note**: At this level, the students do not need to know that **like** can also be followed by the infinitive. **Like + ing** is used with the meaning of *enjoy*. **Like + infinitive** with **to** means to be in the habit of doing something, to choose to do it, e.g. *I like to see my family whenever I can.* It is incorrect to use an infinitive after **enjoy**.

Direct students' attention to the four questions and encourage them to discuss the rules with their partners. Then write this on the board:
   like + ?     enjoy + ?
   want + ?    would like + ?
and as a class write the forms after the verbs.

**KEY**

like + *ing*   enjoy + *ing*
want + infinitive with *to*   would like + infinitive with *to*

### Extra practice

Prepare some visuals or write some word prompts on the board, e.g. *a cup of tea, dancing*. The students work in pairs and interview each other using the prompts on the board and the four question forms.

## EXERCISE 5

Copy the verbs in a list on the board and ask the students to copy them into their books. Point to *watch* and ask *Which noun?* Elicit *television* and write it next to *watch*. Students then work in pairs and do the same. Check their answers as a class and write the nouns next to the verbs.

**KEY**

watch television    play the piano/computer games
learn English/the piano    discuss politics
take photographs    tidy your room
make dinner/cakes    do homework/some exercise
give parties    wash the dishes    go dancing/home

## EXERCISE 6

Write the two questions on the board and underline *do* and *don't*. Play the tape and ask students to listen for which word is stressed (*don't*). Discuss why it is stressed (because it makes a contrast with the previous question) and drill it chorally and individually. Ask a student to read question 1 from the book, stressing it carefully. Students can practise reading questions 1 and 2 in pairs, then play the tape for them to check. Finally, play the questions on tape again for them to repeat.

**TAPESCRIPT**

What do you enjoy doing? What don't you enjoy doing?
1  What do you like eating for breakfast? What don't you like eating?
2  What do you like watching on TV? What don't you like watching?

## EXERCISE 7

Direct the students to the exercise and write the prompts for the example exchanges on the board. Point to the prompts and elicit the first question and answer. Drill the exchange chorally and individually. Then do the same with the other exchanges. Next, divide the students into pairs and they practise the exchanges in closed pairs. Indicate the other two pictures and they make similar conversations. Monitor and correct any errors you hear. For feedback, ask two volunteer pairs to roleplay their conversations. The others listen and correct any errors they hear. If necessary, write the exchanges on the board as they roleplay them and allow the students to copy them at the end.

**KEY**

1  What does he enjoy doing in the evening?
   He enjoys playing the piano and discussing politics.
   What doesn't he like doing?
   He doesn't like making dinner or washing the dishes.
   What would he like to do after class?
   He would like to go home.

2  What does she enjoy doing in the evening?
   She enjoys learning English and taking photographs.

What doesn't she like doing?
She doesn't like going to/giving parties or making cakes. What would she like to do after class?
She would like to do some exercise.

## EXERCISE 8
Direct the students back to the questions in Exercise 7 and tell them to ask their partners. Make sure they make notes. They then write three sentences about their partner. To check their writing, they can either swap texts and check for errors or they can read their sentences out to the whole class.

### Extra practice
To revise the verb and noun collocations, write them out on separate pieces of paper, e.g. *go, home*. The students mingle and must find the appropriate noun or verb to complete their expression. Alternatively, you can read out the noun and the students must shout out the verb.

## EXERCISE 9
Refer the class to the seven questions and check that the students understand *popular*. Next, play the tape until 'weekend workshops' and elicit the answer to the first question. Then play the complete conversation. The students compare their answers in pairs. If necessary, play the tape again and then check answers as a class.

### KEY
1 It's usually open five days a week, Monday to Friday, and sometimes at the weekend.
2 450 – 500 students.
3 All ages. Young children, teenagers and adults – the oldest is 82.
4 Art classes.
5 Yoga, foreign languages, furniture making, philosophy.
6 From the town and from other towns and villages.
7 Because they want to study the subjects, to meet people and to make friends, to get out of their houses.

### TAPESCRIPT
MANAGER: The centre's usually open five days a week – that's from Monday to Friday ... though we do sometimes have weekend workshops. A lot of our classes are in the evening, but there are quite a few during the day, too.
INTERVIEWER: And how many people attend classes here?
M: Um, ... in any one term we can have between 450 and 500 students coming to classes, and they're all ages. Of course, most of the students are adults – in fact, the oldest this term is eighty-two – but we do run playgroups for very young children during the day. Next year we're going to provide more facilities for teenagers, because they don't really have a place to go in a small town like this.
I: Which are your most popular classes?
M: Well, they're probably our art classes because that's what we specialise in. After all, students of all ages really enjoy painting and drawing. Yoga and foreign languages are also extremely popular. But we offer a very wide range of courses – everything from furniture making to philosophy.
I: Are your students all local people?
M: Er, a lot of our students aren't actually from the town. They come from other towns and villages because they want to do a particular subject or because they'd like to be with a particular teacher. And then they also come for other reasons. Of course the subject interests them, but people who are new to the town come to meet people and some people just want to get out of the house ... young mothers and old people in particular enjoy making new friends.

## COMPARING CULTURES EXERCISE 10
Direct the students to the four questions. They can discuss them in groups of three or as a class. Encourage students to talk about any courses that they have experience of.

# Young lives

> **Focus**
> - Describing experiences
> - Expressing feelings
> - Past simple, all forms (regular and irregular verbs, *was/were, could*)

## EXERCISE 1
If your students' listening skills are quite good, ask them to listen to the five people to find out what they are talking about. Alternatively, write A–E on the board and direct the students to the pictures. As they listen, they write the number of the speaker next to the letter of the appropriate picture. Allow them to check their answers in pairs and then as a class. Play the tape again and the students read the texts while they listen.

### KEY
1 C   2 B   3 E   4 A   5 D

### TAPESCRIPT
1 ROSIE
Oh, I hated it. I was five years old, very small and shy.

My mother took me inside and there were a lot of other children. Did I cry? Well, I certainly cried when she left and I was unhappy all day. I felt awful.

2 ALAN
My parents were worried about moving, but I wasn't. I was very excited. Of course, when we moved I lost some of my friends and I changed schools, but it was an adventure.

3 RACHEL
I felt wonderful on the first day. I was only fifteen but I had a job and some money. I didn't work on schooldays – only on Saturdays. And I sometimes worked in the holidays. Of course, the job was actually quite boring. Did they pay me much money? No, but I loved it – I really did.

4 BECKY
They taught me at school and I took the test when I was sixteen. Then my mother lent me her car twice a week. Was I frightened? Well, the first time I drove alone I was frightened for about five minutes, but then I felt fine.

5 MARCO
I love my parents but I was very happy to be free. When I left the house with all my suitcases, I thought, 'I'm an adult!' I went to the airport and caught a plane to Britain. I didn't know then that I would stay here for so long.

## EXERCISE 2
Refer the students to the comments again. Write *good experiences* and *bad experiences* on the board and ask the students to categorise the texts under these headings. Check their answers as a class. Tell students to go through all the texts identifying the adjectives. Then direct them to the first text and ask them to find the adjectives which describe Rosie's feelings. Elicit them from the students and write them in the correct column (good or bad experiences). The students then do the same for the other experiences. Encourage them to check their answers in pairs and then check as a class by asking the students to make full sentences. Drill the adjectives for pronunciation if necessary.

### KEY
Example: unhappy, awful (bad experience)
1 very excited (good experience)
2 wonderful (good experience)
3 frightened, fine (good experience but with bad moments)
4 happy (good experience)

## DISCOVERING LANGUAGE EXERCISE 3
If you think that some of your students may not know/remember how the past tense is formed in English, bring in some pictures of everyday actions, e.g. *get up, have breakfast, go to work*, and use them to elicit your routine for yesterday. Drill each sentence and use the pictures to elicit question forms which the students can practise in closed pairs.

Then draw two columns on the board, like this:

| REGULAR | IRREGULAR |
|---|---|
| hate – hated | be – was |

and direct the students to the verbs in the exercise. They read the comments again and find the first past tense form (*hated*). Elicit whether it is regular or irregular and write it on the board with the students' help. Do the same with *to be*. They then do the same in pairs with the other verbs in the texts. Check their answers on the board.

Then copy the outline of the grid below onto the board and ask the students to copy it into their notebooks. Ask the students to complete the grid and to discuss questions 2 and 3 with their partner. Then check as a class.

### KEY
1 Regular: hated, cried, moved, changed, worked, loved
Irregular: be–was/were, take–took, leave–left, feel–felt, lose–lost, have–had, teach–taught, lend–lent, drive–drove, think–thought, go–went, catch–caught

| | AFFIRMATIVE | NEGATIVE | QUESTION |
|---|---|---|---|
| REGULAR All persons | I hated. (+ed) | I didn't hate. | Did I hate…? |
| IRREGULAR All persons | I went. | I didn't go. | Did I go…? |
| TO BE I/he/she/it We/you/they | I was. We were. | I wasn't. We weren't. | Was I? Were we? |

2 Questions and negative statements are made in the simple past tense using *did* for questions and *didn't* for negatives with all persons.
3 The past tense of the verb *to be* is **was/wasn't** for *I, he, she, it* and **were/weren't** for *we, you* and *they*. There is no auxiliary (e.g. *did*) used in the formation of the past of the verb *to be*.

### Extra practice
1 Prepare a story containing simple past tenses,

about ten to twelve sentences. Tell the class that you are going to dictate a story to them and that they must write it down. Read it once at a reasonably normal speed for them to listen. Then tell them that they can stop you any time you're dictating and ask you to repeat phrases so that they control how fast you speak. When you have dictated all the story, they check their texts in pairs and then dictate it back to you. You write it on the board exactly as they say it and then together correct any errors.

2 Give the students six verbs. In groups of three, they write a short story in the past which includes the verbs and then read it out to the other students.

3 They work in pairs and interview each other to find out six things that they did in the past, with exact dates.

4 Prepare four cue cards with a short biography of a person on it, e.g. born 1962, school 1967–1979, Paris 1980, journalist 1981, etc. They work in groups of four and exchange information about the four people and write a short paragraph about each one to read out to the class.

## EXERCISE 4
To demonstrate the task, direct the students to the instructions and get them ask you the questions. Answer their questions and then divide them into pairs to do the same. Monitor and correct any errors. Then refer the class back to your experience and together write a short text about it on the board. The students then write about their own or their partner's experience. Monitor and help.

## EXERCISE 5
Direct the students to the picture and the article and say *Nicholas is an unusual child. What do you think is different about him?* Students read the text quickly to check their answer. Write the example prompt on the board and ask the class to make a question, which another student answers. Divide the class into pairs to ask and answer about the text. For feedback, ask volunteer pairs to roleplay their exchanges. If necessary, write the questions and answers on the board if the students find the exercise difficult. Ask students if they think Nicholas and his parents are happy.

### KEY
Example:
Where does Nicholas have computer lessons?
He has computer lessons at the West London Institute.
1 When did he start to speak well?
  He started to speak well before he was one.
2 When did he begin to learn French?
  He began to learn French when he was two.
3 When did he learn to read?
  He learnt to read before he could speak.
4 Why did he leave school?
  He left school because he was bored and unhappy and his teachers did not have time to prepare special lessons for him.
5 What instrument does/can he play?
  He plays/can play the violin.

## DISCOVERING LANGUAGE EXERCISE 6
Write *can* and *can't* on the board and ask students to find their past forms in the article (*could/couldn't*).

## EXERCISE 7
The students read the article again and complete the sentences about the text. Encourage them to compare their answers and then check as a class.

### KEY
1 could take   2 could read   3 could speak
4 couldn't stay   5 couldn't prepare

## EXERCISE 8
Write *when/speak in sentences?* on the board and select a student to ask you the question (*When could you speak in sentences?*). Answer and drill the exchange chorally and in open pairs. Then refer the students to the exercise and they do the same in pairs. Monitor and make a note of any errors. Use the board for correction at the end of the activity.

## EXERCISE 9
The students write sentences about themselves based on their discussion in Exercise 8. Monitor and help. They can read out their sentences to the whole class or in groups of four and compare at what ages they could and couldn't do these things.

## ENGLISH AROUND YOU
Focus students' attention on the cartoon. Ask the students *Can he do it, do you think?* and elicit that it is very unlikely!

# Development

## READING EXERCISE 1
**Background notes**
**Automotive repair** is American English for **car maintenance**.

**High School** is the American equivalent to the upper part of British secondary schools, i.e. for young people aged 14–18. It is also becoming more common in Britain for vocational subjects to be offered.

Direct the students to the picture and discuss what they think is happening. Do not confirm their guesses yet. Then they read the text to find out if they were correct.

## EXERCISE 2

Write the four phrases on the board. Ask students to read the text again and find explanations of the phrases. Do the first one together as an example, e.g. Academic subjects improve students' minds. Check their answers as a class.

#### KEY

1 Academic subjects improve students' minds and prepare them for college.
2 Vocational courses prepare students for particular jobs.
3 A course in automotive repair teaches students how to repair cars.
4 On a practical course students learn by doing as well as by studying.

## EXERCISE 3

Direct students to the pictures of occupations and ask them to search the text for the names of the occupations. Write the numbers 1–6 in a list on the board and check students' answers. Write the occupations on the board.

#### KEY

1 secretary  2 mechanic  3 salesperson
4 cook  5 waiter  6 receptionist

## EXERCISE 4

Students read the text again to answer the questions. Check the answers around the class.

#### KEY

1 He teaches a course in automotive repair.
2 High school students can attend the vocational courses in the day. People who are not attending the school can attend vocational courses in the evening.

### Extra practice

You may need to revise the names of different occupations from *Look Ahead 1*. Write the occupations as anagrams, e.g. *cmciehan* (mechanic) on the board and the students decipher them.

## 🔊 LISTENING EXERCISE 5

Explain that students are now going to listen to Gene Abbott. Direct the students to the questions and make sure they understand all the vocabulary. Play the tape once, stopping after 'adults' and check the answer to question 1. Then play the complete conversation. Encourage students to compare their answers in pairs and if necessary, play the tape again. Then check their answers as a class.

#### KEY

1 From 16 to adults.
2 15% are girls.
3 5-10 hours a week.
4 It's free (because it's part of their general education).
5 Many of them want to repair their own cars. Some want to work in garages and service stations when they leave school.
6 One lesson a week.
7 Josh likes the course because it's more practical than his other studies and is 'more of the real world'.

#### TAPESCRIPT

GENE: My programme is a course in automotive repair. Er, .. we, er, teach people from the age of sixteen through adults. We're located on a High School campus. It's vocational, which means that we train people in specific skills that they could use in a job.

PRESENTER: There are programmes for adults in the afternoons and evenings, but all the people in Gene's classes are students at San Rafael High School. About eighty-five per cent are boys. They choose to spend five or ten hours a week with him in groups of eighteen to twenty. It's a vocational course, but it's part of their general education, so they don't have to pay. Many of the students want to learn how to repair their own cars.

G: Every student is an individual that comes into my programme. All of them think that they're going to be able to fix their own car. They all have that as a goal that they are going to get out of the programme.

P: Some students, though, want to work in garages and service stations when they leave school. One lesson a week is in a classroom and deals with the theory of car repairs. On the other days, students work with Gene in the workshop next to the school. They do projects and learn practical skills. This is one of Gene's students.

JOSH: I like classes like this because it's more of the real world than it is sitting there reading a text book, not knowing what you are going to be using it for.

P: In other high schools the local education office runs different vocational courses. Students can learn about radio broadcasting, electronics, business technology

UNIT THREE

and restaurant work at the same time as the usual school subjects.

### SPEAKING EXERCISE 6
Students can discuss the exercise in groups or as a class. If possible, bring some information into the class about vocational courses in your country to generate discussion. It does not matter if the text is in your L1 as the discussion will be in English.

### WRITING EXERCISE 7
Get the students to read the letter and discuss any differences in format between this letter and formal letters they write in their countries. Then they discuss questions 1-3 in pairs and as a class. Make sure they understand the conventions before they do Exercise 8.

#### KEY
1 c, b, a
2 a) paragraph 2   b) paragraph 1   c) paragraph 3
3 The writer ends *Yours faithfully* because he begins *Dear Sir/Madam*. If he begins *Dear Mr Smith*, he ends *Yours sincerely*.

### EXERCISE 8
Students write a letter using the information supplied in Exercise 7. If they cannot think of a course, they could use one of those on page 18 of the Students' Book. Monitor and help. Then students swap texts and correct any errors.

## 3 Planning a trip

### Ways of travelling

> **Focus**
> - Means of transport
> - Making comparisons
> - Comparative adjectives (+ *er* and *more*)
> - Comparative adjectives (irregular forms)
> - *Prefer* + *ing*

### EXERCISE 1
**Background notes**
In American English a **coach** (a comfortable bus used for long distances) is called a **bus** and a **taxi** is called a **cab**. In Britain, local councils run bus services but most coach services are now run by private companies.

A **ship** is a larger vessel, a **boat** is smaller. In conversation, large passenger ships which travel short distances (**ferries**) may be referred to as boats, e.g. *When's the next boat to France?*

To introduce the vocabulary, either use the pictures in the book of different types of transport or prepare/draw on the board some visuals of your own. Write the names of the forms of transport on the board and point at one of the pictures that the students will know, e.g. bus. Ask *What's this?* They give the name, or the letter of the item in the picture. Write the letter next to the name on the board. Students complete the exercise in pairs. Check as a class.

#### KEY
boat 2   car 7   helicopter 4   balloon 3
bicycle (bike) 8   bus 9   coach 6   plane 5   ship 1

### EXERCISE 2
**Note**: In this exercise 'private' refers to something owned by a private individual, e.g. a car, not private as opposed to owned by the government.

Draw the outline of the chart at the top of page 35 on the board. The students complete the chart in pairs. Establish that 'short distances' are within a town, of only a few kilometres. If necessary, demonstrate the task. Ask *Do people usually own cars?* (i.e. private) and complete the chart with the word *private* under *car*. Monitor and help. To check their answers, complete the chart on the board with their help. If necessary, drill each item.

**Extra practice**
To revise the verbs and nouns in Exercise 2, prepare cue cards with gapped sentences on them, e.g. *You _____ a bicycle. You _____ a boat.* Each student completes their sentence. They then mingle, read out their sentence to the other students who must give the missing word. Finally, each student reads out their sentence to the whole class (without the word) and the class supplies the missing word.

### EXERCISE 3
**Note**: If you need to revise the adverbs of frequency from Unit 2 before the students do this exercise, get them to stand in line according to how often they have breakfast, from those who never have it, to those who have it every day. They then make a sentence about each student, e.g. *Juan never has breakfast. Sylvie always has breakfast.*

Refer the students to the pictures on the board/in the book and tell them how often you use the forms of transport, following the model given. Make sure

**KEY**

|   | boat | car | helicopter | balloon | bicycle | bus | coach | plane | ship |
|---|---|---|---|---|---|---|---|---|---|
| 1 | private | private | public | private | private | public | public | public | public |
| 2 | short/long | short/long | long | short/long | short | short | long | long | long |
| 3 | sail | drive | fly | fly | ride | drive | drive | fly | sail |
| 4 | * | driver | pilot | pilot | rider | driver | driver | pilot | * |

\* The word for the person who steers a boat or ship depends on the type of boat.

they remember the use of *by* + means of transport and the exception *on foot*. The students then work in pairs and tell each other how often they use the different means of transport. Monitor and make a note of any errors. Use the board to correct them.

### EXERCISE 4
Direct the students to the title of the article. Discuss as a class what they think the article is about. Teach the word *fear* if necessary. If you wish, use the board to note down their ideas. Then the students read the article quickly to check their guesses. Check as a class and tick (✓) the ideas on the board that the article mentions. Finally, find out if the students agree or disagree with the writer.

### EXERCISE 5
Direct the students to the text and the questions. Check they understand the adjectives in the second question. They can work in pairs to answer the questions. Then check their answers as a class. For question 2, draw two columns on the board:

| TRAIN | PLANE |
|---|---|
|   |   |

and write the adjectives in the correct column with the students' help.

**KEY**

1 by train
2
| TRAIN | PLANE |
|---|---|
| safe | dangerous |
| slow | fast |
| comfortable | bad |
| good | expensive |
| convenient | uncomfortable |

### EXERCISE 6
Students read the article again and match the verbs with their meanings. Check the answers and ask which ones go with *plane*, which go with *train*, and which go with both (plane: *to land, to take off*; both: *to catch, to miss*).

**KEY**

1 b   2 d   3 c   4 a

### DISCOVERING LANGUAGE EXERCISE 7
**Note**: Comparative adjectives are used to compare the quality of two things. (Superlatives are used when more than two things are compared. In spoken English, the superlative is often used instead of the comparative when comparing two things, but this is not an acceptable form in written English.) Two-syllable adjectives are formed with either *-er* or *more*, and sometimes both forms are possible.

Ask the class *Which type of transport does the writer prefer?* (Trains) *Why?* (Because they're cheap/safe, etc.) Then point to the pictures of the train and plane and ask *What's the difference between them?* Elicit *Trains are cheaper than planes.* Check the concept by asking, e.g. *Do they cost the same money?* (No) *Which costs less money?* (Trains) Then drill the comparative sentence chorally and individually. Finally, elicit comparative sentences using *safe, comfortable* and *good*.

Direct students to the exercise and encourage them to work in pairs to answer the questions. Monitor and help. Then write the answers on the board with their help and make sure they copy the rules into their notebooks.

**KEY**

1 safe – saf*er*   comfortable – *more* comfortable
  convenient – *more* convenient   cheap – cheap*er*
  slow – slower   important – *more* important
  good – *better*   bad – *worse*
2 The comparative form of most short adjectives is formed by adding *-er* to the adjective and following it with *than*. The comparative form of longer adjectives is formed by putting *more* before the adjective and adding *than* after the adjective. *Good* and *bad* are

UNIT THREE

adjective. *Good* and *bad* are irregular adjectives.
3 Stations are more convenient than airports.

### 🔊 STRESS AND INTONATION EXERCISE 8

Write the two sentences on the board and tell students to copy them into their notebooks. Ask them which words they think will be stressed. Play the tape for them to check their answers. Check as a class and then play the sentences again and ask students to underline the schwa /ə/ sounds. Check as a class and then ask volunteers to practise saying the comparative sentences.

**KEY AND TAPESCRIPT**

1 'Trains are 'safer than 'planes.
2 'Stations are more con'venient than 'airports.

Choose two objects/people in the classroom and ask a student to make a comparative sentence, e.g. *We are younger than the teacher*. Then ask students to write three sentences making comparisons with things in the classroom, which they then read out to their partners. Monitor, concentrating particularly on the pronunciation.

**Extra practice**
Prepare some large cue cards with the following prompts (or similar): South of France/north of France, the Spanish/the English, summer in Saudi Arabia/summer in Britain, etc. Give one cue card to each pair of students. They write their comparison under the prompts and display it for the others to see. They then mingle, look at the other sentences and correct any errors they find. This is fun if the prompts relate to the students' countries.

### 🔊 EXERCISE 9

Copy the chart onto the board. If necessary, teach *reliable*. Play the tape, stopping after the first speaker and complete the chart for Alan as a class. Then play the complete tape. The students compare their answers with their partners and then check as a class on the board.

**KEY**

|  | HOW? | WHY? |
| --- | --- | --- |
| Alan | plane | faster |
| Anna | bus | friendlier, more interesting |
| Becky | car | reliable |
| Sally | bicycle | good exercise, better for the environment |
| Bob | train | more convenient, more comfortable |

**TAPESCRIPT**

1 ALAN
I prefer travelling by plane because I get there faster.

2 ANNA
Actually, I think buses are better than any other form of transport. On a long journey you always meet people and talk to them. People are friendlier on buses. And the journey's more interesting because you can see the countryside.

3 BECKY
I hate travelling by train. There are always problems with trains in this country. They're late or they're cancelled or something happens. I use my car and I always get where I'm going in time. Travelling by car is definitely more reliable.

4 SALLY
Buses are bad but cars are worse. They both cause terrible pollution in towns and cities. I travel everywhere by bicycle because I think it's better for the environment and it's good exercise. Anyway, I'm too young to drive!

5 BOB
People who drive cars long distances to get to work are crazy. They sit for hours in traffic jams; they get angry and frustrated. Trains are much better. I like travelling by train because I can work while I'm travelling. It's more convenient and more comfortable than travelling by car.

### EXERCISE 10

Write on the board *Alan prefers travelling ... because ...* and complete it with the students' help. In pairs, they write a sentence about Bob. To check their answers, volunteer pairs read out their sentences and the others check that they are correct.

**KEY**

Bob prefers travelling by train because it's more convenient and more comfortable/he can work while he's travelling.

**Extra practice**
1 In their pairs, students write similar sentences about Anna, Becky and Sally.
2 Write these groups of items on the board as prompts: *winter, summer, spring; tea, coffee, coke; beef, chicken, fish; dogs, cats, horses; cities, villages, seaside; reading, dancing, watching TV*, etc. In groups of three, the students interview each other about their preferences and the reasons why they prefer one of the things from each

group, e.g. *I prefer winter because I like cold weather*. You can choose categories according to your students' interests.

## COMPARING CULTURES EXERCISE 11
Write *short distances* and *long distances* on the board and display your transport visuals or refer students to the pictures in the book. In groups, the students discuss which are the usual ways to travel these distances in their countries and why. They then write sentences. They can either do this individually and then swap sentences to compare or they can work with students from the same country and write the sentences in pairs, finally reading them out to the whole class.

# Travel arrangements

> **Focus**
> - Travel
> - Talking about intentions for the future
> - Making decisions
> - Inviting someone
> - Making promises
>
> - Modal: *will* for decisions
> - *I'll* + infinitive for promises
> - *Let's* + infinitive
> - Further practice: *going to* for intentions, *would you like* + infinitive with *to*

## EXERCISE 1
**Background notes**
**Edinburgh** is pronounced /ˈedɪnb(ə)rə/. It is the capital of Scotland and is a centre of business, education, the law, book production, engineering and other industries. It is sometimes called 'the Athens of the North' because it is a centre for the arts, e.g. music and theatre. It has a famous festival of musical and theatrical events for three weeks every summer. It is also a tourist centre.

**Glasgow** / ˈglæzgəʊ / or / ˈglɑːzgəʊ / is the other main city in Scotland. It is very close to Edinburgh.

Direct the class to the picture of Julia and James and elicit who they are. Then copy the questions onto the board and ask students to listen with books closed. Play the tape once. Encourage the students to compare answers and then check by reading/as a class. To check the use of the *going to* future, ask *Does James intend to go to Edinburgh?* (Yes) *How do you know?* (He uses *going to*.) Then play the conversation again and the students shadow it in their books.

### KEY
1 James   2 Julia   3 James – to see some clients in Edinburgh, sightseeing; Julia – to see some clients in Glasgow

## EXERCISE 2
Direct students to the calendar. Tell them to find the day and date when James is going to visit his clients and write it on the board. The students then work in pairs to find the other days and dates.

### KEY
1 Monday 20th   2 Wednesday 15th   3 Friday 17th
4 Wednesday 15th

## DISCOVERING LANGUAGE EXERCISE 3
Refer students to the dialogue in Exercise 1 and ask *When does Julia decide to fly to Glasgow?* Point out the use of the simple future for making spontaneous decisions. If you wish, present this further by using the situation of a class party. Say *We're going to have a party for the class this weekend. What do we need to bring?* and brainstorm a list of things on the board. Then write your name next to one item and say *I'll bring some juice. What about you, Susanna?* (indicating a student) and the student responds in the same way. Ask *Are you deciding now?* (Yes)
When you are sure the students understand the concept of deciding now, ask *What you will bring?* and go around the whole class. As each students says an item, cross it off the list. Next, the students discuss the exercise in pairs. Monitor and help and then check their answers as a class.

### KEY
1 *going to* + infinitive and *will* + infinitive.
2 *will* + infinitive: I'll go by car too, I think. No, I won't drive. I'll fly.
3 *going to* + infinitive: I'm going to see some clients on the 20th. I'm going to visit clients in Glasgow on Wednesday. I'm going to drive there on the Friday before.

## EXERCISE 4
- In pairs, the students brainstorm what you need for a camping holiday. Then discuss as a group and check they know the meaning of *borrow, tent, sleeping bags, guidebook*.
- Divide the class into pairs. Direct the As to page 26 and the Bs to page 117. Point to 'buy the plane tickets' and get the As to ask the Bs a question with *Who?* Then, to check the concept, ask *Is this an intention?* (yes) and, if necessary, drill the

exchange. The students then do the exercise in pairs. Monitor and make a note of any errors. For feedback, volunteer pairs roleplay conversations for each task. Finally, use the board to correct any errors you heard.

**KEY**

Paula is going to borrow the tent. Paula and John are going to get the passports. Penny is going to buy the plane tickets. John is going to change some money. Tim is going to buy the sleeping bags. Penny is going to find the guidebook.

## EXERCISE 5
To introduce the exercise, discuss how well organised the students are before they go on holiday (e.g. *When do you pack your suitcase? Do you clean the house before you go?* etc). Then direct them to the notes and ask *Can they do all these things before they go?* (No) Direct the class to John and Penny's first decision and ask *What's their first decision?* Elicit *We won't clean the bath now. We'll make some coffee.* If necessary, check the use of the simple future by asking *Are they deciding now? Have they already decided?* and drill the sentences. The students then work in pairs and make similar sentences about the other people. Monitor and correct any errors you hear.

**KEY**

JOHN AND PENNY: We won't sweep the floor. We'll have some breakfast. We won't wash the dishes. We'll shut the windows.
TIM: I won't make the bed. I'll pack my bag.
PAULA: I won't phone my mother. I'll phone for a taxi.

### Extra practice
You can use a party situation (if you didn't use one in Exercise 3). The students work in groups of about eight and decide what they will bring. They then regroup and tell the others what they are going to bring (because they have now decided). Another similar situation is buying presents for the students in the class. Divide the class into groups of four. There must be an equal number of groups. Explain that group A is going to buy presents for the students in group B and vice versa. Each student is going to buy a present for **one** member of the other group. In their groups, they decide who they will buy a present for and what it will be (e.g. *I'll buy a gold necklace for Ariane*). They then join groups and tell each other what they are going to buy for them. They are often very interesting presents.

## EXERCISE 6
**Note**: The italic text in the conversation is connected with Exercise 8.

Write these two questions on the board: *Where is Marco going? When and where are Marco and Teresa going to meet?* Play the tape once and check the students' answers. Next, direct the students to the five functions above the conversation and play the tape again for the students to match the functions and expressions. They compare their answers with their partners and then as a class. If necessary, drill each expression chorally and individually.

**KEY**

a) Would you like to come?
b) Let's meet at the ticket office …
c) Don't worry, I'll be there.
d) I'm going to catch the ten o'clock train.
e) I'll see you at the ticket office.

## EXERCISE 7
Ask two students to read the conversation aloud to the class. Concentrate on the stress and intonation. Students then practise reading the conversation in pairs.

## EXERCISE 8
Divide the class into As and Bs. Establish that the As take Marco's role in the activity and the Bs take Teresa's role. Direct the As to the information on page 27 and the Bs to page 117. To check that they understand the task, ask an A to start the conversation. They should say *I'm going to Oxford on Saturday. Would you like to come?* The students then work in pairs. Make sure they change roles for the second conversation. For feedback, elicit the two conversations, drilling them line by line. If students need more practice, write the conversations on the board with their help. They practise them in pairs as you erase words/expressions until there is nothing left on the board and they are practising from memory.

**KEY**

A: I'm going to Oxford on Saturday. Would you like to come?
B: Oh, yes. I'd love to.
A: Oh, good. I'm going to catch the half past eleven coach. Is that OK?
B: That's fine.
A: Don't be late. It's the only direct coach.
B: Don't worry. I'll be there.
A: Let's meet at the coach stop at quarter past eleven. Or earlier at your flat?

B: Er ... no. I'll see you at the coach stop.

B: I'm going to Glasgow on Sunday. Would you like to come?

A: Oh, yes. I'd love to.

B: Oh, good. I'm going to catch the quarter to ten plane. Is that OK?

A: That's fine.

B: Don't be late. It's the only non-stop flight.

A: Don't worry. I'll be there.

B: Let's meet at the airport café at quarter to nine. Or earlier at your flat?

A: Er ... no. I'll see you at the airport café.

**Extra practice**

1 The students draw a blank diary page for next week and fill in three 'social' activities, e.g. cinema, dancing, etc. They mingle and invite the other students to do these things with them and to arrange a place and time to meet. They should try and make arrangements with a different person for every day.

2 Give each student a picture of an activity and tell them this is what they're doing tonight. They mingle and invite other students to do these things and arrange a time and a place to meet.

### EXERCISE 9

Copy Rita's note onto the board. Establish that the students must listen to check that the note is accurate. Play the tape. Encourage the students to compare answers. If necessary, play the tape again and then check as a class.

**KEY**

Book train ticket for Julia. London – Glasgow Central, Tuesday 14th, 12 p.m. Second class, non-smoking, with a restaurant car.

**TAPESCRIPT**

JULIA: Rita, I want to fly to Glasgow early on the 15th, that's this Wednesday, and come back the same day. Can you make the arrangements, please?

RITA: Wednesday. OK, Julia. The plane's expensive, though. Does Tom know about this?

JULIA: Er, no. Oh, all right, I'll go by train the day before. It's more comfortable, anyway. And I'll find a hotel when I arrive.

RITA: What time do you want to leave?

JULIA: At about midday. A second-class, non-smoking seat on a train with a restaurant car, please.

RITA: OK, I'll see what I can do. Oh, do you want Glasgow Central station?

JULIA: Um, yes, I do. Thanks.

### EXERCISE 10

Direct the students to the timetable and ask them to find which train Rita books. They discuss the exercise in pairs. Then check as a class.

**KEY**

Rita books the half past eleven train from King's Cross.

### EXERCISE 11

Still using the timetable, the students answer the questions about Julia's train. Check on the board.

**KEY**

1 11.30  2 London King's Cross  3 17.19
4 eight times  5 yes

**Extra practice**

Do a roleplay based on booking a train. Divide the class into As and Bs. Direct the As to the timetable in Exercise 10. The Bs will need to decide on a destination and time. Before they begin, brainstorm the questions that the As will need to ask, e.g. *Can I help you? What time would you like to leave?* etc. Monitor and make a note of any errors as they roleplay the conversation. If they need more practice, ask them to change roles. Finally, check which trains they decide to catch and use the board to correct any errors you heard.

### ENGLISH AROUND YOU

Focus students' attention on the cartoon and check that they understand the 'joke'. (The person wants to sit on the only seat that is *not* really free!) Ask if this happens in the students' country/countries. Explain that it is unlikely to happen in Britain as people usually avoid sitting next to anyone else!

## Development

### SPEAKING EXERCISE 1

Direct the students to the picture and discuss what they think Sherry's job is. Do not confirm their guesses yet.

### EXERCISE 2

Write the six actions on the board and refer the students to the pictures. They match the actions and the pictures. To check the exercise, say *Picture 1. Which action?* and elicit their answers. To check that the students fully understand the vocabulary, ask questions, e.g. *Who searches luggage?* (security guards) *Why?* (to check there are no bombs, drugs, etc.) *Who issues the tickets?* (the travel agent) *What*

UNIT THREE

*do you do at the airport?* (check in) *When do you get your seat numbers?* (when you check in) *Where do you change your money?* (bank, bureau de change). Finally, ask students which of the six actions they think Sherry does.

### KEY

1 search bags   2 give seat numbers   3 check in luggage   4 change money   5 issue tickets
6 re-confirm flights

### 📼 LISTENING EXERCISE 3

Play the first part of the tape for students to check which tasks Sherry does.

### KEY

She issues tickets, checks in luggage, re-confirms flights and gives seat numbers.

### TAPESCRIPT

SHERRY
A passenger will step up and tell me which flight they intend to be taking that day – whether they have a ticket or not. If they've not got a ticket I can issue the ticket right there at the ticket counter, re-confirm their itinerary for the round trip, check in their luggage for them, and make sure they're satisfied with their seat selection.

### 📼 EXERCISE 4

Direct the students to the questions for the second part of the recording. Play the tape. The students compare their answers with their partners and then as a class.

### KEY

1  coach/economy class; business class; first class.
2  a) false    b) true    c) false

### TAPESCRIPT

SHERRY
The three classes of service that we offer are coach class, which is the economy class; business class, which is better than coach class, and first class, which is the premium service and the best way to travel.

Each transaction is really different. There's never anything that's um, boring, about the job, and for the most part the people that I come into contact with are really pleasant and the people that I work with at the airport are really pleasant.

### 📼 EXERCISE 5

Indicate the conversations for part three of the tape and establish that students must choose the correct answer for the first one, and supply details for the others. Play the third part. Encourage the students to compare answers and then check as a class.

### KEY

Conversation 1:   1 b)    2 b)
Conversation 2:   3 flight 52   4 K19    5 K6B
Conversation 3:   6 Sunday    7 ten past six
                  8 half past eight

### TAPESCRIPT

**Conversation 1**
SHERRY: Hello. Good afternoon.
PASSENGER: Good afternoon.
S: Would you like to check that piece of baggage?
P: Yes, I would.
S: OK. And your destination?
P: Ontario.
S: Ontario, Canada?
P: No, ... er ...
S: Ontario, California?
P: Yes.
S: All right.

**Conversation 2**
SHERRY: OK. In Chicago the flight number right now, flight 52, is gate K19 ...
PASSENGER: OK.
S: And you will be coming into the airport at gate number K6B so it's only a matter of walking in the same terminal, thirteen gates.
P: OK.

**Conversation 3**
SHERRY: And, er, it's just a one way as of now. Did you want to return also with American Airlines?
PASSENGER: Yes, Sunday travel would be fine.
S: OK. Thanks. In the morning, afternoon or evening?
P: Er, I prefer evening.
S: Prefer evening, OK. That would be our American flight non-stop service out of Vancouver, Sunday night at 6.10 in the evening and you'll arrive back here in San José at 8.30.
P: Perfect.

### READING EXERCISE 6

To introduce the article, establish that the distance between London and Edinburgh is about 800 kilometres. Either discuss as a class or in groups of three the ways of making the journey, e.g. plane, train, etc. and the advantages/disadvantages of each means of transport. Then copy the chart onto the board and students read the article quickly to complete the chart. They compare their answers in their groups of three. Finally, complete the chart on the board with their help.

**KEY**

LONDON — EDINBURGH
Means of transport: taxi, plane, coach
Total time: 3 hours, 45 minutes
Total cost: £138.80

EDINBURGH — LONDON
Means of transport: taxi, train
Total time: 4 hours, 51 minutes
Total cost: £93.70

**EXERCISE 7**
Direct the students to the questions and the article. They discuss their answers in groups and as a class.

**KEY**
1 Trafalgar Square, London and the Scott Monument, Edinburgh.
2 a) King's Cross   b) Waverley   c) Heathrow Airport
3 a) False.   b) False. It was free.   c) True.   d) True.
  e) True.   f) False. It was nearly empty.

**WRITING EXERCISE 8**
If necessary, remind the class of the comparative forms. First, they discuss which way they will travel and why. Then they write the paragraph individually or in groups. Monitor and help. They exchange their writing with another student or group who has written about the same means of transport to check for errors. Finally, find out which means of transport was the most popular.

# Progress check 1

## Vocabulary

### EXERCISE 1
1 walk   2 sit   3 jump   4 queue   5 dance   6 drive

### EXERCISE 2
1c   2f   3e   4b   5g   6h   7a   8d

### EXERCISE 3
1 Japanese   2 German   3 Portuguese   4 Spanish
5 Arabic   6 Bengali

### EXERCISE 4
1 a cook   2 a waiter   3 a receptionist   4 a dentist
5 a mechanic

### EXERCISE 5
1 cheap   2 convenient   3 uncomfortable   4 difficult
5 safe   6 reliable

### EXERCISE 6
difficult – easy   safe – dangerous   uncomfortable – comfortable   reliable – unreliable   cheap – expensive

### EXERCISE 7

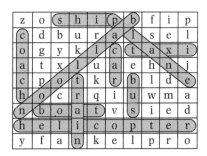

## Grammar and functions

### EXERCISE 8
1 visit   2 is travelling   3 start, finish   4 likes
5 is waiting

### EXERCISE 9
1 How often do your parents eat in restaurants?
2 What are you going to do in July?
3 When did she have/get her first computer?
4 How well can Jim speak Portuguese?
5 Why does she go to discos?

### EXERCISE 10
1 doing   2 to do   3 to buy   4 swimming   5 come

### EXERCISE 11
1 didn't work/'m not working   2 doesn't study
3 aren't playing   4 didn't go   5 can't hear

### EXERCISE 12
1 more comfortable   2 slower   3 better   4 cheaper
5 more expensive   6 worse   7 more convenient
8 older

### EXERCISE 13
1 you like to come?   2 'd love to   3 let's meet
4 'll be

## Common errors

### EXERCISE 14
1 I'*ll* meet you at the station at five.
2 I'm going to go *to* evening classes.
3 How *do* you say 'agua' in English?
4 He visits his parents three *or* four times a year.
5 She can'*t* speak Arabic at all.

UNIT FOUR

## EXERCISE 15
1. We play basketball twice a week.
2. I can write English very well.
3. They do the housework together.
4. She's going to paint her flat next week. *or* Next week she's going to paint her flat.
5. We will book a flight to Berlin.

# 4 Shopping for clothes

## Describing clothes

> **Focus**
> - Clothes
> - Describing clothes
> - Asking about problems
> - Saying what is wrong
> - Adjectives and order of adjectives
> - *Too* + adjective
> - *Not* + adjective + *enough*
> - Further practice: present tenses

### EXERCISE 1
It would be useful to bring into the class examples of the different clothes in the unit (or those which are not usually worn by the students). Write the names of the clothes on the board and make sure students understand each one, by asking them to identify each item. In pairs, they name the clothes in their books. Then point to the words on the board and drill each one chorally and individually. Place the visuals next to their names on the board.

**KEY**

Person 1 is wearing trousers, shoes, a shirt, a tie and a scarf, and he is holding a coat and a pair of gloves.
Person 2 is wearing jeans, a belt, a blouse and a cardigan.
Person 3 is wearing a hat, a dress, tights and sandals.
Person 4 is wearing shoes, jeans, socks, a T-shirt and a jacket. Person 5 is wearing trousers, a T-shirt, a waistcoat, a sweater, boots and earrings.

### EXERCISE 2
Direct the students to the pictures of people in Exercise 1. Play the tape, stopping after the second speaker, and elicit which person is speaking. Then play the complete tape. The students compare their answers with their partners and then as a class.

**KEY**

Stephanie 3   Jo 2   Mark 4   Winston 1   Emma 5

**TAPESCRIPT**

EMMA: So what are you wearing to the fashion show, Stephanie?
STEPHANIE: Well, I'm wearing a big straw hat, a long blue flowery dress, oh, with white buttons, tights and black sandals.
EMMA: And Jo?
JO: I'm wearing tight dark jeans, with a black belt, a long brown cardigan with a zip and a white blouse.
EMMA: What are you wearing Mark?
MARK: Blue jeans, a red T-shirt, white socks and white trainers, a grey sweatshirt and a baggy black jacket.
EMMA: Winston?
WINSTON: Well, I'm wearing grey school trousers, big black shoes and a white shirt, matching green gloves and scarf and a striped tie and I'm holding a black coat.
EMMA: Well, I'm wearing black trousers, this really nice waistcoat with flowers on it, over a white T-shirt and a sweater tied around my shoulders. I'm wearing black boots and gold earrings.

### EXERCISE 3
Check that the students remember the use of the present progressive tense for description by getting them to describe what you are wearing. If necessary, drill each sentence chorally and individually. To demonstrate the task, ask *Who am I describing?* and describe the clothes of one of the students in the class. The students then work in pairs and describe other students in the class for their partner to guess.

**Extra practice**

1. To revise the clothes vocabulary, draw three columns on the board, like this:

   | MEN | WOMEN | BOTH |
   |-----|-------|------|
   |     |       |      |

   The students categorise the items according to who usually wears them.

2. To revise the pronunciation of the clothes vocabulary, write the words on the board. The students must find ones that have the same vowel sound, e.g. *boots, shoes, suit*.

## EXERCISE 4

Display one of your items of clothing or draw one on the board, e.g. a long blue scarf. Ask *What colour is it?* (Blue), *Is it long or short?* (Long) and then get students to describe it to you: *It's a long blue scarf.* Establish that the adjective order is quality + colour + noun and drill the sentence chorally and individually. Check that the students understand the meaning of *tight, loose, ugly, attractive* and point out the other adjectives in the exercise. Then they choose a picture of a person in the book and describe the clothes they are wearing. Monitor and help. For feedback, volunteers describe the pictures to the whole class. (They can do this without naming the person, and other students can search for them. If you do this, restrict the choice to units studied so far.)

## EXERCISE 5
**Background note**
The word **boutique** comes from French. It is used to describe a small shop, or a department in a larger shop, which sells fashionable clothes and accessories for younger people and adult women.

Direct the students to the picture and discuss where Julia is (In a shop/boutique) and what she is doing. (She's trying on a coat) Drill each answer. Then ask *Is the coat OK?* (No) *Why not?* and teach/elicit *It's too small*, providing *too* if necessary. To check the concept, ask *Is the coat the right size for Julia?* (No). Drill the sentence chorally and individually. Then say *Make a sentence with 'big'* and teach/elicit *It's not big enough*. Ask the same concept question, then drill both sentences again.

## EXERCISE 6
Copy this chart onto the board:

|        | PROBLEM |
|--------|---------|
| Coat 1 |         |
| Coat 2 |         |
| Coat 3 |         |

The students listen to the tape and find out the problem with each coat. Then the students check their answers against the ones in the book. Finally, elicit their answers in full sentences and write the problems on the board.

**KEY**

1c It's too small.
2a It isn't long enough.
3b She doesn't like the colour.

**TAPESCRIPT**

ASSISTANT: Can I help you?
JULIA: Yes, I'm looking for a coat. Um, can I try this on?
ASSISTANT: Yes, of course.
JULIA: It's too small. Here.
ASSISTANT: Yes, it is.
JULIA: Do you have any others?
ASSISTANT: Yes, over here.
Try this on. It's your size.
JULIA: Yes, it is my size, but ... it isn't long enough.
ASSISTANT: Right.
JULIA: I prefer longer coats.
ASSISTANT: What about this one? This is your size and it's longer than the other coat. Would you like to try it on?
JULIA: No, I don't like the colour.

## DISCOVERING LANGUAGE EXERCISE 7

**Note**: *Very* cannot be used in front of *too*. If you wish to give emphasis, use *far* or *much*, e.g. *The coat is far/much too long*. It is possible to use *too/enough* in affirmative or negative sentences depending on the meaning, e.g. *It's too warm* (so you feel uncomfortable) or *It isn't too warm* (and you feel comfortable). *It isn't warm enough* (so you feel cold) or *It's warm enough* (and you feel comfortable). Depending on your students' level, it may be necessary to explain this if they ask.

Refer the students back to the three sentences from Exercise 6 on the board and elicit the rules for the position of *too* and *enough*. Then direct them to the three pictures and ask two students to read out the example exchange. The students work in pairs and practise similar exchanges using the pictures.

**KEY**

1. *Too* is placed before the adjective. *Enough* is placed after the adjective.
2. B They're too short./They're not long enough.
   C It's too tight./It's not loose/big enough.

## EXERCISE 8

Direct the class to the adjectives and check that they understand. Ask a student to read out the example sentences. Then ask *Which clothes would/wouldn't you buy?* and elicit some sentences. The students then work in pairs and discuss the ones they like/don't like and the reasons why. Monitor and correct any errors you hear. Then they each write a sentence about one item of clothing they don't like. Either they read their sentences out to the whole class to correct any errors or they read them out in groups of four.

UNIT FOUR

**Extra practice**

1 Write headings on the board that are appropriate to your students, e.g. *seasons, food, sports, TV programmes, cities,* etc. They work in groups of four and discuss which things they don't like and why, e.g. *I don't like winter because it's too cold. I don't like Indian food because it's too hot,* etc.

2 If your students are having problems with the use of *too* and *enough*, prepare about twelve grammatically correct and incorrect sentences, e.g. *It's enough hot in here. This exercise is too difficult,* etc. Divide the class into teams. Each team takes two pieces of paper and writes a large **C** (for correct) on one and a large **W** (for wrong) on the other. Read out your first sentence. Each team quickly confers and then holds up the appropriate card depending on whether they think the sentence is correct or wrong. Give each team a point if they have a correct answer. You can give another point to one team if they correct the sentence and explain why it is wrong.

### STRESS AND INTONATION EXERCISE 9

Write the six sentences on the board and ask the students to copy them into their notebooks. Play the first one and ask *Which two words have heavier stresses?* (this/that) *Why?* (to contrast the two coats). Drill the sentence chorally and individually. Repeat the same procedure with the second sentence (red/green). Then the students work in pairs and underline the two words in the other sentences that they think are stressed. Next, play the tape for them to check their answers. Mark the stressed words in the sentences on the board with the students' help and then drill each sentence.

**KEY**

3 these/those, big/small    4 nice/expensive
5 coat/jacket    6 black/blue

**TAPESCRIPT**

1 I like this coat, not that one.
2 The red one is cheaper than the green one.
3 These shoes are too big, and those are too small.
4 It's a nice dress, but it's too expensive.
5 I want a coat, not a jacket.
6 I like the black jeans. The blue ones aren't long enough.

**Extra practice**

Write this sentence on the board four times, like this: '*She told him to go. She 'told him to go. She told 'him to go. She told him to 'go.* (Use your usual means of marking stress.) Elicit the different meanings, e.g.

'*She told him to go* (not I), etc. and then drill each sentence, giving special stress to the emphatic word.

### EXERCISE 10

Direct the students to the text and pictures and elicit that the man and woman are a married couple. The students read the text and answer the questions. Then they compare their answers with their partners and discuss question 4. Check as a class and discuss what kind of clothes they wear and why.

**KEY**

1 a) She wears a uniform.
  b) She usually wears casual clothes.
2 Jean chooses a lot of his clothes.
3 He wears smarter clothes.

### EXERCISE 11

Refer the students to the questions and get them to ask you. Then they use the same questions to interview each other in pairs. Make sure they make notes. Monitor and write down any errors you hear. Then, using their notes, they tell the class about their partner. If you have a large class, they can give feedback in groups of six. Finally, use the board to correct any mistakes.

## The right clothes

> **Focus**
>
> • Clothes sizes
> • Countries
>
> • Saying what size clothes someone takes
> • Buying clothes
>
> • Superlative adjectives (*-est, most* and irregular forms)
> • Further practice: comparative adjectives (irregular forms)

### EXERCISE 1

Direct the class to the picture of the shop. Ask *What does it sell?* and elicit one or two things and write them on the board. The students then work in pairs and finish the list. Elicit their answers, drill each item if necessary and write them on the board.

**KEY**

It sells shoes, T-shirts, jackets, blouses, shirts and dresses.

### EXERCISE 2

Direct the class to the four T-shirts or draw four

similar ones on the board. Use them to elicit the sizes and drill each one.

**KEY**

S small  M medium  L large  XL extra large

## EXERCISE 3

If you think some of your students may be embarrassed about talking about the size of clothes they wear, draw some simple pictures on the board. Point at a picture and ask *What size T-shirt does he take?* and elicit the answer. Drill the exchange chorally and individually. The students then work in pairs and ask and answer about the pictures/the sizes of clothes they take. Alternatively, you can do this as a mingling activity and the students stand up and interview each other.

## EXERCISE 4

Direct the students to the charts and to the information about Teresa and Marco. Ask *What size shirt does Marco take?* and elicit the example response. Drill the exchange chorally and individually. Then write *jacket: 52* on the board and elicit a similar exchange. The students then work in pairs and do the same with the other information. Monitor and correct any errors. For feedback, volunteer pairs roleplay their exchanges to the whole class. If they are having problems with the form of the present simple or pronunciation of measurements, they can do a 'half-and-half' drill: divide the class into two, half asks the questions and the other half replies using the same information.

**KEY**

What size jacket does Marco take? He takes size 42. What size shoes does Marco take? He takes size 8. What size blouse does Teresa take? She takes size 10. What size dress does Teresa take? She takes size 10. What size shoes does Teresa take? She takes size 6.

### Extra practice

Direct the students to the chart and check that they don't use the same sizes in their countries as in Britain. Then write these prompts on the board: *dresses/suits/blouses, shoes, suits and jackets, shirts.* Point to *shoes* and ask a student *In Britain, what size shoes do you take?*, elicit a reply and drill the response chorally and individually. Divide the students into pairs and they interview each other using the prompts. Monitor and correct any errors you hear.

## EXERCISE 5

Before the students read the dialogue, use the board and pictures to build it orally. Set up the situation of a customer in a shoe shop – use a visual if you have one. Then write a dialogue framework on the board, like this:

CUSTOMER: *black shoes*
ASSISTANT: *size?*
CUSTOMER: *8*
ASSISTANT: *try them on?*
CUSTOMER: *small. 8½ please?*
ASSISTANT: *yes*
CUSTOMER: *fine. how much?*
ASSISTANT: *£24.99*

Display a picture of some shoes and point to the customer's first line. Elicit *I'd like a pair of (black) shoes, please.* Drill the sentence chorally and individually. Then point to *assistant* and elicit the next line of the conversation. Drill both lines and continue using the word prompts and mime. You do not need to write the dialogue on the board. The students then practise the conversation in pairs. Finally, play the tape and the students shadow the conversation in their books.

**TAPESCRIPT**

MARCO: I'd like a pair of black shoes, please.
ASSISTANT: Certainly. What size?
MARCO: Um, eight, I think.
ASSISTANT: Here you are. Would you like to try them on?
MARCO: Yes, please. ... I'm afraid they're too small. Can I try eight and a half, please?
ASSISTANT: Certainly. Here you are.
MARCO: Thanks. They're fine. I'll take them. Oh, how much are they?
ASSISTANT: They're £24.99.

## EXERCISE 6

Direct the students to the picture of the shop and elicit the items of clothing they can see. Next, divide the class into As (customers) and Bs (shop assistants) and get the Bs to look at page 117 for the prices. To demonstrate the task, take the role of a customer and roleplay it with a B student. The students then do the same in pairs. Monitor and make a note of any errors. For feedback, either find out what the customers bought or ask some volunteer pairs to roleplay their conversations for the whole class. Finally, use the board to correct any errors you heard.

### Extra practice

Each student writes a 'stocklist' for their shop. They can only have one of each item from the picture, e.g. one dress – size 42, one blouse – size 46, etc. They decide a price for each item and write it on their list.

UNIT FOUR

They then make a shopping list of four items of clothing that they want to buy for themselves and their own size. (This should be different from their 'stocklist'.) Next, divide the class into shop assistants and customers and the shop assistants sit at their desks/shops. The customers try to buy the clothes they want with the correct size and price. When a shop assistant sells one of their items, they must cross it off their stocklist. They then change roles and repeat the activity.

### 🔊 EXERCISE 7

To remind students of comparisons, draw two coats on the board or display two pictures. Ask *How many coats are there?* (Two) Then write a different price next to each one (e.g. £50, £100) and elicit the different prices. Then ask *What is the difference between the two?* and elicit *The first one is cheaper than the second one.* Drill the sentence chorally and individually.

Then write these questions on the board: *Which jacket does Marco like? Why? What about the price?* Play the conversation and elicit their answers to the questions. (Marco likes the brown one because it's the nicest but it's the most expensive.) Then play the tape again and the students make notes to describe the jacket.

#### KEY

It's brown. It's size 42. It's good quality. It costs £130.

#### TAPESCRIPT

ASSISTANT: Do you like this blue jacket?
MARCO: Yes, it's nice, and I like the green one too. But I think this brown jacket's the nicest. Have you got it in a size, er, 42?
ASSISTANT: Yes, sir. Here you are. Try it on.
MARCO: Thanks ... Oh yes, I like this one very much.
ASSISTANT: I'm afraid it's quite expensive – in fact it's the most expensive jacket in the shop – but it's also the best quality. It really suits you.
MARCO: How much is it?
ASSISTANT: It's £130.
MARCO: Mm. That's OK. Jackets are more expensive in Italy. I'll take it.

### DISCOVERING LANGUAGE EXERCISE 8

**Note:** It is not necessary for this exercise to explain that some two-syllable adjectives take *est* and some take *most*. Others can take either form.

Ask students how many jackets Marco looked at (three), and if they can remember any comparisons between the brown one and the others. If they do, write on the board *It's the nicest.* Copy the chart onto the board and ask the students to copy it into their notebooks. Get them to complete the comparative column and then check as a class on the board. Next, play the conversation again and get them to complete the superlative column. Check as a class. They discuss questions 2 and 3 in pairs and as a class. Establish that usually when there are two things, they use the comparative and when there are more than two, they use the superlative.

#### KEY

1

| ADJECTIVE | COMPARATIVE | SUPERLATIVE |
|---|---|---|
| nice | nicer | (the) nicest |
| cheap | cheaper | (the) cheapest |
| expensive | more expensive | (the) most expensive |
| beautiful | more beautiful | (the) most beautiful |
| good | better | (the) best |
| bad | worse | (the) worst |

2 *good* and *bad*
3 One-syllable adjectives take *the* + adjective + *-est* or *-st* if the adjective ends in *e*, e.g. *nicest*. Adjectives with three syllables or more take *the most* + adjective, e.g. *the most beautiful.*

### EXERCISE 9

Direct the students to the sentences. Together expand the first one and write it on the board. Then they write complete sentences in their notebooks. Encourage them to compare their answers with their partners. Ask them to dictate their sentences to you, and you write them on the board exactly as they say them. Correct any errors as a class.

#### KEY

1 most attractive  2 best  3 worst  4 most difficult
5 longest

### EXERCISE 10

Point to the first sentence on the board and say *I think X is the most attractive American actor.* Encourage some disagreement and then get the students to write five sentences using the same prompts but with their own experiences (*My best friend ..., My worst mistake ..., The most difficult thing about English ..., My longest journey ...*). Then they work in pairs and read out their sentences. Monitor and correct any errors you hear.

### Extra practice

1 Divide the class into groups of four. Give each group a cue card with three or four things to compare in a category, e.g. animals (cobra,

46

cheetah, mouse, dog), famous people, household objects, holidays, etc. Each group produces as many comparisons as possible concerning their prompts. They then regroup and share their comparisons with the others. Alternatively, this can be done as a team activity. Give each team the same prompts and three minutes to brainstorm as many sentences as they can. They read out their sentences – the group with the most correct ones wins ten points. Then they do the same with the other prompts.

2 Lining-up activities can revise comparatives/ superlatives and provide a lively beginning/ ending to the lesson, e.g. the students line up according to age (from youngest to oldest), distance of their homes from the school (nearest to furthest). An alternative to lining up is grouping. Divide the classroom into areas, e.g. the four seasons, and the students stand in the area they like or dislike the most and discuss why. This can be done with types of food, books, sports, etc. depending on what you want to revise.

## EXERCISE 11

Write the eight adjectives on the board and get the students to read the example sentences. In groups of three, they write similar sentences using each adjective. To compare their answers, they either read them out to the whole class or regroup so that they work in groups of four (one student from each of four different groups) and read out their sentences to each other.

## COMPARING CULTURES EXERCISE 12

If necessary, revise the clothes vocabulary from the beginning of the unit. Write the countries on the board and, if necessary, check that the students know them. Next, direct them to the pictures and drill the names of the clothes (see below). In groups, they then match the clothes and the countries and discuss whether they wear the clothes in their own countries. Then discuss as a class.

### KEY

1 kilt / kɪlt /– Scotland  2 kimono / kɪˈməʊnəʊ / – Japan  3 sari / ˈsɑːrɪ / – India  4 sarong / səˈrɒŋ, ˈsærɒŋ / – Indonesia  5 poncho / ˈpɒntʃəʊ / – Peru

## EXERCISE 13

Direct the class to the example paragraph and ask them to read it. They can either write a similar text on their own or with a student of the same nationality. They can then swap texts with each other to check for factual differences. If your students find writing difficult, copy the example paragraph onto the board and underline the parts that they need to change, e.g. *In my country the winter is <u>very cold</u>. I <u>usually</u> wear <u>a sweater, thick trousers and boots</u>*, etc.

# Development

## SPEAKING EXERCISE 1

If necessary, pre-teach/revise *casual, overalls, stylish, uniform, suit, smart*. Refer students to the picture of five people in their book and ask them to deduce each person's occupation from their clothes. They should justify their answer, e.g. *I think 1 is a student. Her clothes are very casual and comfortable.*

Ask students to give as many justifications for their answers as possible, and encourage disagreement and discussion.

## LISTENING EXERCISE 2

Explain that students are going to listen to a British woman doing the same exercise. They must make notes about the woman's choices. Play the first part of the tape, stopping after *I'd say she's a student, that one* and elicit the first choice and reason. Write it on the board. Then play the whole tape. Encourage the students to check their answers in pairs. Then, with the students' help, write the woman's reasons on the board next to their reasons and discuss the differences.

### KEY

1 student – wild hair, casually dressed, quite young
2 gardener – scruffy, dirty boots
3 fashion designer – smart, flash suit, strong body language, in control
4 bus driver – scruffy, uniform, cap with badge
5 business woman – smartly dressed, nice hair-do, looks smart and official

### TAPESCRIPT

OK, well, um, right the girl on the end on the left, um sitting on the floor, she's sort of really casually dressed and she's sort of got quite sort of wild hair, she's quite young, um I'd say she's probably, she could be a play school teacher perhaps, or maybe, maybe a student. Yeah, I'd say she's a student that one. Um OK, right now next to her there's this sort of scruffy chap, with um dungarees on and overalls I suppose they are, and big boots and they're dirty and he's, sort of, he's got a sort of checked shirt on. I'd say he's a labourer of some sort um a builder perhaps, or maybe, he certainly works in the outdoors, a gardener, yes I think he's probably a gardener. OK, now next to him, oh, now he's really smart this chap here, with his legs crossed and this flash suit and his sort of really strong body language taking up all this space. Um, I think he's really in control, he's probably quite artistic, something like, I don't know, a fashion designer maybe, something like that, yeah. He obviously spends a lot of money on clothes anyway. Right, now next to him is this guy with a suit on, sort of, bit scruffy though, a uniform of some sort and this cap with a badge on the front of the cap I'd say, mm, something like, um, is he in transport? Probably something like a bus driver! Maybe, yeah, er yeah I'd say so. Now the last one, the woman on the right. OK, she's really smartly dressed and, and she's got a sort of a nice hair do and she's really sort of, she looks really smart and official, you know, like a sort of business woman, of some sort. Um, she obviously has to dress really well for work every day. Sort of padded shoulders and looks her best. Yeah an executive business woman I'd say! Definitely. No question.

## READING EXERCISE 3
Direct students to the prompts in the exercise and to the photographs of Niki in the article. Ask *What kind of work do you think Niki does?* and elicit their answers. Then they work in groups of three and use the words to make sentences about Niki. Get quick feedback as a class and then they read the article to see if their guesses were correct.

## EXERCISE 4
Indicate the sentences and ask *Is the first sentence true or false?* (False) and correct the sentence as a class. They then do the same with the other sentences.

### KEY
1 False. She doesn't lead the life of a normal American schoolgirl. She is director of her own company and is a multi-millionaire.
2 True.
3 False. She is seventeen.
4 True.
5 True.
6 False. People expect her to eat in expensive restaurants all the time but sometimes she just wants to eat pizzas with her friends.

## EXERCISE 5
Copy the words and phrases onto the board. Do the first one together. Students do the exercise in pairs. Check as a class and write the answers on the board.

### KEY
1 average   2 schoolkid   3 a contract   4 the cover
5 (high school) diploma   6 make-up

## WRITING EXERCISE 6
To introduce the exercise, discuss as a class or in groups the types of clothes students like wearing and don't like wearing and the reasons. Then tell them about one item that you like wearing and why. Next, copy this onto the board:

ITEM: _____ REASONS: _____

and ask them to read the extract from the letter. Check their answers as a class.

Students choose one item that is important to them, make notes about the reasons and discuss their choices in pairs. Then they use their notes to write a short paragraph. They can swap their texts with their partners to check for errors. If your students enjoy displaying their writing, divide them into groups of about eight and give each group a large piece of card/paper and the heading 'Our favourite clothes'. They stick their texts onto the card and then display for the others to read, with pictures if possible.

# 5 The rules of the road

## Problems with vehicles

> **Focus**
> - Traffic signs
> - Parts of a motorbike
>
> - Talking about what is possible or permitted
> - Talking about rules and obligations
> - Explaining a problem
>
> - *Have to/don't have to* + infinitive
> - Further practice: *can/can't* + infinitive

### EXERCISE 1
**Background notes**
Large towns and cities in Britain have strictly regulated parking restrictions because of the large volume of traffic and the need to keep it flowing smoothly. In the centres of towns, parking is usually only allowed in **car parks** or at **parking meters**, although certain restrictions are lifted after about half past six in the evening. Parking restrictions are monitored by **traffic wardens**, who will give the drivers of illegally parked cars **parking tickets**.

This means that the driver will have to pay a **fine**.

**Note**: In this unit *can* is introduced as a way of expressing permission and *can't* for expressing prohibition. The students also learn *have to/don't have to*. At this level it is not necessary to explain the difference between *have to* and *must*, but if students ask about it, point out the use of *have to* here, i.e. for 'rules' imposed by an external authority. *Must* is used more for obligations the speaker imposes on him/herself (or others), e.g. *You must do your homework tonight* (I insist) and *You have to do your homework tonight* (It is a school rule). Native speakers tend to make this distinction less these days.

To introduce the lesson, either display or draw a sign on the board which shows 'no smoking' e.g. 🚭 Point to the sign and ask *Is it possible for you to smoke in the classroom?* (No) *Why not?* (It's a rule) and elicit the sentence *We can't smoke in the classroom*. Then ask *Is it OK for you to use dictionaries?* and elicit *Yes, we can use dictionaries*.

Direct the students to the picture and ask *Do you think everything is OK?* (No). Check they understand *taxi rank*. Write the two questions on the board and play the tape. Encourage the students to check their answers in pairs and then check as a class on the board, writing the answers in full. Finally, play the tape again and the students shadow the conversation in their books.

**KEY**

1 Rita can't park in the taxi rank.
2 She can park in the car park round the corner.

**TAPESCRIPT**

WARDEN: Excuse me.
RITA: Yes?
WARDEN: You can't park here.
RITA: But it's only for a few minutes. I'm waiting for a friend.
WARDEN: This is a taxi rank. You can park in the car park. It's just round the corner.

## EXERCISE 2 DISCOVERING LANGUAGE

Direct the students to the two sentences on the board and ask *Which one is a rule? Which one is a possibility?* Then direct them to the exercise and they match the sentences with the explanations. Check as a class. Drill the two sentences, paying particular attention to the pronunciation of *can* / kən / and *can't* / kɑːnt /.

**KEY**

1 a   2 b

## 📼 EXERCISE 3

To introduce the idea of obligation, ask the students *Do you do your homework every day?* (Yes) *Why?* (It's a rule) *Do you always want to do your homework?* (No) *Why do you do it?* and give/elicit *Because I have to do it*. Then ask *What about a uniform? Is it necessary for you to wear a uniform at school/work?* (No) and elicit *I/We don't have to wear a uniform*.

Next, refer the students to the picture of Rita in Exercise 1 and explain that the conversation with the traffic warden is continuing. Write the two questions on the board. Play the tape. Encourage the students to check their answers in pairs and then write their answers on the board. Check that they have made the transformation from *have to* to *has to*.

**KEY**

1 She has to be at work at nine o'clock.
2 No, you don't have to pay.

**TAPESCRIPT**

RITA: But I have to be at work at nine o'clock.
WARDEN: The car park is very near here and you don't have to pay. Are you going to move or do you want a parking ticket?
RITA: No, no, I'll move. I'm going now. Sorry.

## EXERCISE 4 DISCOVERING LANGUAGE

The students discuss the exercise in pairs. Then check as a class. Drill the two sentences.

**KEY**

1 b   2 a

### Extra practice

If the concepts are still a little unclear, draw this chart on the board:

| OBLIGATION (RULE) | has/have to |
| --- | --- |
| PERMISSION (CHOICE) | can |
| NOT POSSIBLE (FORBIDDEN) | can't |
| NOT NECESSARY | don't/doesn't have to |

Elicit the language students have learnt in this unit to express these ideas and complete the grid as a class. Then the students write sentences which are true about themselves using each modal verb.

### EXERCISE 5

Indicate the pictures and ask *Does car A have to leave now or can it stay?* Elicit *It doesn't have to leave now* and a reason (there is more time on the meter). Then they work in pairs to complete the sentences about the other car. Monitor and help. Get feedback as a class and check the concepts using similar questions to those in Exercise 3.

**KEY**

1 Car A doesn't have to leave now.
2 It can stay here.
3 Car B has to leave now.
4 It can't stay here.

## PRONUNCIATION EXERCISE 6

**Note**: The aim of this exercise is show students that *have to* is pronounced /hæf/ rather than /hæv/, e.g. *I have to* /hæftə/ *go* vs *I have* /hæv/ *a car*, and that the *s* in *has* is pronounced /hæs/ rather than /hæz/, e.g. *He has to* /hæstə/ *stay here* vs *He has* /hæz/ *six children*. The sound changes because *ve* and *s* are followed by the unvoiced consonant /t/.

Copy the two questions onto the board. Ask the students to listen for the sound in *have to* and play the four sentences on the tape. Discuss as a class which sound they hear. Then do the same with *has to*. Then play the tape a second time, stopping for the students to repeat. Drill the sounds.

**KEY**

1 /f/   2 /s/

**TAPESCRIPT**

1  1  Do I have to go?
   2  She doesn't have to park there.
   3  We have to turn here.
   4  They have to use the car park.

2  1  She has to move her car.
   2  He has to do his job.
   3  She has to shop now.
   4  There has to be a rule.

## EXERCISE 7

Copy this dialogue framework onto the board (TW = traffic warden, R = Rita).

TW: *sorry/park here*
R: *few minutes*
TW: *taxi rank/car park/the corner*
R: *work/nine*
TW: *car park/very near/not pay. Move or parking ticket?*
R: *move/now/sorry*

Divide the students into As (Rita) and Bs (traffic warden) and explain that they are going to act out the conversation between Rita and the traffic warden that they heard in Exercises 1 and 3. Elicit the first line to demonstrate the task and then they work in pairs. Monitor and make a note of any errors. Make sure they change roles. For feedback, one pair can act their conversation for the whole class. Finally, use the board to correct any errors.

**Extra practice**

1  In groups, students brainstorm their school rules, using the verbs they have learnt. Check them as a class.

2  Display more signs/word prompts on the board, e.g. *no dogs, keep off the grass, no left turn, 30 kph, camping, litter*. In groups, students write two sentences for each sign, e.g. *Your dog can't come into the restaurant. It has to stay outside.* This makes the students contrast the concepts.

3  Divide the class into groups. Give each group a place (e.g. library, school, prison, aeroplane, beach, etc). They must write a list of rules about the things they can/can't do in these places. Make sure that all the students in the groups write the sentences down. Then regroup them. They read out their sentences and the others guess the place. They can do the same with jobs.

## COMPARING CULTURES EXERCISE 8

Draw a sign on the board which shows 'right turn only' e.g. ⬤ Ask *Do you have to turn right?* (Yes) *Why?* (Because it's a law) Get the students to ask you the question and give a short answer (Yes, I do). Drill the exchange chorally and individually. Then ask *Can you turn left?* (No, you can't) *Why not?* (Because it's a law) Drill this exchange. Do the same with a picture of red traffic lights. *(Do you have to stop? Can you go?)* Next, direct the students to the picture and teach *moped* and *crash helmet*. Copy the chart onto the board and divide the students into pairs. Direct the As to their chart and the Bs to page 118. To demonstrate the task, ask one of the Bs *Do moped riders have to wear crash helmets in the UK?* and elicit the answer. Write *Yes* in the chart on the board. Check that they realise that they use *can* for the last three questions. The As then interview the Bs about the other laws in the UK. Then they ask each other about the laws in their countries. Monitor and make a note of any errors. For feedback, get volunteer pairs to roleplay their exchanges and complete the chart with their answers. Then discuss the differences between the UK and their countries. Finally, use the board to correct any errors you heard.

**KEY**

They have to: wear crash helmets, have a driving licence and be sixteen years old.
They can't: ride on motorways, ride on cycle paths or carry more than one person on the back.

### Extra practice

If your students enjoy talking about laws in their countries, write these prompts on the board: *when/get married? get married/church? do/military service, girls/do military service? how long/military service? when/vote? when/learn to drive? how many tests/do?* The students interview each other in pairs. If you have a multinational class, they can use the prompts as the basis for a class survey.

### EXERCISE 9
**Background note**
In American English **tyre** is spelt **tire**.

If possible, draw a simplified picture of a motorbike on the board. Direct students to the picture of the motorbike in their books. In groups, they name the different parts. Elicit their answers and together label the picture on the board. Drill each item.

**KEY**

1 handlebars   2 seat   3 engine   4 brakes   5 lights
6 indicators   7 petrol tank   8 wheel   9 tyre

### EXERCISE 10
**Note:** Both *could* and *couldn't* are used to make polite requests. The use of the negative makes it more 'persuasive/assertive' and so more difficult to refuse.

Write the question *What's wrong with Alan's motorbike?* on the board and play the tape. Elicit the answer. Then play the conversation again, stopping after each line for students to repeat. Make sure their intonation remains 'polite' especially with *Couldn't you repair it now?* If necessary, ask questions to check the concepts as you go along (e.g. *Can the mechanic look at it now? What does he say he will do? How does he say this?*).

**KEY**

There's something wrong with the brakes.

**TAPESCRIPT**

MECHANIC: Can I help you?
ALAN: Yes. There's something wrong with the brakes.
MECHANIC: What's the matter with them?
ALAN: I don't know. They're not working.
MECHANIC: OK. Leave the bike here and I'll look at it later.
ALAN: Oh. Look, I need it this afternoon. Couldn't you repair it now?
MECHANIC: I'm sorry, I can't. I'm busy at the moment.

### EXERCISE 11
To introduce the exercise, use the pictures to elicit the different problems. Divide the class into pairs and direct them to the instructions and the example exchange. Build up the dialogue and elicit different ways of suggesting a solution, e.g. *OK. Leave it here. I'll look at it later* or *Would you like a new one?* They then roleplay the conversations in pairs. Monitor and make a note of any errors. Make sure they change roles. If you wish, some students can roleplay their conversations for the whole class. Use the board to correct any errors.

### Extra practice

You can extend the exercise by dividing the class into customers and about five/six shop assistants. Give each customer a problem (e.g. a broken glass, shoe has a hole in it, radio not working, etc). They go to each shop to complain and get a solution. They must go to all the shops. To check the activity, find out who was the most helpful shop assistant and who got the best 'solution'.

## On the road

> **Focus**
> - Roads and driving
> - *Had to/didn't have to* + infinitive
> - Further practice: past simple

### EXERCISE 1
Direct the class to the four cartoons and ask *What do you think is happening in each one?* They should not look at the articles. They discuss their ideas in pairs and then as a class. Do not confirm their guesses yet.

### EXERCISE 2
Focus students' attention on the headlines and discuss what they think the articles are about. Before they start reading, establish that the first time they read, it is only for general understanding and that they should read very quickly. Then they read the five articles and, with their partner, match the headlines and cartoons to the article. Check their answers as a class.

## UNIT FIVE

**KEY**

Article 1: cartoon D, headline 4
Article 2: cartoon A, headline 2
Article 3: cartoon C, headline 1
Article 4: cartoon B, headline 3

### EXERCISE 3

Divide the class into As and Bs. Tell the As to read articles 3 and 4, and the Bs to read articles 1 and 2. Then direct the As to the questions about articles 1 and 2 and the Bs to the questions about articles 3 and 4. They use these questions to interview each other. If necessary, teach the more difficult vocabulary: *heart attack, accident, crash (vb)*.

**KEY**

**Article 1**
1  It means 'learner'.
2  Richard is a driving instructor. Jeff is his pupil.
3  He had a heart attack during Jeff's lesson.
4  He had to drive him to hospital (five miles through the city centre) and he had only 90 minutes' experience.
5  He's going to give Jeff free driving lessons.

**Article 2**
1  He drove the wrong way down the fast lane of a motorway at 30 kph.
2  He missed his exit and did a U-turn when he realised his mistake.
3  He had to pay 1,000 DM.
4  He can't drive for a year.
5  He has to take another driving test.

**Article 3**
1  She had her eleventh accident.
2  She painted her car yellow.
3  Because yellow cars have fewer accidents.

**Article 4**
1  Tommy is Sandy and Ken's baby son. Joan is their neighbour.
2  It was in its carrycot on the roof of Sandy and Ken's car. They put it there because Ken had to open the car door.
3  She screamed at Ken.
4  The baby was fine.

### EXERCISE 4
Write this on the board:

| REGULAR PAST TENSE | IRREGULAR PAST TENSE |
|---|---|
| 1 | drive – |
| 2 | do – |
| 3 | lead – |
| 4 | go – |
| 5 | put – |
|   | find – |

Direct the students back to the articles. They work in pairs to find five of the regular forms and the six irregular past tense forms. Check as a class and write their answers on the board.

**KEY**

Regular: saved, realised, contacted, happened, crashed, painted, turned, screamed, stopped.
Irregular: drove, did, led, went, put, found

### DISCOVERING LANGUAGE EXERCISE 5

Direct the students to the first article and ask *What did Jeff have to do?* and elicit *He had to drive Richard to hospital.* Establish that *had to* is used to talk about the past. Then, to elicit *didn't have to*, ask *In the end, Jeff had to pay for his driving lessons, didn't he?* and elicit *No, he didn't have to pay for his lessons*. Drill both sentences.

### EXERCISE 6

Direct the class to the gapped sentences and they complete them with the correct tense of *have to*. Monitor and help. Encourage the students to check their answers in pairs and then as a class. Write their complete answers on the board and highlight the use of the auxiliary, *did/didn't*.

**KEY**

1  These days she often has to work until six o'clock.
2  You don't have to go if you don't want to.
3  I didn't have to move, but I liked the new flat.
4  Do we have to go home now?
5  They had to catch a train because the plane was too expensive.

### EXERCISE 7

Write the words on the board and refer the students to the definitions. Ask them to find the words in the texts and match them with their definitions. Encourage them to check their answers with their partners and then check as a class.

**KEY**

1 c  2 a  3 f  4 d  5 b  6 e

### EXERCISE 8

The students work in pairs to complete the sentences without looking at the text. Then check as a class. If they have made quite a few mistakes, direct them back to the articles. Check they understand the meaning of each verb.

**KEY**

1 had  2 had to  3 drove  4 contact  5 pay  6 take
7 happen  8 paint, painted

## ENGLISH AROUND YOU

Focus students' attention on the cartoon and discuss the situation. Ask about other ways of apologising.

# Development

## SPEAKING EXERCISE 1

Direct the students to the photographs and the three questions. They discuss them in groups of three. Then discuss as a class but do not confirm their answers yet.

## READING EXERCISE 2
**Background note**

The **M25** is the orbital motorway around London. It is always very busy and has a reputation for being dangerous because people drive very fast on it. The **M1** is the major motorway from London to the north of England and is also a very busy road.

To introduce the text, find out if any of the students drive, if they have seen any accidents and if they think people drive well or badly in their countries. As you discuss these things, check that they understand *overtake, a shift, injured*. Then direct the students to the questions and the text. Encourage them to check their answers in their groups. Then check as a class.

**KEY**

1 They each work an eight-hour shift.
2 There are nine to twelve (three to four per shift).
3 He does b and c.
4 People drive too fast, especially when the roads are wet.

## EXERCISE 3

Copy the chart onto the board. Ask students *Can cars use motorways in Britain?* Students look at the text to find the answer. Tick *Cars* in the chart on the board. Students work in pairs to complete the chart. Check by asking students to tell you some of the rules concerning motorways in Britain. Discuss whether the rules are the same in their country.

**KEY**

| Cars | ✓ |
| Lorry drivers | ✓ |
| Pedal cyclists | ✗ |
| Motorcyclists | ? |
| Buses | ✓ |
| Agricultural vehicles | ✗ |
| Pedestrians | ✗ |

## EXERCISE 4

Students look at the diagrams and work out the law for overtaking in Britain. Discuss it, and how it differs (if it does) from the law in their country.

**KEY**

You can only overtake on the right.

## 🎧 LISTENING EXERCISE 5

Direct the students to the three pictures and explain that the radio announcement is about one of them. Play the tape once. Encourage students to check their answers in their groups. If necessary, play the tape again and then check their answer as a class. If your students' English is quite good, draw the diagram on the board, and elicit a description of what happened from the students and draw it on the diagram.

**KEY**

3

**TAPESCRIPT**

A message for drivers going north up the M1. Traffic is not moving at all on the northbound carriageway of the M1 after a major accident involving a lorry and four cars near Northampton, between junctions 15 and 16. Drivers going north have to take the A508 at junction 15 in the direction of Northampton and join the motorway again at junction 16. The other side of the motorway is clear, so no problems for drivers going south. I'll just repeat that message. An accident on the M1 between junctions 15 and 16 is blocking the northbound carriageway. Drivers should take the A508 at junction 15 towards Northampton and rejoin the motorway at junction 16 via the A45 from Northampton. That's all the traffic news for now. Next news at 2 o'clock. Until then, drive carefully.

## SPEAKING EXERCISE 6

Ask your students to draw a picture of an incident they have seen. If they cannot think of anything they have seen or read, they can draw an imaginary incident. They show their picture to their partner,

UNIT SIX

who asks them questions. Monitor and correct any errors you hear. You can extend this activity by regrouping the students and getting each student to explain their partner's incident to the other students in the group.

## WRITING EXERCISE 7
Write the four questions on the board and if necessary, refer the students back to the articles on page 40. They write a short article about their partner's incident. They can give the article to their partner to check for factual and language errors.

### Extra practice
Divide the students into pairs and ask them to sit back to back. One student has an account of a road accident and the other has to draw it. Alternatively use the account to do a 'running dictation'. One student is the 'scribe' and the other is the runner. Put the text on the wall. The runner has to look at the text, remember as much as possible, run to the scribe and dictate what they can remember. The scribe must write it down accurately. The pair with the most accurate text wins.

# 6 How things work

## Victorian inventions

> **Focus**
> - Inventions
> - Talking about function: *for + ing*
> - Giving instructions
> - Imperatives
> - Sequence words: *first, then*
> - *For + ing*

## EXERCISE 1
To introduce the lesson, hold up your copy of *Look Ahead* and ask *What's it for?* Elicit *Learning English* and say *It's for learning English*. Drill the exchange chorally and individually. Do the same with a pen (*It's for writing*) and a dictionary (*It's for learning new words*). Then direct the students to the pictures and encourage some discussion about what the objects are and establish that they were invented in the nineteenth century. Teach *invention/to invent*. Then the students work in pairs to match the two pictures with their descriptions. Check as a class.

### KEY
1 D   2 A

## DISCOVERING LANGUAGE EXERCISE 2
Direct the students back to Picture D, ask *What's it for?* and write their sentence on the board. Elicit the form that comes after *for* (*ing*) and highlight it on the board. Use your examples (book, pen, etc.) from Exercise 1 to elicit more examples of the form and write the students' sentences on the board.

### KEY
*For* is followed by the *ing* form.

## EXERCISE 3
**Note:** Students may have problems with the spelling of the *ing* form. Here are some rules:
- one vowel + one consonant: the final consonant is doubled, e.g. *swim → swimming*.
- vowel + *y*: there is no doubling of the final consonant, e.g. *play → playing*.
- consonant and silent *e*: the *e* is dropped, e.g. *serve → serving*.
- one vowel + two consonants: the final consonant is not doubled, e.g. *climb → climbing*.
- two vowels and one consonant: the consonant is not doubled, e.g. *rain → raining*.

Look at the example with the students and ask one student to do it. Students complete the sentences, then check their answers with their partners. Write the correct sentences on the board. Next, direct them to the pictures and they match the sentences with the pictures. Do not check their answers yet.

### KEY
Example: keeping – picture E
1  washing – picture B
2  printing – picture C
3  serving – picture A

## 📼 EXERCISE 4
Play the tape for the students to check their answers from Exercise 3. Then play the first sentence again and direct them to it on the board. Ask *How do you pronounce 'for'?* Elicit that it is the weak form /ʃər/ rather than the strong form /ʃɔːr/. Play the next three sentences. Then ask *Why is it weak?* and establish that it is because *for* is a preposition and it is in the middle of the sentence. Play the tape again, stopping to allow the students to repeat. Then write the two questions from Exercise 4 on the board and tell the students to listen to the pronunciation of *for*. Play the tape and

encourage them to discuss the pronunciation in pairs. Then discuss as a class the reasons for the change in the pronunciation of *for*.

**KEY**

*For* is usually unstressed and therefore pronounced /fə$^r$/. At the end of a sentence, it is pronounced /fɔː$^r$/ because it is stressed.

**TAPESCRIPT**

1 Example: It's for keeping your moustache dry.
2 It's for washing yourself.
3 It's for printing advertisements on the street.
4 It's for serving food.

What's it for? What's that for?

## EXERCISE 5

Divide the students into pairs and direct them to the four pictures. Check that they know the names of the objects. To demonstrate the task, ask a student *What's the first object for?* and elicit *It's for opening bottles*. If necessary, drill the exchange. Then the students work in pairs and take turns to ask and answer about the pictures. Finally, they write a sentence about each object. To check students' answers, write the sentences on the board with their help.

**KEY**

1 A bottle opener is for opening bottles.
2 A coffee maker is for making coffee.
3 A fax machine is for sending or receiving faxes.
4 A camera is for taking photographs.

## EXERCISE 6

Ask two students to read out the example exchange. Then quickly brainstorm as a class other objects they can see in the classroom and write them on the board. They then work in pairs to ask and answer about the objects. Monitor and correct any errors. For feedback, point to the objects on the board and ask pairs to roleplay exchanges for the whole class.

### Extra practice

1 Bring in a few household objects or pictures, e.g. knife, saucepan, towel, tennis racket, etc. (or the students can find pictures). Display them in the classroom and the students work in pairs and ask and answer about them using the language from the exercise. This is more fun if you can find unusual household gadgets, e.g. a garlic press.

2 Prepare small pictures of household/leisure objects (as in the first activity). The students work in groups of three or four. They place the cards in a pile face down on the desk. The first student picks up the top card and describes the use of the object without saying its name, e.g. *It's for cooking food. It's for heating water.* The student who guesses the object correctly takes the card. Then the next student does the same. The aim of the exercise is to 'win' the most cards.

3 Write a list of ten objects for a weekend camping trip on the board, e.g. penknife, bottle opener, sleeping bag, etc. The students work in groups and choose four objects that are the most important. They compare their choices as a class. This should also revise comparatives / superlatives as well as *It's for + ing*. You can change the activity according to the interests of your students, e.g. an evening at the disco, a day at the seaside.

## EXERCISE 7

Direct the students to the text and ask them to match it with the correct picture. Check their answer as a class. Then write the four vocabulary items on the board and get the students to identify them in the picture. Check as a class.

**KEY**

The instructions describe Picture B.

### Extra practice

The students work in pairs. One reads out the text from Exercise 7, the other 'does' the actions. This will help students to distinguish the instructions from the other information in the text and also check understanding of the vocabulary.

## DISCOVERING LANGUAGE EXERCISE 8

**Note**: In formal English *do not* is used to express negative imperatives but in spoken and informal written English, *don't* is more common. Imperatives can often sound rude or abrupt so it is important that the students practise a 'polite' intonation (rising on the imperative rather than falling) and that you emphasise that they are used in this unit for giving instructions. For requests, suggestions, invitations and advice, they should use the language that is presented in *Look Ahead 1* and *2* rather than the imperative form.

Write *instructions* and *negative instructions* on the board and refer the students to the text. Get them to read the first sentence. Elicit that *pull down* is an instruction and write it on the board under instructions. The students then work in pairs and

UNIT SIX

do the same with the other imperatives in the text. Write their answers on the board and discuss how the imperative is formed.

**KEY**

Instructions: pull down the lever, climb in, hold the rails, put your feet on the pedals, press down, climb out, push the lever up.
Negative instructions: don't get in, don't press too hard.
The imperative form of the verb is formed with the base form of the verb (the infinitive without *to*) and the negative imperative is formed with *don't* + the base form of the verb.

**Extra practice**
To revise imperatives, draw some simple stick pictures on card/paper of people in different positions, as in the illustration below.

Give each student two or three pictures. They work in pairs and give instructions to their partners in order to put them in the same position as in their picture, e.g. *Put your left hand on your head and your right hand on your leg.*

### EXERCISE 9
Copy the verbs onto the board and check that the students understand their meaning. Next, direct the students to Picture A. They work in pairs or groups of three to write the instructions for the people who are going to use the train. Monitor and help. Then two groups swap texts to compare. Finally, get the students to dictate their texts to you and write a model text on the board.

**KEY**

Put the food on the train in the kitchen and start the train. The train moves into the dining room. Stop the train when it reaches the table. Take the food and then send the train back to the kitchen.

### EXERCISE 10
Direct students to the two questions. They discuss them in pairs. Monitor and make a note of any errors you hear. Then get feedback as a class and discuss which are the most/least practical of the inventions and why. Finally, use the board to correct the errors.

### EXERCISE 11
Hold up a watch and discuss when they think watches were invented (over a hundred years ago). Then, either in groups or as a class, the students brainstorm other things that were invented over a hundred years ago. Write them on the board.

### EXERCISE 12
Ask each student to choose one of the objects on the board and make notes on how it is used. Students then use the notes to give instructions to their partner. Make sure they work with a partner who has chosen a different object and that they keep their notes. They will need them later in the unit.

## Machines around us

**Focus**
- Machines and equipment
- Controls

- Explaining how things work
- Making offers
- Further practice: giving instructions

- Phrasal verbs (separable)
- Position of object pronoun
- Sequence word: *next*
- Further practice: imperatives

### EXERCISE 1
Direct the class to the picture of Karl and the instructions. Elicit who he is and where he is. Next, direct them to the conversation and the three pictures. Play the tape, stopping after 'thermostat', and check the first answer. Then play the complete conversation. Check their answers as a class.

**KEY**

1 C  2 B  3 A

### EXERCISE 2
**Note**: A *knob* is a round button which you *turn*; a *button* is something you *press* and a *switch* is moved *up/down* to operate something electric.
Write the words *button*, *switch* and *knob* on the board and ask the students to identify them in the pictures. Then ask *What's the button for?* and elicit *It's for turning on the TV*. Drill the answer chorally and individually. Do the same with *switch* and *knob*.

Next, copy the grid onto the board and do *turn* as an example with the class. They then work in pairs and complete the grid. Discuss their answers as a class and complete the grid on the board. (Some students may point out that lights *with dimmer switches* can be turned up and down. Accept 'yes' answers to this question.)

**KEY**

|  | TURN | TURN ON/OFF | TURN UP/DOWN | PRESS |
|---|---|---|---|---|
| the heating the TV the radio | no | yes | yes | no |
| the lights | no | yes | no | no |
| the button the switch | no | no | no | yes |
| the knob | yes | no | no | no |

**Extra practice**
To revise the verbs, read out these prompts: *What do you do if you can't hear the TV/you want to listen to the radio/the room is dark/you want to listen to the answerphone/you want to bake a cake/you want to have a bath/your cake is ready/your bath is almost full*, etc. Pause after you have read each prompt and the students write down the action, e.g. *You turn it up.* They then check with their partners and as a class. You can also use these prompts for students to test each other in pairs or teams.

### DISCOVERING LANGUAGE EXERCISE 3
Write the question on the board and discuss the exercise as a class.

**KEY**

*You* refers to a person. It is the impersonal *you*, i.e. it refers to people in general, not the listener specifically.

### EXERCISE 4
Copy this onto the board:
A: the heating, TV, radio, lights
B: button/switch/knob
Divide the students into As and Bs and direct them to their roles on the board. Ask a pair to read out the example exchange and point to the prompts on the board. The students then use these prompts to practise similar exchanges in pairs. Monitor and make a note of any errors. For feedback, get volunteer pairs to roleplay their exchanges. Finally, use the board to correct any errors you heard.

**KEY**
How do you turn on/off the heating? You turn this knob.
How do you turn on/off the television? You press this button.
How do you turn up/down the television/the radio? You turn this knob.
How do you turn on/off the radio? You turn this knob/press this button.
How do you turn on/off the lights? You press the switch.

### EXERCISE 5
Try to bring in some pictures of machines. Brainstorm the machines the students can see in the classroom and your pictures and make a list of them on the board. Then direct students to the example exchange and ask two students to read it out. If necessary, drill the exchange chorally and individually. Students then work in pairs to ask and answer about the machines. Monitor and make a note of any errors. For feedback, get volunteer pairs to roleplay their exchanges for the class. Finally, use the board to correct any errors you heard.

### EXERCISE 6
Refer the students back to Karl in the hotel room and ask *What do you think he did when the porter left the room?* Play the first sound and write their sentence on the board. Then play all the sounds, stopping after each one to give the students time to write a sentence. They check their answers in pairs. Write the answers on the board with their help.

**KEY**

2 He turned up the radio.
3 He turned on the main light.
4 He turned off the main light.
5 He turned off the heating./He turned down the heating.

**TAPESCRIPT**

1 Karl: A bit of music ...
2 Karl: Hmm. It's not loud enough.
3 Karl: Now, where's the main light switch? Ah ...
4 Karl: No, I don't need that. It's not very dark.
5 Karl: Oh, it's too hot now. Now, where's that thermostat?

### DISCOVERING LANGUAGE EXERCISE 7
**Note**: At this level it is not necessary for your students to know that these multi-word verbs are formed with a verb + particle (preposition or adverb), but the position of the object is important.

If your students enjoy identifying mistakes, copy the eight sentences on the board. Get them to work

UNIT SIX

in pairs and identify the two sentences which are incorrect. Then they discuss the rule in pairs and as a class.

**KEY**

The *noun* can go either *between* the verb and the particle, e.g. *Turn the radio on*, or *after* the verb and the particle, e.g. *Turn on the radio*. The *object pronoun* must be placed *between* the verb and the particle, e.g. *Turn it on*.

### EXERCISE 8

Copy the sentences onto the board and get the students to copy them into their notebooks. Play the first sentence, stop and mark the main stresses on the board with the students' help. Then play the other sentences, stopping to allow the students time to mark the stress. They then check their answers with their partners and as a class on the board. Finally, play the tape again, stopping after each sentence for the students to repeat.

**KEY AND TAPESCRIPT**

Turn it off.
Turn off the radio.
He turned off the radio.
He turned the radio off.
Turn it up.
Turn up the heating.
She turned up the heating.
She turned the heating up.

**Extra practice**

The aim of this activity is to give some controlled oral practice of the stress and intonation patterns. Copy the chant below and give one copy to each student. Divide the class into pairs.

First, students practise the dialogue in pairs. Then the As read together and the Bs answer together. Practise this a few times, concentrating on the stress, rhythm and intonation. Then write the dialogue on the board with the students' help and erase two words from each line (not key words). Students do the chant as a class. Continue erasing words until nothing is left and the students can do the chant from memory.

**CHANT**

| A | B |
|---|---|
| Turn the radio up. | What? |
| Turn the radio up. | Why? |
| I can't hear it. | What? |
| I can't hear it. | Oh right.(*pause*) Turn the radio down. |
| What? | Turn the radio down. |
| Why? | It's too loud. |
| Why? | It's too loud. |
| Oh right.(*pause*) Turn the TV up. | What? |
| Turn the TV up. | Why? |
| It's too quiet. | What? |
| It's too quiet. | No it isn't. It's just right. |

### EXERCISE 9

It may be necessary to revise the use of the simple future for making offers. If possible, turn off the lights in the classroom and say *Is it OK? Can you see?* Elicit the problem (I can't see). Then say *I'll turn the lights on*. If this is not possible, use the cassette recorder, turning the volume very low. Ask questions to check that students understand the concept of the simple future used to make offers, e.g. *Who's going to turn on the lights?* (You) *Do I want to?* (Yes, it's an offer). Drill the exchange chorally and individually. Then direct the students to the pictures and get two students to read the example exchanges. They then do the exercise in pairs. Make sure they change roles. Monitor and make a note of any errors. To check their answers, select pairs to roleplay their exchanges for the whole class. Make sure they use the pronoun correctly, i.e. if A mentions the TV, it's natural for B to use the pronoun rather than repeat the noun. Finally, use the board to correct any errors you heard.

**KEY**

1  A: It's very hot.
   B: I'll turn the heating down./I'll turn down the heating.
2  A: I can't hear the radio./The radio is too quiet.
   B: I'll turn it up.
3  A: I can't study./The television is too loud.
   B: I'll turn it off./ I'll turn off the television.
4  A: I can't see./It's too dark.
   B: I'll turn the light on./I'll turn on the light.

### EXERCISE 10

Direct the students to the picture and discuss what the object is for. Use the picture to check that the students know *lens cap*, and *eject button*. Students work in pairs to write instructions on how to use it. Make sure they both write the instructions. Monitor and help. If you wish, get quick feedback but do not confirm their answers yet.

### EXERCISE 11

Play the tape, stop after Rosie's first instruction and allow the students to make any corrections to their first instruction. Check whether any students used the sequencers *First*, *Next*, etc., and ensure that they use them in their corrections. Then play the whole tape, stopping after each instruction for the students to edit their notes. They then check their answers in pairs. If necessary, play the tape again. To check their answers write the instructions on the board with their help.

### KEY

First, press the switch and turn the power on. Next, take off the lens cap. Then hold the camera up to your eye and press the red button. Then, when you finish your video, press the eject button and take out the cassette.

### TAPESCRIPT

ALAN: So how does this work?
ROSIE: It's easy. I'll show you. There's a cassette in the camera, OK? First, press this switch here and turn the power on.
ALAN: Right.
ROSIE: Next, take off the lens cap so you can see.
ALAN: Uh-uh.
ROSIE: Then hold the camera up to your eye and press the red button.
ALAN: It's recording! That's easy. And when I take my finger off the button, it stops recording! Does it focus automatically?
ROSIE: Yes, it does. Then, when you finish your video, press the eject button.
ALAN: ... and take out the cassette. Lovely. Thanks.

### COMPARING CULTURES EXERCISE 12

The students read the text about Britain. If necessary, write these questions on the board before they read to check their understanding: *When do people in Britain use video cameras? Why do people use video cameras?* Then they discuss what happens in their countries in groups or as a class.

### EXERCISE 13

Refer the students back to the notes they made about their invention in Exercise 12 on page 45. They write instructions for its use. Monitor and help. If two students have chosen the same invention, they can write their instructions together.

### Extra practice

If you wish to extend this activity, divide the class into groups of four (A, B, C, D) and each group into pairs (A/B, C/D). Each student dictates the instructions to his/her partner, who writes them down. They can only say each instruction twice. Then regroup the students (A/C, B/D) and this time they dictate their previous partner's instructions to their new partner. Finally, regroup the students a third time so that they compare their texts with the student who originally wrote the instructions (A/D, B/C). As the grouping can be quite complicated, give each student a piece of paper with their letter on it to make sure they know which letter they are. Each time you regroup the students, just call out the letters. This activity provides them with useful practice for speaking, listening and writing.

### ENGLISH AROUND YOU

Direct students' attention to the cartoon and ensure that they understand by asking *Where is the child? What does he want to know? What happens if he presses the button?*

## Development

### SPEAKING EXERCISE 1

Write the three questions on the board and direct the students to the pictures. They discuss the questions in groups of three and then as a class. Confirm what Bronco is doing in the pictures (question 1) but not their other answers.

### KEY

1 He's acting in a film.

### LISTENING EXERCISE 2
**Background notes**

The films that Bronco mentions are all 'action/adventure' films. **Sean Connery** /ʃɔːn ˈkɒnərɪ/ is a Scottish film actor who is especially famous for playing James Bond. **Robert de Niro**, /ˌrɒbət də ˈnɪərəʊ/, **Charles Bronson**, /tʃɑːlz ˈbrɒnsən/, **Sylvester Stallone** /sɪlˌvestə stəˈləʊn/ and **Arnold Schwarzenegger** /ˌɑːnəld ˈʃwɔːtsənegə/ are all American film actors. **Richard Harris** /ˌrɪtʃəd ˈhærɪs/ is an English film actor.

Direct the students to the three questions and play the tape once. They check their answers with their partners. If necessary, play the tape again and then check as a group. Finally, compare the things Bronco says he does in his job (question 3, Exercise 1) with their ideas from Exercise 1.

### KEY

1 He's a stunt man. (He does fights, jumps off and on trains, falls off buildings, falls down stairs.)
2 a, c, d
3 a, c, d, f, g, h

UNIT SIX

**TAPESCRIPT**

INTERVIEWER: What do you do, Bronco?
BRONCO: I'm a stunt man by trade. That means I fall off horses, I get shot, blown up – all things like that in movies and television. I've worked in quite a lot of films – all the Indiana Jones series, *Rambo III*, *Total Recall*, and such. So I work with a lot of stars, including Sean Connery, Robert de Niro, Charles Bronson, Sylvester Stallone, Arnold Schwarzenegger, Richard Harris, and so on.
I: So what kind of stunts do you do?
B: All kinds of stunts, really. I do fight scenes, jumping off trains, jumping onto trains, falling off buildings, falling down stairs and so on.

## READING EXERCISE 3

Pre-teach *cattle ranch* and *rodeos*. Write a–i in a list on the board and direct the students to the events. They read the text and put the events in the correct order. Encourage them to check their answers in pairs and then check them as a class on the board.

**KEY**

a 7   b 4   c 9   d 5   e 1   f 2   g 8   h 6   i 3

## SPEAKING EXERCISE 4

To introduce the exercise, discuss with the class if they know/have seen the film *Robin Hood, Prince of Thieves* and what they thought of it. Use the pictures to teach *cable*, *gallop* and *arrow*. Revise *harness* from Unit 1. Then they work in pairs to discuss the order of the pictures and match the pictures and the captions. Get quick feedback and write all their suggested picture sequences on the board but do not confirm their answers yet.

**KEY**

1 – picture C, caption d)      4 – picture D, caption c)
2 – picture F, caption f)       5 – picture E, caption e)
3 – picture B, caption a)      6 – picture A, caption b)

## LISTENING EXERCISE 5

Play the tape, stopping after 'I put a harness on' and establish that Picture F shows the first action. Then play the complete tape. Finally, check answers and write the correct sequence on the board.

**TAPESCRIPT**

INTERVIEWER: Can you describe one particular stunt and how it works?
BRONCO: Yes, there was one in *Robin Hood, Prince of Thieves*, where I had to be shot off a horse with an arrow. So in order to do this, I put a harness on, fixed a cable to the harness from a tree, about twenty-five yards of cable. I got on my horse, remembering that the arrow was fixed on my chest and when I lift my arm the arrow pops up. So I gallop straight to the end of the cable, which stops me in mid-air. The horse gallops on, the arrow pops up and I hit the ground.

## WRITING EXERCISE 6

Refer the students back to the captions and write the four sequencers on the board. Choose a student to read out the beginning of the text and write it on the board. Then divide the students into pairs/groups and they write about the stunt. Remind them to use the past tense and sequencers. Monitor and help. The groups either swap texts to correct them or dictate their texts to you and together you write a model text on the board.

**KEY**

(Other uses of the sequencers are possible.) First, he tied a cable to a tree. Then he put on a harness and fixed the other end of the cable to his harness. Next, he got on his horse. After that he galloped to the end of the cable. He reached the end of the cable and it stopped him in mid-air. The horse galloped on and he fell off. Then the arrow popped up from his chest and he hit the ground.

**Extra practice**

Elicit this mime story from the students. As you elicit each line, drill it and then get the students to repeat the story from the beginning. Students then retell the story in pairs. Finally, they dictate the story to you and you write it on the board exactly as they say it. Encourage peer correction. *I was asleep in bed. I woke up suddenly. I turned on the light. It was four o'clock. I turned on the radio. I couldn't hear anything. I turned the knob. I couldn't hear anything. I turned it off. I heard a noise. I went downstairs. Somebody was in the living room! I opened the door. I saw ... the television! It was on. I pressed the button and went back to bed.*

# Progress check 2

## Vocabulary

**EXERCISE 1**
1 socks   2 a tie   3 earrings   4 a dress   5 a belt
6 gloves

**EXERCISE 2**
1 No, they aren't. They're loose.
2 No, it isn't. It's beautiful.
3 No, they aren't. They're his casual clothes.
4 No, they aren't. They're dry.

**EXERCISE 3**
1 seat   2 handlebars   3 mirror   4 brake   5 lights
6 wheel   7 tyre

**EXERCISE 4**
1 pull   2 turn on   3 press   4 turn up   5 push

## Grammar and functions

**EXERCISE 5**
1 the oldest   2 the most dangerous   3 the highest
4 the worst   5 the most beautiful   6 the best
7 the most expensive   8 the most important

**EXERCISE 6**
1 The roads are too busy.
2 The houses are too old.
3 The houses aren't large enough.
4 The area isn't quiet enough.
5 The traffic is too noisy.
6 The streets are too dirty.

**EXERCISE 7**
1 What size are you/do you take?
2 Would you like to try it on?
3 How much is it?/How much does it cost?
4 I'll take it.

**EXERCISE 8**
1 True   2 True   3 False. You can leave a tip if you want to.   4 False. You can pay by credit card.   5 True

**EXERCISE 9**
1 do the teachers have to   2 didn't have to   3 had to
4 don't have to   5 Did you have to

**EXERCISE 10**
1 drove   2 did   3 led   4 went   5 saved   6 put
7 found   8 took   Saved is regular.

**EXERCISE 11**
1 What's it for?
2 How do you turn the heating on/up?
3 How does it work?
4 What's the matter with it?
5 Can I park here?

**EXERCISE 12**
First, write your letter. Then/Next, put it in a stamped, addressed envelope. Next/Then, put the letter in a letter box.

## Common errors

**EXERCISE 13**
CUSTOMER: Are you *a* mechanic?
MECHANIC: Yes. Can I help you?
C: There's something wrong *with* the lights on my car.
M: What's the matter with them?
C: I don't know. They *are* not working. Can you look *at* them now?
M: No, I *am* busy at the moment.

**EXERCISE 14**
1 I take size six shoes.
2 Look at those beautiful brown sandals!
3 It's the most expensive suit in the shop.
4 This coat is not long enough.
5 Here's the video recorder. You turn it on here.

**EXERCISE 15**
I think the best – and the oldest – thing that I have is some/a pair of brown leather trousers. They are comfortable and they suit me. They weren't too/very expensive. I bought them from a friend and they cost only a hundred francs.

# 7 Getting around town

## Sightseeing

> **Focus**
> - Waxworks
> - Taxis
> - Tipping
> - Describing manner
> - Adverbs of manner (-*ly* and irregular forms)

## EXERCISE 1

**Background note**
**Joan Collins** /ˌdʒəʊn ˈkɒlɪnz/ is an English actress who has appeared in many films. She is famous for playing the part of Alexis Carrington in the American soap opera *Dynasty*. **Paul Gascoigne** /pɔːl ˈgæskɔɪn/ is an English footballer, also known as **Gazza** /ˈgæzə/. He now plays for Lazio, Italy. He is famous for crying after scoring a goal in the 1990 World Cup. **Anthony Hopkins** /ˌæntəni ˈhɒpkɪnz/ is an English actor who has appeared in many films. He is particularly renowned for his performance in *The Silence of the Lambs*, for which he won an Oscar. **Madame Tussaud's** is pronounced /ˌmædəm tʊˈsɔːdz/.

To introduce the reading text, write *Madame Tussaud's* on the board and find out what the students know about it. Discuss as a class if they have similar museums in their countries, what kinds of people they have in these places, etc. Pre-teach *waxwork* and *wax models*. Next, direct students to the pictures. In pairs they name the famous people. Check as a class.

**KEY**

1 Anthony Hopkins   2 Paul Gascoigne ('Gazza')
3 Joan Collins

**Extra practice**
Write the names of eight famous people who your students will know on the board, e.g. a politician, a pop singer, an actor, Einstein/famous scientist, Marie Curie/famous doctor, etc. Tell students that they (i.e. the students) work for a waxwork museum and they have enough money to make models of four of the people on the board. They work in small groups and decide which four models should be made, giving reasons for their decisions. They compare their answers with the other groups. This revises comparatives and superlatives.

## EXERCISE 2

Direct students to the questions and to the article about Madame Tussaud's. First they read it, answer the questions and then check their answers in pairs. Next, check as a class and write their answers on the board. Highlight the use of the prepositions in the first five answers.

**KEY**

1 She was from Paris.
2 She opened the London museum in 1835.
3 They are made of wax.
4 It takes about six months to make a model.
5 They come from the celebrity/famous person.
6 They replace the models when the celebrities are no longer popular, because it's important that people recognise them.
7 They are planning to show figures that can walk and talk.

**Extra practice**
If your students need further revision of prepositions, copy this 'Find someone who' questionnaire onto the board. You can change the prompts according to your students. The students mingle and interview each other. They write the names of the people next to the prompts which are true for them.

| FIND SOMEONE WHO: | NAME |
| --- | --- |
| 1 takes about one hour to do their homework. | Naomi, Pablo |
| 2 was born in 1971. | |
| 3 comes from a village. | |
| 4 comes from a large city. | |
| 5 has a birthday in June. | |
| 6 has a watch made of gold. | |
| 7 goes dancing on Fridays. | |
| 8 goes shopping at the weekend. | |

## EXERCISE 3

Copy the explanations in the Students' Book onto the board. Students work in pairs to find the words in the text. Check as a class on the board.

**KEY**

1 exhibition   2 a team   3 a sculptor / ˈskʌlptəʳ /
4 a celebrity

## DISCOVERING LANGUAGE EXERCISE 4

To introduce the language, draw or display pictures of two people and write *five words a minute* next to one and *forty words a minute* next to the other picture. Point at the first picture and ask *How fast does this person type?* Elicit *He types slowly*. Drill the sentence chorally and individually. Do the same with the second picture and elicit *He types quickly*. Drill both sentences. You can mime other things, e.g. walk quickly/slowly, speak softly/loudly, if the students need more practice. Then copy the chart onto the board and they work in pairs to complete the chart with adverbs from the text. Check as a class and discuss the rule for the formation of regular adverbs from adjectives.

**KEY**

| REGULAR | | IRREGULAR | |
|---|---|---|---|
| Adjective | Adverb | Adjective | Adverb |
| slow | slowly | good | well |
| careful | carefully | fast | fast |
| quick | quickly | | |

Regular adverbs are formed from adjectives by adding *-ly* to the adjective.

## EXERCISE 5

Direct the students to the exercise and copy the adverbs onto the board. Make sure students realise that there are more adverbs than sentences and that more than one may be possible for some answers. They complete the exercise and check their answers with their partners. Check as a class.

**KEY**

1 carefully/well  2 beautifully  3 well  4 easily/fast
5 quietly

## EXERCISE 6

Direct the students back to the adverbs on the board. Say *She sings ...* and get the students to complete your sentence with one of the adverbs, e.g. *well, beautifully, badly*. They then work in pairs to write ten sentences, one with each of the adverbs. Encourage the pairs to compare their sentences.

**Extra practice**

1 Write these prompts on the board: *cook? drive? work? speak? walk? sleep? sing? write?* Make sure students know the question form *How do you* + verb? (e.g. *drive*). They work in pairs and interview each other. Monitor and supply adverbs as needed, e.g. *speak clearly, drive carelessly, sleep lightly/deeply*.

2 Give each student a cue card with a verb and an adverb on it, e.g. walk slowly, shake hands slowly, drink a cup of tea sadly, ask politely, drive dangerously, write a letter quickly, etc. Each student mimes their action and the others guess what it is. If you have a large class, divide the students into groups of six or eight.

## EXERCISE 7

Erase some of the adverbs from the board to leave only those ending *-ly*. (See the tapescript below.) Make sure that students have copied them into their notebooks. Play the first one, stop the tape and mark the stress together. Then play all the adverbs, pausing after each one for the students to mark the stress. Encourage them to check their answers in pairs. Then get the students to say the words to you and mark the stress on the board according to their pronunciation. Encourage peer correction if any are incorrect. Drill each adverb if necessary. Finally, discuss as a class the stress rule for adverbs ending *-ly*.

**KEY AND TAPESCRIPT**

'beautifully  'dangerously  po'litely  'easily  'badly
'carefully  'quietly

The adverb retains the same stress as the adjective; the suffix *-ly* is never stressed.

## EXERCISE 8

The aim of this listening exercise is to introduce the topic of taxis and tipping, which is continued in Exercises 9, 10 and 11. Write the three questions on the board. Do not pre-teach *tip* as the meaning is made clear in the conversation. Play the tape once. The students check their answers in pairs. If necessary, play the tape again and then check as a class.

**KEY**

1 They are black.
2 It is the extra money you give to taxi drivers.
3 They usually expect about ten per cent (of the fare).

**TAPESCRIPT**

JULIA: Right. What do you want to do now, Karl?
KARL: I'd better get back to the hotel. I'm meeting someone this evening.
J: Oh, OK. How are you going to get back?
K: I think I'll take a taxi. Do you know where I can get one?
J: Oh, just wait by the side of the road. Taxis just drive past. I'll wait with you.
K: OK. Thanks. Um, are all the taxis in London black?
J: Yes. Well, nearly all of them. Is this your first time in a London taxi?
K: Yes, it is. Do you give extra money to taxi drivers here?
J: You mean a tip? Oh, yes. They usually expect about ten per cent.
K: Yes, it's the same in Germany.
J: Oh, look, there's one. Taxi!

## COMPARING CULTURES EXERCISE 9
**Background notes**

There are two types of taxi in most large British towns. There is the black cab – the licensed, registered taxi service. These can be stopped on the

UNIT SEVEN

street. They have a yellow *For hire* sign. If it is lit, they are available for hire. Once they have stopped, they have to take the passenger anywhere within six miles, and they have to charge the amount shown on the meter. The other type of taxi is the minicab – these are people with private cars who work for a minicab company. They can be hired by telephoning the company; they cannot be hailed on the street. They do not have meters, so a price can be negotiated before the journey, or the driver states a price at the end of the journey.

Direct students to the statements. Tell them that they are true for London black cabs. The students then discuss the statements in groups to decide whether they are true about their country/ countries. Discuss the answers as a class.

### EXERCISE 10
Direct the class to the photographs of the taxis. Draw this grid on the board.

|   | COUNTRY | REASON | SIMILAR TO |
|---|---------|--------|------------|
| 1 |         |        |            |
| 2 |         |        |            |
| 3 |         |        |            |
| 4 |         |        |            |

This acts as a prompt for the discussion. Students look at the pictures and discuss the photographs in groups of three. Monitor and make a note of any errors. Check their answers as a class and discuss which are most similar to taxis in their countries.

**KEY**

1 India (a rickshaw)   2 the United States (a New York yellow cab)   3 Britain (a black cab)   4 Indonesia (a bemo)

### EXERCISE 11
Direct the class to the chart. If you wish, copy it onto the board (without the answers) and discuss what the students think happens in Britain. Then complete it with the correct answers. Next direct students to the three questions. They discuss the first one in groups and complete the chart. They then discuss the other two questions. Monitor and note down any serious errors. Discuss as a class. If your class is multinational, compare the different countries.

## Getting to work

> **Focus**
> - Means of transport
> - Times and distances
> - Maps and directions
> - Talking about distance, time and frequency
> - Giving directions
> - Questions: *How far? How long? How much? How often?*

### EXERCISE 1
The aim of this section is to revise the language for directions and talk about journeys to work from *Look Ahead 1*. Write Rosie's questions on the board. Play the tape. Allow the students to check their answers in pairs and then elicit their answers and write them on the board.

**KEY**

I walk to the station and take the underground. Five or six miles (I suppose). About forty-five minutes (on a good day). Twenty pounds.

**TAPESCRIPT**

ROSIE: Would you like some more coffee, James?
JAMES: Oh, yes, please. Another day's work. I like the job; it's the travelling around London I hate. It's just awful.
R: Oh, come on, James. Surely it's not that bad. How do you get to work?
J: I walk to the station and take the underground.
R: How far is it? The office, I mean.
J: Er, five or six miles, I suppose.
R: So how long does the journey take?
J: About forty-five minutes on a good day.
R: That's not too bad. How much does it cost?
J: It's twenty pounds a week. I think that's quite a lot.
R: Oh, James. Stop complaining. And hurry up. You'll be late.

### EXERCISE 2
Refer the students to the questions on the board. They interview each other in pairs and make notes about their partner's answers. Then they write sentences. For feedback, they can read out their sentences to the class or, if you have a large class, they can give feedback in groups of about eight.

**Extra practice**

Draw the grid at the top of the next page on the board:

|  | SIMON | SARAH | PETER | RUTH |
|---|---|---|---|---|
| How? | car | bike | train | walk/underground |
| Distance? (in miles) | 10 | 2 | 57 | 6 |
| Time? (in minutes) | 30 | 20 | 70 | 50 |
| Cost? (a week) | £8 | – | £60 | £10 |

The students work in pairs and use the information to ask and answer about each person, e.g.
A: How does Simon get to work?
B: He gets to work by car.
A: How far is it?
B: It's about ten miles.
A: How long does it take?
B: It takes half an hour.
A: How much does it cost?
B: It costs £8 per week.

## EXERCISE 3
Direct the students to the four photographs and write *advantages* and *disadvantages* as headings on the board. Elicit the different methods of travelling shown in the photographs. In pairs they discuss the advantages and disadvantages of travelling to work in these ways. Discuss the exercise as a class, encouraging students to make comparisons between the methods.

## EXERCISE 4
Divide the students into As and Bs. Direct the As to the two articles on page 54 and the Bs to the two articles on page 118. Students read their articles and match them with the pictures.
Draw this grid on the board:

| NAME |  |  |  |
|---|---|---|---|
| How/work? |  |  |  |
| How far? |  |  |  |
| How/take? |  |  |  |
| How/cost? |  |  |  |

The students first complete the first two columns in the grid with information from their articles. Then, using the prompts to make questions, they interview their partners about the other people in the photographs. If necessary, elicit the first question and drill for the correct pronunciation of *does* /dəz/. Monitor and correct any errors you hear. For feedback, volunteer pairs roleplay their conversations. Complete the grid on the board. Finally, you can compare the advantages that the people mention in the texts with the ones that the students thought of in Exercise 3.

### KEY

Text A (Picture 1): He gets to work by rowing boat/He rows to work. It's half a mile. It takes twenty minutes. It doesn't cost him anything.
Text B (Picture 3): He gets to work by helicopter and bicycle. It's thirty miles. It takes twenty minutes and it costs him ten per cent more than the cost of using his car.
Text C (Picture 4): She runs to work. It's four miles. It takes forty-five minutes. It doesn't cost anything apart from the car on Monday.
Text D (Picture 2): He roller-skates to work./He goes to work on roller skates. It's four miles. It takes ten minutes. It doesn't cost anything.

### Extra practice
Divide the class into four groups. Direct them to the information in the completed grid and each group writes four sentences about each person. Then check as a class or direct them back to the texts to check their answers.

## EXERCISE 5
### Background notes
The London underground is often called the **tube** /tjuːb/. **Holborn** is pronounced /ˈhəʊbən/, **Earls Court** /ˌɜːlzˈkɔːt/, **Piccadilly** /ˌpɪkəˈdɪli/.

Direct the students to the London underground plan and get them to find Wimbledon underground station. Then play the conversation on tape. Check that everyone is following the underground journey on the map. The students check their routes in pairs. If necessary, play the tape again.

### KEY

The nearest underground station is Holborn.

### TAPESCRIPT

ROSIE: So where exactly is MAP? I'll meet you there when you finish work.
JAMES: Er, well, to get to Wimbledon tube station you go out of the building and turn left. Then take the er, second street on the left.
R: Left and second left.

UNIT SEVEN

J: Yes, keep walking and you'll see the station. Now, I've got an underground map here somewhere. Look. Here's Wimbledon station. Umm here, you take the District Line – that's the green one – to Earls Court and then change to the Piccadilly Line ... that's this dark blue line here. It's nine stops to Holborn station and MAP is five minutes' walk from there.

R: I see. So from Wimbledon to Earls Court and then Earls Court to Holborn. I've got it. And where's MAP from there?

J: It's a bit difficult to explain. I'll write down the address. Just ask someone.

R: OK.

## EXERCISE 6

Write *directions* on the board as a heading. Play the tape again, stopping after 'go out of the building'. Elicit the directions from the class and write them on the board. Then play the complete tape, stopping briefly to give the students time to make notes. Next, they work in pairs and write the instructions for Rosie. To check their answers, get them to read out their instructions and write them on the board.

### KEY

Go out of the building and turn left. Then take the second street on the left. Wimbledon station is straight ahead. Take the District Line to Earls Court and then change to the Piccadilly line. Get off at Holborn station. MAP is five minutes' walk from there. Ask someone for directions at Holborn.

## EXERCISE 7
**Background notes**
**Buckingham Palace** is pronounced /ˈbʌkɪŋəm ˈpælɪs/, **Trafalgar Square** /trəˈfælgə skweə$^r$/.

**The Hard Rock Café** is part of a chain of international restaurants which sell American style food. They are very fashionable particularly with young people and you often have to queue for a long time to get a table.

**The Tate Gallery** is an art gallery in London, which is known especially for its collection of British art, particularly of the artist Turner.

Copy the sentences onto the board and get the students to copy them into their notebooks. Play the example sentence, stop and mark the main stresses on the board with the students' help. Then play the four sentences, stopping after each one to give the students time to mark the stress. They check their answers with their partners and then as a class on the board. Play the tape again, stopping after each sentence for the students to repeat.

### KEY AND TAPESCRIPT

Example: Ex<u>cuse</u> me. <u>How</u> do I get to <u>Ma</u>dame Tu<u>ssaud's</u>?
1 Ex<u>cuse</u> me. <u>How</u> do I get to Tra<u>falgar Square</u>?
2 Ex<u>cuse</u> me. <u>How</u> do I get to <u>Buckingham Palace</u>?
3 Ex<u>cuse</u> me. <u>How</u> do I get to the <u>Hard</u> Rock Café?
4 Ex<u>cuse</u> me. <u>How</u> do I get to the <u>Tate Gallery</u>?

## EXERCISE 8

Divide the class into pairs. Establish that they are both at Holborn underground station. Direct the As to their underground maps and the Bs to page 119 and their street maps. In pairs they practise the example exchange about Madame Tussaud's. Then the Bs ask the As for directions using the questions in Exercise 7. If you wish, they can change roles after the first two exchanges. Monitor and make a note of any errors. For feedback, get pairs to roleplay their conversations and the others to follow on their maps.

### KEY

1 Buckingham Palace: nearest tube station is St James's Park; Take the Central Line to Tottenham Court Road, then change to the Northern Line and go to Embankment. Change to the Circle or District Line and get off at St James's Park.
2 Trafalgar Square: nearest tube station is Charing Cross; Take the Central Line to Tottenham Court Road, then change to the Northern Line. Get off at Charing Cross.
3 The Hard Rock Café: nearest tube station is Hyde Park Corner; Take the Piccadilly Line straight there.
4 The Tate Gallery: nearest tube station is Pimlico; Take the Central Line to Oxford Circus and change on to the Victoria Line. Get off at Pimlico.

### Extra practice
1 Using the same underground plan, divide the students into pairs. Each student chooses a starting and a finishing station. Then they ask their partner *How do I get from A to B?* and their partner gives them instructions. The other student follows on their map.

2 Bring in maps of your own area or, if possible, tourist ones of London. Divide the students into groups of three or four. Give each group three places to incorporate into a day's sightseeing. They work out a route and write it down. Then they regroup and explain their routes to the others who follow it on their maps.

3  The students work in pairs and give exact directions to get to their homes from the school, including any use of public transport. If you wish to extend the activity, they then work with another partner and tell them how their first partner gets to his/her home.

## EXERCISE 9
Direct students to the matching activity. First, they match the questions and answers on their own and then check their answers with their partners.

### KEY
1  How far is (the station)? Not far./A long way.
2  How long does (the journey) take? A long time./Not long.
3  How often do (the buses) go? Quite often./Not very often.
4  How much is (the fare)? Not much./A lot.

### Extra practice
1  For controlled practice of the question/answer forms, the students work in pairs. Student A says one of the answers and Student B must give the correct question form.

2  Write between ten and fifteen questions based on your own neighbourhood, e.g. *How far is it to the station? How much is the fare into the city centre? How often do the buses go to …?*, etc. Read each question out and the students write down true answers using the forms in the exercise. They can work in pairs. As an extension of this activity, they can write their own questions in groups and then 'test' the other students.

## ENGLISH AROUND YOU
Focus students' attention on the cartoon. Check that they understand *prison*, and ask them to try to guess what *single* and *return* mean. Then, ensure that they understand the joke. (The prisoner is unlikely to need a return.)

# Development

## READING EXERCISE 1
Use the picture and brochure to introduce the topic. Discuss with the class what the brochure is advertising, if the students have been on trips like this or would like to go on one. Then direct them to the four questions and they read the brochure. Encourage them to check their answers in pairs and then as a class.

### KEY
1  It takes one and a half hours.
2  It's Warwick Avenue /ˌwɒrɪk ˈævənjuː/.
3  Bus numbers 6 and 46.
4  a) £4.50 + £4.50 = £9
    b) £4.50 + £4.50 + £3.25 = £12.25 (the younger child travels free)

## SPEAKING EXERCISE 2
Divide the class into As and Bs. Direct the As to the instructions on page 56 and the Bs to the maps on page 119. Establish that the As must ask for directions. Monitor and correct any errors you hear. For feedback, get the students to give you instructions and write/draw them on the board.

### KEY
Take the Jubilee Line from Bond Street station to Baker Street, then take the Bakerloo Line. Get off at the fourth station, Warwick Avenue. From the station turn left into Clifton Villas, then right into Blomfield Road. It's on the right.

## LISTENING EXERCISE 3
### Background notes
**Camden Town** is a residential area in North London. It is famous for **Camden Lock Market** where you can buy clothes, accessories and antiques. **Little Venice** is an expensive residential area on the Regent's Park Canal. The **Aviary** is part of **London Zoo**. The aviary houses much of the zoo's collection of birds. It has become a famous landmark.

Direct the students to the map and draw an outline of it on the board with the place names. Play the tape, stopping after 'Little Venice' and mark it together on the map on the board. Then play the complete monologue. Encourage the students to check their answers in pairs and then check them as a class on the board.

### KEY
1 Little Venice   2 Maida Hill Tunnel   3 London Zoo
4 Camden Town

### TAPESCRIPT

PAUL MONEY
They go from Little Venice, which is where we are today, down to Hampstead Road Lock, which is in Camden Town. The journey down to the Hampstead Road Lock is a distance of about two and a half miles, that's five miles in total, and the return journey takes one and a half hours.

UNIT EIGHT

There isn't really a typical passenger. Um, tourists from all countries of the world, groups of old-age pensioners who book the boat and they're our favourite customers for sure, um, all sorts of people.

The journey goes from here through the tunnel under Maida Hill, which is about 250 metres long. By canal standards it's quite short. It's one of the shorter tunnels on the system. The fastest that the boat travels is probably about four and three quarter miles an hour although the speed limit is actually four miles an hour.

The journey makes its way around the north-west edge of Regent's Park through the London Zoo. There's a beautiful aviary and a few antelope to be seen and sometimes we get to see the elephant walking around. And then winds down in a very narrow channel past some beautiful old houses and down to Hampstead Road Lock.

In the high summer we make four trips a day. The return fare for an adult is £4.50, or single fare £3.50 and then there are reductions for children and pensioners.

I love boats, um, the fresh air is a great attraction. If there's a sunny day I'm out in it, and yes, meeting people too is very important to me.

### EXERCISE 4
Direct the students to the questions and check that they understand *antelopes*, *bears*, and *fresh air*. Play the tape again. The students check their answers in pairs and then check as a class.

**KEY**

1 It's two and a half miles.   2 c   3 It's four miles an hour.   4 b, e   5 b, d, f

### WRITING EXERCISE 5
Draw an outline of the postcard on the board. Ask the students to dictate the beginning to you. Then using the information from the listening, they write about their trip. They can swap their postcards to check for factual and grammatical differences/errors. If you want the students to have a model text, get them to read out their postcards to you. The class chooses the sentences for you to write on the board.

### Extra practice
To extend the writing activity, bring in some postcards of different places or get the students to bring in one postcard each. They each write the postcard (in pencil, if you want to use them again) to one of the students in the class, using the picture on the front to talk about their holiday/trip, etc. Then they 'send' the postcard to the student, who must write a short reply, either on another postcard or on a piece of paper. If one student does not 'receive' a postcard, give them one of the others to reply to. Alternatively, to make the exercise more communicative, divide the class into pairs. Give each student a postcard. They think about who they want to send their card to and what they want to say. They then tell their partner what they would like to say and who they would like to send their card to. The partner listens (without writing anything down) and then writes the postcard, finally giving it to their partner, who corrects any factual or grammatical errors. They then 'send' their postcards. They can write replies to the ones they receive in the same way.

## 8 Cooking a meal

### Shopping for food

**Focus**

- Supermarkets
- Food and household goods
- Prices

- Asking polite questions
- Saying what someone has to pay
- Asking about forms of payment
- Asking about quantity

- Indirect (polite) questions
- *Some* and *any*
- Countable and uncountable nouns
- Questions: *How much? How many?*

### EXERCISE 1
**Note:** This exercise is very useful for revising word stress and the schwa. You can point out the different stress in *dessert* /dɪˈzɜːt/ (the sweet part of a meal) and *desert* /ˈdezət/ (dry wasteland, e.g. the Sahara), the schwas in *bakery* /ˈbeɪkəri/, *ingredients* /ɪnˈɡriːdɪənts/ and *vegetables* /ˈvedʒtəbəlz/.

To introduce the lesson, brainstorm the items a supermarket sells and how they organise them. This can be done as a class or with the students in pairs. Get feedback and elicit the vocabulary for the different sections of a supermarket. Write the sections on the board (make sure you include the ones from the exercise) and drill each one, concentrating particularly on the stress. Next, direct the students to the picture of Teresa and the items in her basket, teaching new vocabulary as necessary. In pairs, they match the items with the sections and make sentences based on the model.

**KEY**

She found the lamb in the 'meat' section.
She found the milk in the 'dairy products' section.
She found the carrots in the 'vegetables' section.
She found the chocolates in the 'sweets' section.

### Extra practice

1 To extend the activity and revise food vocabulary, bring in some pictures of other food items. The students work in groups and match the items with the sections in the supermarket.

2 To revise food containers and quantities, write two lists on the board, one of containers/quantities (e.g. a box of, a pound of) and one of food/household items (e.g. crisps, soap). The students work in pairs to match the containers/quantities with as many of the food items as possible. This could also be done as a team game, with a time limit. The team with the most correct phrases wins the game.

3 First revise containers, using the above exercise or by bringing pictures/realia to revise them. Prepare a list of containers and food items, e.g. a box of chocolates, a carton of milk. Draw a 'bingo' card on the board, like this:

|  |  |  |
|---|---|---|
|  |  |  |
|  |  | a box of chocolates |

Get the students to write a different container in each box of the grid. Then read out your list of different containers and the students put a cross through each one they hear which is on their bingo card. Keep a check of which ones you have read out. The student who is first to cross out all the squares is the winner. The students can also do this activity in pairs. One says the containers and the other crosses them off their card as they hear them. It is important here to work with a limited number of containers and food items all of which should be on the board so that the students' choice is restricted.

### EXERCISE 2

Before the students do the exercise, you may need to revise the use of *much* and *many*. Hold up some pens and write *How ...?* on the board. Elicit the question *How many pens have you got?* Answer and drill the exchange. Next, show the students some paper and repeat the procedure. To check the concept, ask *Can you count pens?* (Yes, one pen, two pens, etc.) Then ask *Can you count ink?* (No). If the students need more practice, write some classroom items on the board, e.g. lights, books, space, furniture. The students work in pairs and ask and answer about the items, e.g.

A: How many students are there?
B: There are 20/a lot.

To check the idea of *needs* + noun, ask *What do you need to learn English?* Using realia, elicit *We need a book, a dictionary, a teacher*, etc. To check the concept, ask *Is ... necessary? Why?*

Direct students to Teresa's incomplete shopping list and ask them to add to it the items from her shopping basket. Then divide the class into pairs and direct the B students to page 120. Explain that the As have to complete Teresa's shopping list with more items, and with quantities for the items already there. The Bs have the complete list. Get one pair to read the example exchanges to the class. Then the As interview the Bs to complete their lists. Make sure they write the information on their lists (in their notebooks). If you wish, ask students to change roles halfway through so that the Bs interview the As to complete the lists. To check their answers, the students can look at the completed list on page 120. Make sure they keep a copy of the list as they will need it in Exercise 7.

### EXERCISE 3

Write these two questions on the board: *What does Teresa want? Where are the items?* Play the tape. Students check their answers in pairs and then as a class.

**KEY**

Teresa wants olive oil and pizzas. The olive oil is in the 'cooking ingredients' section, and the pizzas are in the 'bakery' section.

**TAPESCRIPT**

TERESA: Excuse me. Can you tell me where the olive oil is?
ASSISTANT: Yes, it's over there in the 'cooking ingredients' section, next to the canned food.
T: Right. And what about pizzas? Can you tell me where they are?
A: Pizzas. Er, let me think. Oh yeah, they're in the bakery section. Can you see that over there at the back?
T: Oh yes. Thank you.
A: That's all right.

### EXERCISE 4

Tell the students to listen to the conversation again and write down Teresa's two questions. Play the tape, pausing if necessary to give them time to

UNIT EIGHT

write. They check with their partners. Then elicit their questions and write them on the board.

**KEY**

Can you tell me where the olive oil is?
Can you tell me where they are?

## DISCOVERING LANGUAGE EXERCISE 5

Direct the students to the first three questions. Ask them to read them and say which question in each pair is more polite (and why), and to say what the difference in verb forms are. Discuss their answers as a class, and how the indirect questions are formed. Then ask students to look at questions 4 and 5, and to compare their formation with the first three. Discuss the answers as a class. For further practice, ask students to make a few simple questions more polite, e.g. *What time does the train arrive?* and analyse each one.

**KEY**

Question b in each pair is more polite, because of the use of *Can you tell me ...?* They are more indirect.
In the direct questions the verbs are in the question form, e.g. *How much does it cost? How do you cook this?*
In the indirect (polite) questions the verbs are in the statement form, e.g. *Can you tell me how much it costs?*
Polite questions without a question word (*Who? When?*) are formed with *if*, e.g. *Can you tell me if there are any peas?*

### ▣ EXERCISE 6

First play the drill on tape, pausing to allow the students to repeat. Next, drill the complete question chorally and individually, focusing on the stress and rhythm. Then direct them to the sentences in the book. In pairs they practise the drill, e.g.
A: Can you ...?
B: Can you tell me ...? etc.

**TAPESCRIPT**

Can you ...?   Can you tell me ...?   Can you tell me where the ...?   Can you tell me where the carrots are?
Can you ...?   Can you tell me ...?   Can you tell me if there's ...?   Can you tell me if there's any bread?

### Extra practice

Write these prompts on the board: *where/bank? if/cheese? when/shop? if/peas?* Point to the first prompt and build up a polite question – *Can you tell me where the bank is?* Build up all four on the board. Then divide the class into two groups and they do a 'table tennis' drill as they did in Exercise 6.

## EXERCISE 7

Divide the students into pairs. Direct the As (customers) to the lists they wrote in Exercise 2 and the Bs (shop assistants) to the supermarket sections in Exercise 1. To demonstrate the task, get two students to read out the example exchange whilst the others shadow it in their books. Drill the exchange chorally and individually. The As then interview their partners. Monitor and make a note of any errors. To check their answers, volunteer pairs can roleplay their exchanges.

**KEY**

ice cream – frozen desserts   carrots – vegetables   flour – cooking ingredients   shampoo – body and hair care
pizza – bakery   olive oil – cooking ingredients
chocolates – sweets   peas – canned food
cucumber – vegetables   lamb – meat   bread – bakery
milk – dairy products   toilet paper – general household goods

## EXERCISE 8

The students continue to work in the same pairs but change roles. Direct the As (customers) to the pictures on page 59 and the Bs (shop assistants) to those on page 120. To demonstrate the activity, point to the first picture and ask the As *What do you ask the shop assistant?* Elicit *Can you tell me how much this (shampoo) is?* Ask the Bs to answer *Yes. It's £1.50.* If necessary, drill the exchange. Students then work in pairs. Monitor and make a note of any errors. For feedback, volunteer pairs roleplay their exchanges. Finally, use the board to correct any errors you noted from Exercises 7 and 8.

**KEY**

1  A: Can you tell me how much this (shampoo) is?
   B: Yes. It's £1.50.
2  A: Can you tell me how many tissues there are (in a box)?
   B: Yes. There are 200.
3  A: Can you tell me if you have any yoghurt?
   B: Yes, we have. It's in the 'dairy products' section.
4  A: Can you tell me where the manager is?
   B: Yes. He's in his office, behind you.
5  A: Can you tell me when the shop closes today?
   B: Yes. It closes at 7 p.m.
6  A: Can you tell me what this fruit is?
   B: Yes. It's a kiwi fruit.

### Extra practice

1  Prepare ten questions using the polite question form, some correct and some incorrect, e.g. *Can you tell where the sugar is? Can you tell me when*

*does the bank open?* The students write the numbers 1–10 on a piece of paper. They can work in pairs or individually. Read the first question out. They quickly decide if it is right (**R**) or wrong (**W**) and write down (**R**) or (**W**) next to number 1. Do the same with each question. Then read the questions again and the students decide as a group which are right or wrong. The students keep score of how many they get right. Finally, read them out again and the students write down the correct form for the incorrect questions. Check as a class. Alternatively, they can do this as a team activity. Give one point when they identify if the question is right or wrong and one point if they can correct the mistakes.

2 If you have access to tourist information brochures or 'What's on' magazines, bring them into the class. Divide the students into As (tourist information guides) and Bs (tourists). Write some prompts on the board for the information that the tourists want to find out, e.g. *film times, opening hours of banks, prices, location of museums, trips*. The guides must find out the information and answer the tourists' questions. If they do not have the information in their brochure, they must ask the other tourist guides, e.g. *Pablo, can you tell me when the bank opens?*

### 🔲 EXERCISE 9

Copy the example list onto the board. Play the tape, stopping to elicit the stress and intonation and mark it on the board. Discuss the list intonation pattern (rising on all items except the last, where it falls). Next, copy the three lists onto the board. The students work in pairs and practise saying them together. Then they mark the stress and intonation patterns. Play the tape again, stopping after each list to check their answers. Finally, play the tape again, pausing for the students to repeat.

**KEY AND TAPESCRIPT**

Teresa: ... ice cream, lamb, carrots, milk and chocolates.

1 I need some cheese, some eggs, some flour and a loaf of bread.
2 Some sugar, some biscuits, and a packet of tea.
3 Jam, marmalade, butter and milk.

### Extra practice

1 Bring in some pictures of items that you can buy from the supermarket. Display them on the board. The students work in groups of four. Using the pictures, they practise saying shopping lists with four items, e.g.
   A: *I need some sugar ...*
   B: *a box of tissues ...*
   C: *some coffee ...*
   D: *and some bananas.*
   Then the second student begins the list. Each student in the group practises rising and falling list intonation.

2 You can use the activity of 'I went shopping yesterday and I bought ...' to practise food/clothes items and list intonation. You begin by saying *I went shopping yesterday and I bought a bunch of bananas* and then indicate that the student nearest to you should continue. Make sure they begin with your item, e.g. *I went shopping yesterday and I bought a bunch of bananas and a bottle of coke*. The students must remember all the items and add one of their own.

### 🔲 EXERCISE 10

Direct the students to the picture and establish where Teresa is. Discuss as a class the different ways of paying for goods at a supermarket. Get two students to read out the conversation, then explain that there are some mistakes in it. Play the tape once. Encourage the students to compare their answers with their partners, then ask students to supply the corrections line by line.

**KEY**

It costs £40.20, not £14.20. She's paying by cheque. The assistant gives her back her card. She doesn't need any more bags.

**TAPESCRIPT**

ASSISTANT: That's £40.20, please. How are you paying?
TERESA: By cheque. Here you are.
A: Thank you. Here's your card. Do you need any more bags?
T: No, no more, thank you. Goodbye.
A: Goodbye.

### ENGLISH AROUND YOU

Focus students' attention on the cartoon and ask them to find a trolley in the picture. Check that they understand the play on the phrase *take a trolley*. The sign points out that shoppers should take a trolley into the supermarket to do their shopping; the woman has interpreted it as meaning *take a free gift*.

UNIT EIGHT

# The food we eat

> **Focus**
> - Food and its characteristics
> - Saying what you think
> - Responding to argument
> - *A lot (of)*, *(not) much* and *(not) many*
> - Question: *What kind?*
> - Further practice: *How much? How many? some, any*

## EXERCISE 1

To introduce the exercise, discuss as a class the most popular food in their country/countries and the reasons. Check that the students know *taste* and *keen on*. Next, copy the definitions of the adjectives on the board and direct the students to the four pictures and texts. Point out the first definition and get them to read the first text to find the adjective (*fresh*). Write it next to the definition. The students then do the same with the other adjectives. Encourage them to check their answers in groups and then check as a class and write their answers next to the definitions on the board. If necessary, drill the adjectives for correct pronunciation.

### KEY

1 fresh   2 raw   3 healthy   4 unhealthy   5 sweet
6 fatty   7 revolting   8 fattening

## DISCOVERING LANGUAGE EXERCISE 2

Direct the students back to the texts. Ask them to find and underline the phrases with *much*, *many* and *a lot (of)*. Establish that *much* is followed by uncountable nouns *many* by countable nouns and *a lot (of)* can be followed by both.

Draw this grid on the board for further practice:

| MUCH | MANY | A LOT (OF) |
|------|------|------------|
|      |      |            |

Say *Fruit. Which columns does it go in?* and elicit their answer (*much/a lot of*). Then, in pairs, they read through the texts and place the different items in the appropriate columns. Check as a class and establish that the students understand the difference between countable and uncountable nouns. If necessary, use the concept questions from Exercise 2 on page 58 and bring in pictures to show the difference between *chocolate/cake* (as uncountable) and *chocolates/cakes* (as individual, countable ones). Then ask *What about 'a lot of'? Is this for countable or uncountable nouns?* and establish that it is used for both kinds of nouns in positive sentences and that *much* and *many* are used in questions and negative sentences.

### Extra practice

1 Draw the outline of this grid (without the information) on the board:

|  | TONY | SARAH | RICHARD | HEATHER |
|---|---|---|---|---|
| Job | factory worker | accountant | musician | teacher |
| Salary | £13,250 | £30,500 | £17,000 | £15,750 |
| Hours (a week) | 40 | 45 | 30 | 40 |
| House/Rooms | 6 | 10 | 5 | 6 |
| Children | 3 | 1 | 0 | 2 |

The students work in groups of four. Give each student information about one of the people. Practise the question forms as a class. They interview each other and complete the grid, e.g. *What does ... do? How much does ... earn? How many hours does ... work? How many rooms has ... got in his/her house? How many children has ... got?*

2 Prepare four cue cards, like this:
Yesterday: lemonade – postcards – biscuits – money
Yesterday: homework – apples – phone calls – milk
Yesterday: Coca-Cola – shopping – newspapers – friends
Yesterday: photographs – English – English books – bread

The students work in groups of four. They each have one cue card. First, they look at the prompts on the cue card and decide on the quantity, e.g. how much lemonade they drank yesterday, how many postcards they wrote yesterday, etc. Then draw this on the board:

| YESTERDAY | |
|---|---|
| What? | How much/How many? |
| 1 lemonade<br>2<br>3<br>4 | two glasses |

To demonstrate the task, write *lemonade* on the board and build up an example conversation, e.g.
A: *What did you do yesterday?*
B: *I drank some lemonade.*

A: *How much did you drink?*
B: *I drank two glasses.*

Drill the conversation chorally and individually. Write their answers on the board. The students interview each other about what they did yesterday. Make sure they make notes about each person in the group. Then, using their notes, they give feedback as a class. If they need written practice, they can use their notes to write sentences, e.g. *Luis drank two glasses of lemonade yesterday.*

## EXERCISE 3

Ask students to copy the questionnaire into their notebooks. Get two students to read the example exchange and write the two questions on the board. To demonstrate the task, get the students to interview you. Then they interview each other. Make sure they make notes about their partner. For feedback, discuss which are the most and least popular types of food.

## EXERCISE 4

Direct the students to the example paragraph. Then, using their notes from Exercise 3, they use the paragraph as a model to write about their partner. Monitor and help. They can swap texts for their partner to check for grammatical and factual errors. If your students find writing difficult, get the students to dictate the example paragraph to you and write it on the board. To guide them in their writing, underline the things they must change, e.g. *Gina is very keen on junk food*, etc.

## EXERCISE 5

Direct the students to the photographs and see if they know who the people are. Then point out the questions and ask them to read the article. The students read and then discuss the questions with their partner. Check as a class and discuss which person's eating habits they prefer.

**KEY**

1  Dannii Minogue doesn't eat meat, fish or dairy products. Brian Harvey eats meat and doesn't like vegetarian food.
2  A vegetarian can't eat meat (and often fish). A vegan can't eat meat, dairy products or fish.

## EXERCISE 6

Write *Eating meat is ...* on the board and direct the students to the exercise. If necessary, do the first one together as an example. They work in pairs and match the arguments and the reasons. Then check as a class. Insist on students giving full sentences, e.g. Eating meat is unkind to animals *because* ... If necessary, check that they have understood the four adjectives.

**KEY**

1 b   2 d   3 a   4 c

## EXERCISE 7

To introduce the language, say an extreme statement to the class, e.g. *I think all animals are dangerous*. Encourage the students to disagree with you. Then draw two columns on the board like this:

| GIVING OPINIONS | DISAGREEING |
| --- | --- |
|  |  |

Elicit the expression you used to give your opinion (*I think*) and the ones they used for disagreeing and write them on the board. Add others from the exercise. Drill each one chorally and individually.

Divide the students into As and Bs. Group the As together to make a list of reasons for being a vegetarian and the Bs together to list the arguments for eating meat. Then regroup them into As and Bs. They must try to convince each other of their ideas. You can tell them that the students who keep going win the argument! For feedback, discuss as a class what they really think about the topic. They can use their lists of reasons in Exercise 7 on page 63.

**Extra practice**

Write some statements on the board that you think your students will disagree with, e.g. *Pop music is bad for young people. Vegetables are bad for you.* etc. The students work in groups of four. The first one says the statement, the others must disagree, each using a different expression and reason.

## COMPARING CULTURES EXERCISE 8

Direct the students to the pictures. If you have a multinational group, students of different nationalities work in groups to discuss which food they eat or don't eat in their countries and the reasons. With a monolingual class, they can work in groups and discuss the food in relation to their country and other countries that they know about. Get quick class feedback. Then, if possible, the students work with another student of the same nationality. Direct them to the example sentences. They write similar ones about their country.

If you have a mixed nationality class, write each food item on a separate piece of paper. Give each student one of the pieces of paper. If you have several students from one country, they can work together. They write a sentence about the food in

UNIT EIGHT

their country, e.g. *A lot of people in France eat snails because they are delicious.* Then they pass the paper onto the next nationality group who write a sentence about their country. At the end of the exercise, display the pieces of paper on the noticeboard and the students can compare the different eating habits.

## Development

### 🔊 LISTENING EXERCISE 1
Indicate the picture of Dennis Malone and his wife and discuss where the students think they are. Say that Dennis and Margaret own a restaurant and encourage students to guess which type. Then they read the introduction to the listening.

Next, direct them to the six pictures and check they understand the instructions for the stew. Establish that the instructions are in the wrong order. Play the tape. Encourage the students to compare answers with their partners. If necessary, play the tape again. Check as a class.

**KEY**

Correct order: 5, 3, 4, 1, 6, 2

**TAPESCRIPT**

DENNIS
One of the favourite dishes in Milly's that we've been making a lot er, is, a stew and we do it as a special and it's called O'Malleys Stew. We get all of the seasonal vegetables that we buy at farmers' market and we wash them and we chop them on our preparation board. Ah, then we get a pot and fill it with water and begin to blanch the carrots and the leeks. After they've been simmering for a couple of minutes we add the Shii-taki mushrooms and the smoked tofu. We continue then to add the remaining ingredients and simmer a while longer, add some fresh herbs and let it simmer for a few more minutes and then the dish is complete.

### Extra practice
Find a picture of a recipe that you have made or that the students will recognise. Write out the instructions for the recipe. Then prepare two worksheets for 'a mutual dictation': take the instructions and delete groups of four or five words in alternate sequences on each worksheet. Copy each 'part recipe' enough times for half the class. Show the students the picture and discuss the ingredients you need to make the dish. Write them on the board. Then divide the students into pairs (As and Bs) and give As one of the 'part recipes' and Bs the other. In pairs, they sit back to back and dictate the recipe to each other. At the end, they will have the complete recipe.

### READING EXERCISE 2
**Background notes**
**Dim sum** is a type of Chinese food which consists of various mixtures of small pieces of meat, fish and vegetables, wrapped in rice or a kind of light bread and steamed or fried.

Direct the students to the four advertisements. Check the names of the four restaurants. Copy the questions onto the board. Encourage students to check their answers in pairs. Then check as a class.

**KEY**

1 A, B, C, D   2 A, B   3 A, B   4 A   5 B

### EXERCISE 3
Refer the students back to the advertisements. They discuss the exercise in groups of three.

**KEY**

1 A   2 D   3 B   4 C

### 🔊 LISTENING EXERCISE 4
Direct the students back to the four groups of people in Exercise 3 and establish that they must listen to find out who is speaking to which restaurant. Play the tape. Check as a class.

**KEY**

Julie is speaking to the manager of the Lotus Restaurant.

**TAPESCRIPT**

MANAGER: Lotus Restaurant. Manager speaking.
JULIE: Hello, I'd like to book a table for four, please.
M: Certainly. When would you like to come?
J: Tomorrow lunchtime. One o'clock?
M: That's fine. Would you like a smoking or non-smoking table?
J: Oh, non-smoking, please. Um can I just check. Do you serve vegetarian food?
M: Yes, we do.
J: And can you tell me if you do children's meals?
M: Not normally, no, but we can serve small portions at a lower price.
J: Good. Thank you very much. One o'clock tomorrow, then. Goodbye.

### 🔊 EXERCISE 5
Copy the four prompts onto the board. Play the tape again. The students check their answers in pairs. If

necessary, play the tape again. Elicit their answers and write them on the board as they dictate them to you. Encourage peer correction of errors.

**KEY**

1 I'd like to book a table for four, please.
2 Would you like a smoking or non-smoking table?
3 Do you serve vegetarian food?
4 And can you tell me if you do children's meals?

## SPEAKING EXERCISE 6
Direct the students back to the questions on the board from Exercise 5 and the restaurant information. Divide the students into pairs and ask the As to read their role as customer and the Bs their role as restaurant manager. They act out their telephone conversations. Make sure they change roles. Monitor and make a note of any errors and use the board to correct them.

## WRITING EXERCISE 7
First find out which students are vegetarian, vegan or meat-eaters. Put them into groups according to which category they belong to. Together they make a list of the reasons why they are or are not vegetarians/vegans. They can use their notes from Exercise 7 on page 61. They then write a paragraph explaining their reasons. To check their writing, they can swap texts with other groups who have the same eating habits to compare reasons and check for errors.

# 9 In the country

## Changing places

**Focus**
- Locations
- Country and city life
- Talking about location
- Saying what is best
- Further practice: asking for and giving opinions, making comparisons
- Modal: *should* + infinitive
- Further practice: comparative adjectives

## EXERCISE 1
Revise *in* + place by drawing a rough outline map of your town on the board. Mark about ten places (including 'suburbs') in the north, north-east/west, south, south-east/west, east, west and in the centre. Draw the four compass points next to the map. Point to a place in the north and ask *Where's ...?* Elicit *It's in the north*. Drill the response. Do the same with south, east and west. Then do the same with north-east, etc. Teach the word *suburbs*.

Then direct the students to the exercise and get them to ask you the questions. The students then work in pairs and interview each other. Monitor and correct any errors you hear.

## EXERCISE 2
The students work with the same partner as in Exercise 1. Each student draws his/her family tree (of immediate family only) and gives it to his/her partner who then asks questions about each person. Monitor, make a note of any errors and use the board to correct them at the end of the activity.

**Extra practice**

1 To practise describing location, do a picture dictation with the students. Draw an outline of a town on the board. The students copy it into their notebooks. Describe where the areas and facilities are, e.g. *There are suburbs in the north-west. There's a park in the south.* They write or draw everything in the correct position. To check their answers, they describe the picture to you and you draw it on the board.

2 In a multinational class, the students draw an outline of their countries and mark the position of industrial areas, mountains, lakes, cities, etc. They then draw the blank outline of their country and give it to their partners. They dictate their map to their partner, who completes their blank. If you have a monolingual group, they can draw a map of an imaginary country.

## EXERCISE 3
**Background notes**
**New Age Travellers** is a term in British English for people who have rejected the traditional values of ordinary society. They go from place to place living in a vehicle, e.g. a lorry, van, caravan. They are disliked and distrusted by many people, who think they steal things and cause trouble. They are not the same as **gypsies** (gipsies – /ˈdʒɪpsɪz/), who are members of a dark-haired race which may be of Indian origin. Gypsies are often nomadic – living and travelling in caravans. They live in most European countries and are often treated with mistrust and a lack of understanding.

**Terry** /ˈterɪ/ is usually a man's name, short for **Terence**. Here it is probably short for **Teresa**.

UNIT NINE

**Streak** is a nickname. **Scarlet** is not a common name. It is a very bright red colour. Perhaps the child in the article is called Scarlet after the character of **Scarlett O'Hara** in the film **Gone with the Wind**.

Direct the students to the picture and discuss as a class what kind of people they think they are, e.g. where they live, what they do. Then write the four statements from the exercise on the board and ask the students to read the first paragraph of the article. In pairs, they correct the statements. Check the answers with the whole group and correct the statements on the board. Establish that the students understand *New Age Traveller*.

**KEY**

1 They live in a van.
2 They move around the country.
3 The child does not go to school.
4 Her father wants to stay on the road.

**EXERCISE 4**

Direct students to the first question and ask them to read the rest of the article. Discuss as a class who they think is speaking in each paragraph and why. Then copy the chart onto the board and get the students to copy it into their notebooks. To demonstrate the task, get them to read the first line of the second paragraph. Ask *What are the good points?* Elicit them from the students and write the advantages in note form on the board. The students then read the rest of the article and make notes in the same way. If necessary, teach *survive*, *dangers* and *cough*.

An alternative way of handling the exercise is to divide the pairs into As and Bs. Get the As to read the text and make notes about 'travelling life' and the Bs to make notes about 'city life'. Then using their notes they tell their partner about their topic. Finally, check with the whole group and make notes on the board. Make sure the students copy these notes as they will need them in Exercise 7.

**KEY**

1 Streak is the speaker in Paragraph 2. We know this because he is in favour of the travelling life. In Paragraph 3 we know Terry is speaking because the speaker thinks they should move back to the city. In addition, she says 'Streak and I ...'.

2

|  | GOOD POINTS | BAD POINTS |
| --- | --- | --- |
| Travelling life | good friends<br>live in the open air<br>can keep animals<br>can do what they want<br>safer than cities | difficult in winter<br>Scarlet gets ill<br>problems with farmers and police |
| City life | Scarlet can go to school<br>She can have 'normal' friends | small flats, like boxes<br>terrible jobs<br>can be dangerous |

**EXERCISE 5**

To introduce the language, hold up your copy of *Look Ahead 2* and ask *Is this an interesting book?* Elicit *Yes*, and say *Yes, I think so*. Establish that we use *so* because we don't want to repeat the whole phrase giving the opinion, e.g. *I think* **so** = *I think* **it is an interesting book**. Drill the response chorally and individually. Then ask *Is 'Look Ahead 2' a boring book?* and elicit *I don't think so*. Drill both exchanges. You could also use a film, pop group, etc. that most students like/dislike.

Direct students to the exercise and get two students to read the example exchange. Then they work in pairs, using the statements to practise similar exchanges. Make sure they change roles.

**DISCOVERING LANGUAGE EXERCISE 6**

Ask students to look at the article and find sentences containing *should* and *shouldn't*. Write them on the board.

Direct students to the three jumbled sentences. They use the sentences on the board as models to rewrite the sentences correctly. Check as a class.

**KEY**

I think that we should move to the city.
We shouldn't keep travelling.
Scarlet should go to school.

Now ask the students to choose the correct function of *should*. They can do this by looking at the sentences in context in the article. Discuss their answers.

**KEY**

b

To reinforce the concept of *should* and *shouldn't* display or draw a picture of an unhealthy looking person, like the one on the next page:

Ask *Is Tim healthy?* (No) *Is his doctor happy with him?* (No) *Why not?* Elicit *Because he's fat, unfit and he smokes.* Ask *What does the doctor say to him?* Elicit *You should lose weight/go on a diet.* To check the concept, ask *Is it an order?* (No) *Is it a good idea?* (Yes) *Why?* (Because he's fat and it's bad for his health). Your students may want to use *must* instead of *should*. To establish the difference in concept, ask *Is 'should' as strong as 'must'?* (No) *Which one do we use for an order?* (must) *What do we use 'should' for?* (advice, a good idea). Next, drill *You should go on a diet* chorally and individually. Use the picture to elicit *You should take more exercise. You shouldn't smoke. You should stop smoking. You shouldn't eat cakes.* Establish that *should* remains the same for all persons, i.e. *I, you*, etc. To highlight the third person form, ask one or two students to make sentences about Tim, e.g. *He should go on a diet.* Drill the sentences as necessary.

## EXERCISE 7

To revise the language of agreeing and disagreeing, draw this grid on the board:

| GIVING OPINIONS | AGREEING | DISAGREEING |
| --- | --- | --- |
| I think ... <br> I feel ... | I agree. <br> That's true. <br> You're right. <br> I think so. | I'm sorry, I don't agree. <br> I don't think that's true. <br> I'm afraid you're wrong. <br> I don't think so. |

Elicit the expressions they learnt and write them on the board. Add the ones that they practised in Exercise 5. Drill as necessary.

Next, refer the students back to the notes they made in Exercise 4. Divide the class into As (Streak) and Bs (Terry). Group the As together and the Bs together and get them to discuss their ideas first, using their notes. Make sure they expand their opinions and give reasons. Then regroup them into As and Bs to roleplay the conversation. Monitor and make a note of any errors. For feedback, discuss what they think Streak and Terry should do. Use the board to correct any errors you heard.

### Extra practice

1 Write twelve different problems on separate cue cards, e.g. *You haven't got any friends. You haven't got a job. You want to buy your sister a present*, etc. Divide the students into groups of three. Each group needs a set of cue cards. They put them on the desk face down. The first student picks up the card and explains the problem to the other two, who must give advice. The student with the problem gives the card to the person who gives them the best advice. Then the next student picks up a card and explains the problem. The student with the most cue cards at the end of the activity 'wins' the game. If you have a large class, divide it into groups of about ten. They each have a cue card and mingle to get advice. Again, they give their cue card to the student who gives them the best advice.

2 Divide the students into groups of four. Give each group a different holiday, depending on the interests of your students, e.g. camping in the south of Spain, walking in the French mountains. They discuss the things they should take. Then they regroup and tell each other about their holidays and the items. As a group, they prioritise the three most important items for each holiday and discuss as a class.

3 Brainstorm the things you should know or have before visiting a foreign country, e.g. places to visit, climate, language, injections, typical food and drink to try, things to buy. In a multinational class students work with someone of different nationality and interview each other about what they should do if they visit their partner's country, e.g. *Where should I go? What should I eat?* In a monolingual group, they can work in small groups or pairs to discuss what a visitor should see and do when visiting their country.

4 To revise the language from Exercise 7, get each student to write down an opinion statement that they agree with, e.g. *All children should study two languages at school.* Then elicit their statements and write them on the board, correcting any errors. The students copy them into their notebooks. Then they mingle and make a note of the students who agree with the statements, e.g.
   A: *Do you agree that all children should study two languages at school?*
   B: *No, I don't* or *Yes, I do.*
Finally, they report their findings to the class.

UNIT NINE

## 📼 EXERCISE 8

Discuss the advantages of having an office in the town centre or in the country, e.g. transport, price of rent. Check students understand *rent*. If your students find listening difficult, write these three questions on the board:

1  What does Tom want to do? (Move the company to the country)
2  What does Julia think of the idea? (She doesn't like it)
3  What does James think of the idea? (He's not sure)

Play the tape. Check the answers with the whole class. Next, draw the grid below on the board and get students to copy it:

| MOVING THE OFFICE TO THE COUNTRY ||
|---|---|
| Tom | Julia |

Divide the class into As (Tom) and Bs (Julia). Play the tape again and the As make notes about Tom's opinions in the chart while the Bs make notes about Julia's opinions. The As compare their notes together and the Bs compare their notes together. If necessary, play the tape again.

Reorganise the students into pairs of one A and one B. Using their notes, they recreate the discussion between Tom and Julia. If the students are having problems with the comparison of adjectives, elicit some of the advantages of moving to the country and write them on the board, e.g. *It's quieter in the country than in the town.* Then discuss the rules for the formation of comparatives. Drill each sentence chorally and individually.

### KEY

For: cheaper rent, cheaper houses, cleaner air, quieter, easier parking, better transport (communications), go for walks and horse-riding, good entertainment facilities in a nearby town.
Against: a long way from some clients, nothing to do in spare time.

### TAPESCRIPT

TOM: We have to move the company. To a new office.
JAMES: Move? But ...
JULIA: I think that's a great idea.
T: Good.
J: We should be in the centre of town. We'll be nearer our customers.
T: Julia, I ...
J: The transport is better ...
T: Julia, I ...
J: ... and there are lots of good restaurants.
T: Julia, I think we should move to the country.
J: Oh!
T: For ... against. For: cheaper rent, cheaper houses, cleaner air. It's quieter. There's not so much noise. And parking's easier. Do you agree that these are all good reasons for moving?
J: Yes, I agree. But let's talk about the things against moving. Number one. A long way from some clients. Don't you mean from all of our clients?
T: No, that's not right. One of our biggest clients is in the west, and we have another, in the north.
JAMES: What about communications?
T: There's an airport here and a motorway here. And there are fast trains to everywhere in Britain from this station.
J: So communications are better than they are from here?
T: I think so.
J: But what do we do with our spare time? I know we can go for walks in the country. Perhaps go horse-riding. But we can only do that in summer. What do we do in winter? When it's cold and wet. It's not like London, is it?
T: I agree. But in this town here – twenty minutes by car – there are cinemas, theatres, good restaurants and there's a jazz club. So, I think MAP Advertising should move to the country. Do you agree?
J: No, I don't agree.
T: James.
JAMES: I'm not sure.

### Extra practice

Bring in pictures of pairs of objects for students to compare, e.g. cars, types of food, landscape, types of energy. Number each picture and write appropriate adjectives on the board, e.g. *unusual, expensive, heavy, flat, spicy, fast, comfortable*. The students work in groups and write down sentences giving the advantages/disadvantages of the objects and using comparison, e.g. *The weather is sunnier in .../ Picture 9 than in .../ Picture 10.* Then they regroup and read out their sentences. They write down any different sentences from the ones they have. By the end of the activity, the students should have at least twenty different sentences using the comparative.

## EXERCISE 9

Direct the class to the example letter. Establish that their letter must have a similar beginning to the model, four paragraphs and an ending. Check for errors as the students are writing, then encourage pairs to swap letters and discuss them, making any further corrections. In a multinational class, the students can read each others' letters and decide where they think Penny should live.

# Pets or pests?

> **Focus**
> - Pets
> - Asking questions
> - Checking information
> - Tag questions

## COMPARING CULTURES EXERCISE 1
**Background notes**
The animals in the pictures are all popular pets in Britain. **Budgerigars** are informally called **budgies**. They are small, brightly coloured birds originally from Australia. They are kept in cages in people's houses. **Hamsters** are specially bred as pets. They are small rodents with pockets (pouches) in their cheeks for storing food, and short tails (unlike mice, which have long tails). **Guinea pigs** are small, roundish, furry rodents with short ears and no tail.

If possible, bring in pictures of other pets e.g. snakes, tortoises, frogs, lizards. Make sure the students understand *pet* and then ask *Have you got any pets?* Discuss as a class the different pets that people keep, using pictures to teach their names. Write the names of the animals on the board and drill as necessary. Then direct the students to the exercise in the Students' Book. They discuss the questions in groups of three. Finally, discuss as a class.

## EXERCISE 2
Divide the students into As and Bs. Direct the As to the article and the Bs to the letter. The As read their article, then in groups choose the correct answers to the statements. The Bs do the same with their letter. They may want to make notes of the key points. If they do not have dictionaries, monitor and explain any key words they do not understand, e.g. *stroke, cholesterol, blood pressure*. If they have dictionaries, make sure they don't look up all the vocabulary in their text. Do not check their answers yet.

## EXERCISE 3
Reorganise the students into A and B pairs. Using their notes from Exercise 2, the As tell the Bs about the article. The Bs then read the questions that go with the article and choose the best answers. If they choose the wrong answer, the As must explain the point again. Then the pairs swap roles and the Bs do the same with the letter. Finally, the students discuss what they think about keeping pets.

**KEY**

Text 1:  1 Yes, they are.   2 No, they can't.   3 Yes, it is.
Text 2:  1 No, we shouldn't.   2 Yes, we do.   3 Yes, they do.

## DISCOVERING LANGUAGE EXERCISE 4
Refer the students back to the questions on Text 1 in Exercise 2 and write the first one on the board. Cross out the question tag at the end, like this: People with cats or dogs are healthier than other people, a~~ren't they~~? Ask *Is it a question now?* (No), *How do we make this into a question without changing the word order?* (by adding *aren't they?*). Underline *are* and *aren't* on the board and establish that the verb is positive in the sentence and negative in the question tag. Next, direct students to the third question in the exercise. In pairs, they discuss how question tags are formed. Check with the whole class.

**KEY**

3  The auxiliary of the main verb is used in the question tag, e.g. *like* in the statement takes *do* in the tag. Modal verbs, e.g. *can, should* are used in the tag as well as the statement. Personal pronouns replace the noun subject in the tag, e.g. *People with cats or dogs are healthier than other people, aren't they?*
The verb and personal pronoun are inverted in the tag just as they are in a normal question, e.g. *He eats meat, doesn't he?* If the first verb in the statement is positive, the verb in the tag is negative and vice versa. There is a comma between the sentence and the tag, e.g. *The weather's bad, isn't it?*
There is a question mark at the end of the tag, e.g. *He shouldn't go, should he?* The verb in the tag is in the same tense as the one in the statement.

## EXERCISE 5
Write the numbers 1-7 in a list on the board and get the students to copy it into their notebooks. Do the first one together as an example. They then complete the sentences with question tags and check their answers in pairs. Check with the whole class and write the answers on the board.

**KEY**

1 do we?   2 is she?   3 shouldn't we?   4 aren't you?
5 didn't they?   6 can he?   7 isn't it?

## 📼 EXERCISE 6
As a class discuss why the students think we might use tags in English and if they have them in their languages. Then read out the explanation in the

UNIT NINE

Students' Book and check it against what they thought. Copy the two sentences onto the board and get the students to copy them into their notebooks. Tell students to listen to the speaker's voice at the end of the tag. Play the tape and mark the intonation on the board. Do the same with the second sentence. Elicit a rule for the patterns.

**KEY AND TAPESCRIPT**

1 You're coming on Friday, aren't you?
   The voice goes up at the end.
2 Your birthday's today, isn't it?
   The voice goes down at the end.

The rule is that the voice rises when we are really asking for information with a question tag; and it falls when we are just checking the information.

### EXERCISE 7

Draw this grid on the board:

|   | (1) NOT SURE | (2) CHECKING |
|---|---|---|
| 1 |   |   |
| 2 |   |   |
| 3 |   |   |
| 4 |   |   |

Play the first example and elicit if the speaker is not sure or checking. Students tick [✓] under *not sure* next to 1. Then play the other conversations. Check the answers with the whole group. If there is any disagreement, play the sentence again and discuss the intonation pattern. Then students listen again with their books open. Play the questions again, pausing for the students to repeat.

**KEY**

1 not sure   2 checking   3 checking   4 checking

**TAPESCRIPT**

1
A: Hello, George. Where are you going?
B: I'm going to buy a puppy for my son's birthday.
A: Really? You've got a dog, haven't you?
B: Well, we had one, but it died.

2
C: Hi, George. Have you got the puppy?
B: Yes, look.
C: Oh, it's lovely. You bought some food, didn't you?
B: Yes, I did.

3
D: Mrs Simon is back from holiday.

E: Is she? How do you know?
D: There, on the wall. That's her cat, isn't it?
E: Oh, yes. I think it is.

4
E: I'm surprised Mrs Simon's got a cat.
D: Why? Oh, her husband. He hates animals, doesn't he?
E: Yes, he does.

**Extra practice**

1 To practise the two intonation patterns, prepare two worksheets with statements on them, without the tags. First, the students change the statements into questions, using question tags. Then they work in pairs and 'test' their partners. One says the sentence, the other must complete it with the appropriate tag, e.g.
A: *It's hot,*   B: *isn't it?*
Then they say the question tag again, and their partner must decide if the intonation is 'checking' or 'not sure'. Alternatively, if you do not have access to a photocopier, write each sentence on a cue card, a different one for each student. First, they change their sentence into a question tag, then the students mingle and 'test' each other in the same way.

2 Prepare about twelve question tags, some correct and some incorrect. Divide the class into teams. Read out the first one. Each team must decide if it is correct or incorrect. If the first team says *incorrect*, they must correct it immediately to get a point. Do not repeat your sentence. If they get it wrong, allow another team to correct.

3 Get each student to write down one thing that they think is true about some of the other students in the class, e.g. *Françoise lives in the suburbs*. Then they mingle and go to that person, using a question tag to find out if the information is correct or not, e.g. *Françoise, you live in the suburbs, don't you?* Their intonation will vary depending on whether they think the information is definitely correct or not.

## Development

### READING EXERCISE 1

Direct students to the four questions in Exercise 1 and get them to read the article. They discuss their answers in pairs and then check with the class.

**KEY**

1 Where does milk come from? Where do eggs come from?

2  From the supermarket, of course!
3  Because it wasn't the answer he expected. Because the children did not know where food came from.
4  They live in the city and do not see animals in their natural surroundings.

## SPEAKING EXERCISE 2
Write the two questions in the Students' Book on the board. The students discuss them in pairs and then compare their answers with another pair. Discuss as a whole class.

## EXERCISE 3
Direct the students to the pictures of the animals and birds in the Students' Book. In pairs, they match the pictures and the names. Then say *Picture 1* and elicit their answer. Drill the word if necessary. Do the same with each animal.

### KEY
1 duck  2 sheep  3 lamb  4 chicken/hen  5 pig
6 cow  7 goat  8 goose (geese)  9 horse

## 🔊 LISTENING EXERCISE 4
If necessary, present *farm* by referring students to the text in Exercise 1 and discussing where milk/eggs come from. Introduce the topic of 'Cherry Trees Farm'. Direct students to the questions and check that they understand *collect eggs*. Play the tape once. Students check their answers in pairs. If necessary, play the tape again and then check answers with the whole class.

### KEY
1  cows/cattle, pigs, sheep, chickens, geese, ducks, goats.
2  School children from city areas.
3  c, b, a, d

### TAPESCRIPT

MARY: We keep cattle, which are called Herefords; we keep black pigs; we keep sheep and we keep chickens for laying eggs and various farmyard animals – geese, ducks, goats. The majority of educational visits to Cherry Trees Farm are from schoolchildren aged between four and ten who are from city areas.
MICHAEL: Welcome to Cherry Trees Farm. Now a visit to Cherry Trees Farm is, er, not the usual sort of visit because where practical I ask you to help me.
MARY: After they've had their lunch, they then go to collect eggs, which to many is, is one of the best things they do on the farm because a hen often will be sitting in the box where the egg is laid and the child must slip its hand under the hen and actually touch a warm egg.
CHILD: I've got it, Alex!
MARY: And then usually after they have collected eggs, they will set off to see all the other animals. Part of our philosophy or belief is that animal welfare is as important as the methods by which we farm. So for us freedom amongst the animals is part of the whole system.

## READING EXERCISE 5
Introduce the idea of a 'country code' and discuss what things people should or shouldn't do in the countryside. Use the picture in the Students' Book to teach *litter*, *crops*, *hedge* and *fence*. Ask students to read the Country Code in the Students' Book and check they understand the vocabulary. Then refer them to the *fire* in the picture. Ask *Is the fire OK?* (No). Elicit *They should be careful with fires* and write the sentence on the board. Then they work in groups of three and using the code they make sentences about the picture. Check the answers with the whole group.

### KEY
They shouldn't drop litter. They should take it home with them.
The dogs shouldn't chase the sheep./They should keep their dogs under control./They should keep their pets away from farm animals.
They shouldn't leave their fire unattended./They should be careful with fires.
They shouldn't run/walk on fields where crops are growing.
They shouldn't break branches off trees. They should protect trees and plants.
They shouldn't leave gates open. They should close gates.
They shouldn't damage hedges.

## READING AND SPEAKING EXERCISE 6
Write these two questions on the board:
1  *What is the problem?*
2  *What is Sally going to do now?*
Students read the text. Encourage them to compare their answers. Then check with the whole class.

### KEY
1  Sally makes a lot of noise. (The neighbours and local council officials have complained 77 times).
2  She is going to sell her flat and move to another area where she can make as much noise as she wants to.

## EXERCISE 7
Use the example of Sally from the article to introduce the idea of a 'city code'. Ask *Do you think it's OK for Sally to make a lot of noise?* Discuss as a

class and make a rule, e.g. *People shouldn't make a noise after 11 p.m.* Write the prompts from the exercise on the board and get students to discuss other rules for the city in pairs. Monitor and correct any errors you hear. Do not discuss as a class yet.

### WRITING EXERCISE 8

The students work in the same pairs and write their own City Code. Use the example of Sally to write the first rule, e.g. *Don't make any noise after 11 p.m.* Remind the students that *should* is for giving advice but they need to use the imperative because they are **writing rules** (rather than speaking informally). Monitor and help. They then discuss their City Code with another pair and make any changes to theirs. As a class, decide which rules are the best and write them on the board. Students copy the code into their notebooks.

# Progress check 3

## Vocabulary

### EXERCISE 1
1 carrots, potatoes, peas, cucumber
2 apples, bananas, tomatoes
3 beef, lamb
4 yoghurt, ice cream, milk
5 chocolates
6 shampoo, tissues, soap, toothpaste

### EXERCISE 2
1 west   2 north   3 east   4 south

### EXERCISE 3
1 duck, goose, chicken, budgerigar   2 goldfish
3 cow, sheep, goat   4 horse   5 hamster

### EXERCISE 4
ACROSS
4 celebrity   6 sculptor   7 fatty   8 tube   9 litter
11 crop   12 meter

DOWN
1 vegetarian   2 pet   3 village   5 trolley   6 suburb
10 tip

## Grammar and functions

### EXERCISE 5
1 quickly   2 well   3 easily   4 carefully   5 fast
6 hard   7 badly   8 quietly

### EXERCISE 6
1 How do you go to work?   2 How far is it?
3 How long does it take?

### EXERCISE 7
1 Can you tell me how far the centre is, please?
2 Can you tell me when the bank opens, please?
3 Can you tell me how I get to Oxford Circus, please?
4 Can you tell me how much a large tin costs, please?
5 Can you tell me if there is a train to Paris this morning, please?

### EXERCISE 8
1 fruit, cheese, flour, milk, bread
2 mushrooms, eggs, oranges, carrots, tomatoes, boxes of chocolates

### EXERCISE 9
1 I think we should move to the city.
2 Should the little girl go to school?
3 We shouldn't keep travelling.
4 Should children be near their grandparents?
5 You look ill. You should see a doctor.

### EXERCISE 10
1 I'm sorry, I don't agree./That isn't true.
2 You're right.
3 I'm sorry, I don't agree./That isn't true.
4 I agree./You're right.
5 I don't agree./That isn't true.

### EXERCISE 11
1 British people like cats, don't they?
2 You're coming on Saturday, aren't you?
3 She's late, isn't she?
4 They didn't phone, did they?
5 He can swim, can't he?
6 We shouldn't arrive before eight, should we?

## Common errors

### EXERCISE 12
1 exhibition   2 dessert   3 potatoes   4 delicious
5 typical   6 exercises   7 physical   8 difference

### EXERCISE 13
1 Is life in the country healthier?/Is life healthier in the country?
2 I think so.
3 She always drives very carefully.
4 Here is your change.
5 The journey costs a lot of money.
6 Turn left at the traffic lights.

## EXERCISE 14

1 We haven't got *many* apples.
2 I eat *a lot of* fresh fruit.
3 A lot *of* people go away at weekends.
4 She *shouldn't go*. She's too young.
5 You've got a dog, *haven't you*?
6 *The journey* takes an hour.
7 I *don't* agree with you.
8 She isn't keen *on* junk food.
9 You spend all your money *on* clothes.

# 10 Describing things

## Lost property

**Focus**
- Lost property
- Indefinite pronouns: *someone, anything*, etc.
- Indefinite adverbs of place: *everywhere*, etc.

### EXERCISE 1
**Background note**
Each major railway station in London has a **Lost Property Office**. The **London Transport Lost Property Office** in central London is only for property lost on London buses and underground trains. Railway stations outside major cities have a regional lost property office. In American English, they are called **Lost-and-found offices**.

Direct the students to the pictures in the Students' Book and see if they can find any connection between them. Check that they understand *false teeth* by referring them to the picture. Refer them to the title of the lesson and the article and ask what the article might be about. Direct them to the questions and discuss the first one together. They then read the article and answer the questions. Encourage them to check their answers with their partners. Then check answers with the class.

**KEY**

1 a bus
2 b, d
3 Manager of the London Transport Lost Property Office.
4 She tries to contact the owner of the item and return it to them.
5 The Office keeps it for three months, and if nobody collects it, the Office sells it.
6 It's interesting and people are pleased when they find their lost item.

### EXERCISE 2
To introduce the exercise, ask *What kind of things do people lose when they're travelling?* and elicit one or two items. Write them on one side of the board. Then divide the students into pairs and give them two minutes to write down as many other items that they can think of. They must be items that people are likely to lose. Elicit their answers and write them on the board. Check that the students know all the words and drill as necessary. Keep this list on the board for Exercise 4.

### 📼 LISTENING EXERCISE 3
Copy the questions onto the board. Tell students they are listening for numbers only. Play the tape once. Students check their answers in pairs. If necessary, play the tape again.

**KEY**

1 (as many as) 500 items    2 over 1,000    3 19,000

**TAPESCRIPT**

MAUREEN BEAUMONT
On a typical day we can receive as many as five hundred items, um, if it's been raining we could receive over a thousand umbrellas, um, handbags, purses, cameras, watches, you name it and somebody's lost it at some time or another. As you can see, this is some of the false teeth that we have handed in. We're not quite sure what are tops and what are bottom sets. Probably enough musical instruments here to equip a small orchestra, false hand, part of a skeleton – that's the leg part, I think – quite a large theatrical sword, a stuffed eagle, a beautiful wedding dress. We received nineteen thousand umbrellas last year; ladies' umbrellas, gents', and even the more unusual type – an umbrella for two.

### 📼 EXERCISE 4
Direct students to the list of items in their book. Play the tape again, stopping after 'umbrellas'. Elicit the item and get students to tick it off the list in their books. Next, play the complete tape. Check the answers with the whole class and write those that are mentioned on the board. Then compare this list with the one you compiled on the board.

**KEY**

handbags, purses, umbrellas, watches, cameras, musical instruments

## DISCOVERING LANGUAGE EXERCISE 5

**Note**: There is no difference in meaning between *someone* and *somebody*, *everyone* and *everybody*, etc. We usually use *any+one/thing/where* in negative statements and questions. We can use *some + one/thing/where* in questions if we think the answer is going to be *yes*, e.g. *Did you have something to eat at the party?* = we think you did. *Anyone* can be used as a subject in a positive statement to talk about people in general, e.g. *Anyone can come to the meeting.* (But it is not used in this way in the unit.) *Anywhere* means any place, e.g. *You can park anywhere here*. In American English, *someplace/anyplace* may be used instead of *somewhere/anywhere*.

Direct the students to the words in their book. Write these headings on the board:

| PEOPLE | PLACES | THINGS |
|--------|--------|--------|
|        |        |        |

Tell them to find a sentence with *something* in it from the text. Discuss as a class if *something* is used for a person, place or thing. Write it under *things* on the board. The students then find the other words in the text. In pairs they place them under the headings. Check the answers with the whole class. Next, direct them to the other three questions in the exercise. They refer to the text and discuss them in their pairs. Then check as a class.

**KEY**

| PEOPLE | PLACES | THINGS |
|--------|--------|--------|
| anyone | somewhere | something |
| no one |  | everything |

1 anyone   2 no one   3 singular (collects)

## EXERCISE 6

Copy the chart onto the board and get students to copy it into their notebooks. They use their answers from Exercise 5 to help them complete the chart. Encourage them to check their answers with their partner. Check with the class and complete the chart on the board. Some of the pronouns listed here were not presented in Exercise 5, but students should guess their meanings by analogy with the other pronouns. To check that the students understand them, ask concept questions such as *Which word means 'not anywhere'?* Leave the chart on the board for the next exercise.

**KEY**

| PERSON | PLACE | THING |
|--------|-------|-------|
| everyone | everywhere | everything |
| someone | somewhere | something |
| anyone | anywhere | anything |
| no one | nowhere | nothing |

### Extra practice

Tell the students that you are going to read out a long sentence and they must stop you by using one of the words from the chart on the board. Read out the first sentence:
*It's my brother's birthday. I want to buy him <u>a watch or a clock or a bicycle ...</u>* and elicit *something*. As a further concept check, ask *Do we use 'something' in a positive sentence, negative sentence or a question?* and elicit *positive sentence*. Drill the sentence *I want to buy him something*. Use the sentences below in the same way. If necessary, with each one elicit the pronoun and check that the students know how it is used. Remember to use rising intonation on each of the items in the lists, and falling intonation on the pronoun to finish the list. The underlined words are the final sentences to be drilled.

- I was so hungry that I went to the fridge and <u>I ate the cheese, the meat, the tomatoes ...</u> (*everything*)
- I can't find my glasses. <u>I can't find them in the bathroom, in the kitchen, in the bedroom ...</u> (*anywhere*)
- I don't know where he is. <u>He's in the garden, or in his bedroom or in the kitchen ...</u> (*somewhere*)
- It's important. <u>I need to see Mary or Joe or Ruth or ...</u> (*someone*)
- It's personal. <u>I can't ask Andrew or Peter or Sally or...</u> (*anyone*)
- <u>The room is empty. Paul isn't here, Sarah, isn't here, Roger isn't here. There's ...</u> (*no one*) here
- I couldn't find my glasses yesterday. <u>I looked in the bathroom, in the fridge, in the garden, ...</u> (*everywhere*).
- It's impossible! <u>I don't understand the grammar, the words, the pronunciation, my teacher ...</u> (*anything*).
- The cupboard is empty! <u>There's no coffee, no biscuits, no cake ...</u> (*nothing*)

## WORD STRESS EXERCISE 7

Refer the students back to the chart on the board from Exercise 6. Play the first word and mark the stress on the board. Then play the complete tape, stopping if necessary for the students to mark the stress in their notebooks. Check the answers with the whole class and establish that the main stress always falls on the first syllable of each word. Play the tape again, pausing for the students to repeat.

### KEY

The main stress falls on the first syllable of each word.

### TAPESCRIPT

éveryone sómeone ányone nó one
éverywhere sómewhere ánywhere nówhere
éverything sómething ánything nóthing

## EXERCISE 8

Direct the students to the paragraph in their book and back to the chart in their notebooks (from Exercise 6). They should read the paragraph for gist first. Then do the first sentence together to demonstrate the task. Encourage them to compare their answers with their partners. Then check the answers with the whole group.

### KEY

1 no one   2 something   3 everywhere   4 anything
5 anywhere   6 someone

### Extra practice

1  Prepare twelve correct and incorrect sentences/questions, using the words from the chart, e.g. *I'm not going nowhere. I don't understand nothing.* Read them out or write them on the board. The students work in pairs, identifying those with errors and correcting them.

2  You can use the same sentences in Practice 1 above to do 'an auction'. You divide the class into teams and 'give' each team £1,000. The aim of the activity is for the students to use the money to buy 'correct' sentences. You read out the first sentence twice and then start the bidding, e.g. Team A offers £25, Team B increases it to £40, Team C to £100, and so on until someone 'buys' the sentence. Then you quickly go onto the next sentence. The team to win has bought the most correct sentences. If two or more teams have the same number of correct sentences, the winner is the team with the most money left at the end. If your students are unfamiliar with the idea of 'an auction', you will need to explain it.

3  Draw a 'noughts and crosses' grid on the board, like this:

| somewhere | nothing | everyone |
|---|---|---|
| no one | anything | everywhere |
| something | anywhere | someone |

Make sure the students understand how to play the game. Divide the class into two teams. They decide which team is noughts (0) and which is crosses (X). Then the first team chooses a word from the grid and makes a correct sentence/question using the word, e.g. *My pen is somewhere on this desk.* The other team decides if the sentence is grammatically correct or not. If it is correct, they can put a 0 or a X in the square, over the word. Then the next team chooses a word. The team to win gets the first straight line of words, like this:

| som⨯where | nothing | everyone |
|---|---|---|
| no one | any⨯hing | everywhere |
| something | anywhere | som⨯one |

## EXERCISE 9

Write the four questions on the board and tell the students that you lost something really important last week. Wait until they ask you the first question (point at it if necessary) and then answer it. Do the same with the other questions. Then divide the students into pairs. Get them each to think about the last time they lost something. They use the questions on the board to interview each other. Monitor and correct any errors you hear.

## EXERCISE 10

Direct the students to the pictures and write the names of the items on the board. The students work in pairs and match the pictures with their names. If the students do not have dictionaries, get them to ask other students in the class if they know the answers. Check the answers with the whole class.

### KEY

1  a sword            2  part of a skeleton
3  handcuffs          4  a false hand
5  a wedding dress    6  an accordion

## EXERCISE 11

Ask *Why do you think someone took part of a skeleton on a bus?* and discuss possible reasons. Get the students to read the explanation to see if they guessed correctly. Then divide the students into pairs. They each choose one of the objects in the

# UNIT TEN

picture and make up a story about why they had it on a bus/train and how they lost it. Then they tell each other. For feedback, some of the students can tell their story to the whole class.

## Giving details

> **Focus**
> - Objects
> - Materials
>
> - Describing things
> - Talking about colour, size, weight and material
> - Describing shape
>
> - Questions: *What colour? What shape? How big? How heavy?*
> - Present simple passive: *be made of*

### EXERCISE 1

Bring to the lesson an object which is large enough for everyone to see, e.g. a beach ball, a cake tin. Show the students the object and ask *What colour is it?* Elicit *It's* + colour. Then ask *What shape is it?* If necessary, mime *shape* if the students do not understand. Elicit *It's round.* Do the same with *How big is it?* (It's 20 centimetres wide). *How heavy is it?* (It's 300 grams). *What's it made of?* (It's made of metal). The students practise the five exchanges in open pairs. If you wish, you can do the same with another object.

The students listen to the conversation with books closed. Play the tape once. They make notes about Rosie's present to James, and check their answers with their partners. Then check with the whole class. Discuss what they think the present is. Then play the conversation again with books open. Students shadow the conversation. Point out the use of *wide* and *long* and teach *high*, e.g. with this picture of a house:

**KEY**

It's green and blue and rectangular. It's about 30 centimetres wide and two metres long. It's less than a kilo and is made of wool. It's a scarf.

### EXERCISE 2

Copy the questions onto the board. Play the first question, stopping for the students to repeat.

Discuss where the main stress falls. Then play the other questions, stopping for the students to repeat. Drill the questions if necessary.

**KEY AND TAPESCRIPT**

(Main stresses are underlined.)
1 What <u>colour</u> is it?   2 What <u>shape</u> is it?
3 How <u>big</u> is it?   4 How <u>heavy</u> is it?
5 What's it <u>made</u> of?

### EXERCISE 3

Direct the students to the pictures of the six objects in the Students' Book. Elicit what each one is and write their names on the board. Then refer the students to the descriptions of the objects and get them to read the first description. Ask *Which object is it?* and elicit *a computer disk*. The students then work in pairs and match the other objects and descriptions. To check their answers ask *Which one is the mirror?* and elicit the answer (or get a student to read out the description). Write the number of the description next to the object on the board. Check that the students understand *plastic, in diameter, frame, handles, face* and *strap*.

**KEY**

A – mirror – 2   B – lamp – 3   C – case – 4
D – computer disk – 1   E – watch – 5   F – rug – 6

### EXERCISE 4

Direct the students to the pictures of the five shapes. If you have a large class, you may want to draw the shapes on the board. Point to the first shape and ask *What shape is this?* Elicit *It's square.* Students can refer to Exercise 3 to work out the shapes. Drill the answer, noting the stress. Do the same with the other shapes.

**KEY**

1 It's square   2 It's round   3 It's <u>o</u>val
4 It's rec<u>tan</u>gular   5 It's tri<u>an</u>gular

### EXERCISE 5

Remind the students of the five questions in Exercise 2. If necessary, drill them again and remind them of *long, wide* and *high*. Then divide the class into As and Bs. Direct the As to the pictures in Exercise 5 and the Bs to page 121. Check that they know the names of their objects but make sure they do not look at each other's pictures. They can sit back to back to do the exercise if you wish. Establish that they each have three objects to ask about. Tell the As to ask the questions first. Monitor and correct any errors you hear.

86

## EXERCISE 6

To demonstrate the task, think of an object and tell the class they must ask you questions to guess what it is. Do not answer if they ask *What is it?*! Next, tell each student to think of an object. The students work in groups of about five. One student 'starts' and the other students ask questions to find out what his/her object is. Monitor and make a note of any errors. Get feedback as a class and find out what objects the students chose. Use the board to correct any errors you heard.

### Extra practice

The students work in groups of six, each group subdivided into two groups of three. One group of three has a list of four people to buy presents for, e.g. a parent, teacher, student in the class, sister. The other half of the group has either twelve colour pictures of different objects, or the names of twelve objects. They cannot show these objects to the students who are buying the presents, who must find out what the objects are and choose a present for each person by asking questions, e.g. *What's the first object?/ It's a ... . What colour is it?* etc. If the second 'group' has names only, not pictures, they must decide on the details.

## COMPARING CULTURES EXERCISE 7

Check the students understand the term *second-hand*, e.g. describe or show a picture of a second-hand car. Then direct them to the exercise. In groups they discuss if they buy these items second-hand in their country/countries. Then discuss as a class. Explain that it is quite common in Britain to buy second-hand cars, bicycles, etc. and that there are a large number of second-hand shops for clothes, most of which receive the clothes free and give the profits to a charity.

## EXERCISE 8

Divide the students into pairs. The As look at the advertisement in the exercise. The Bs turn to page 121 and look at the information about the things they are selling. Establish that the As are going to phone the Bs because they are interested in buying B's items. Check that the students understand the vocabulary in their information. Get the pairs to read the example exchange and then continue the conversation. Then they change roles. Make sure they make notes for Exercise 9.

## EXERCISE 9

Refer the students back to their notes about the objects from Exercise 8. To demonstrate the task, use the carpet as an example. Elicit the beginning of the description from the class and write it on the board, following the model in their books. The students write about their partner's objects. They then exchange texts and check for any grammatical or factual errors.

### KEY

The colour TV is rectangular. It's 45 cm high, 45 cm wide and 42 cm deep. The screen is 40 cm wide. It's black and it's got a remote control.

The computer desk is 69 cm high, 100 cm wide and 70 cm deep. It's made of metal. It's grey and white with wheels and special shelves for a printer and paper.

The tent is one m high, 120 cm wide and 190 cm deep. It is for two people. It's blue and green and it's made of nylon.

The portable CD player is 16 cm long, 13 cm wide and 6 cm deep. It weighs two kilogrammes. It has got a radio, stereo headphones and a case.

The shelves are rectangular; they are 2 m long and 20 cm wide. They're black and they're made of wood.

### ENGLISH AROUND YOU

Focus students' attention on the cartoon. Check that they understand the humour: the impossibility of answering the question *What's it like?*

## Describing clothes

> **Focus**
>
> - Clothes
> - Materials
>
> - Describing clothes
> - Asking what something is like
> - Talking about possessions
>
> - Adjectives and order of adjectives
> - Possessive pronouns: *mine*, *yours*, etc.

### EXERCISE 1

Bring in pictures of clothes or use the students' clothes to teach/revise vocabulary of colours and material. Make sure you teach *cotton*, *cashmere*, *woollen*, *plastic*, *leather* and possibly *silk* and *polyester*. Then direct students to the pictures of the five sweaters in the Students' Book. Write the names of the people on the board. Point to Gene and play the first description. As a class decide which sweater he is describing and write the letter of the picture next to his name. Then play the complete tape. Do not confirm their answers yet.

UNIT TEN

**TAPESCRIPT**

1 PAUL MONEY
Almost all my sweaters are dark blue and wool or cotton – I have a number.
2 MARK HILL
My favourite sweater is red, and it's made of wool, with my golf club's emblem on it.
3 GENE ABBOTT
My favourite sweater is blue, it's made of wool and I bought it in Scotland.
4 JOSH LOFRANO
My favourite sweater is a mint green colour and it's made of 100% cotton.
5 MILDRED COOKSON
Grey and cashmere.

**KEY**

Gene Abbot – Sweater 1    Josh Lofrano – Sweater 2
Mark Hill – Sweater 3    Mildred Cookson – Sweater 4
Paul Money – Sweater 5
Note that in the first edition of the Students' Book, Gene's sweater is incorrectly referred to as dark blue and sweater 5 shown as patterned instead of dark blue.

### EXERCISE 2

The aim of this exercise is for students to work with their partners to check their answers to Exercise 1. Play the tape again if necessary, then get them to read the example exchange. If necessary, drill it, concentrating on *Whose?* and the *'s*. They practise similar exchanges to check their answers.

**Extra practice**

If you wish to revise vocabulary of clothes from Unit 4 with your students, write the words as anagrams on the board, e.g. *cskso* (socks), *tlbe* (belt). The students work in groups and decipher the words. If you like, they can do it in teams. The fastest team wins as long as their answers are correct!

### DISCOVERING LANGUAGE EXERCISE 3

To remind the students of the rule they learnt in Unit 4 for adjective order, write this sentence on the board: *It's a blue large vase*. Ask *Is it OK?* (No) *Why not?* and elicit that the order of adjectives is incorrect and that it should be quality followed by colour. Then copy the first sentence onto the board and draw this grid:

| ADJECTIVE 1 ? | ADJECTIVE 2 ? | ADJECTIVE 3 ? | + NOUN |
|---|---|---|---|
| large | blue | woollen | sweater |

Ask students to copy the grid into their notebooks. Do the first sentence together as an example. Get the students to do the same with the other sentences. Write their answers in the columns. Then as a class make a rule for the order of adjectives and add the types of adjectives next to the question marks in the chart, i.e. quality + colour + material.

### EXERCISE 4

Direct the students back to the pictures in Exercise 1. To demonstrate the task, write a sentence about the first picture on the board. The students then write sentences for the other sweaters. They compare their answers with their partners and then check the answers with the whole class.

**KEY**

1 It's a long, blue, cotton sweater.
2 It's an old, green, cotton sweater.
3 It's a new, red, woollen sweater.
4 It's a (small), grey, cashmere sweater.
5 It's a large, dark blue, woollen sweater.

### EXERCISE 5

Direct them to the two pictures in the Students' Book. Get them to read the descriptions and match the descriptions with the pictures. Then, draw simple sketches of the jackets on the board. In pairs, the students name each labelled item, using dictionaries if available. Check the answers with the whole class. To check understanding, point to the items on the students and elicit the vocabulary.

**KEY**

Jacket 1 – Description 032    Jacket 2 – Description 031
A – collar    B – button    C – pocket    D – hood
E – zip    F – belt

**Extra practice**

To practise the order of adjectives, copy this list onto the board: j*acket, leather, woollen, short, long, blue, black, cashmere, sweater, dress, silk, cotton, navy, warm, hat, new, heavy, light, trousers, thick, coat, beautiful, old*. The students work in groups and write down as many combinations as they can, e.g. *a long, black, woollen coat*.

### EXERCISE 6

To focus on more vocabulary relevant to clothes ask students to find the opposites of the following words/phrases in Exercise 5: *cool* (warm), *at the back* (at the front), *heavy* (light), *short* (long).

To introduce the question form say *I've got a lovely new sweater.* and pause. Elicit/teach the question *What's it like?* Give a short answer. Establish that this is a question you ask when you want a description and that like is only used in the question not in the answer. Drill the question chorally and individually. Then say *I've got some lovely new shoes* and elicit *What are they like?* Point out the plural form of the verb *to be* and drill both questions.

Divide the students into As and Bs. Get two students to read out the example exchange. The students then work in pairs and interview each other about their favourite clothes. Monitor and correct any errors you hear.

## EXERCISE 7
Direct the students back to the descriptions in Exercises 3 and 5. Get each student to choose one piece of clothing that another student is wearing. Individually, they write a short description of the item. Monitor and help. Then they read out their description and the other students guess who is wearing it. If you have a large class, they can read out their descriptions in groups of six.

## EXERCISE 8
You may need to revise the use of the present progressive for description. Point to a student and ask *What is he/she wearing?* Elicit a description and drill the question form. Then write the names of four other students on the board or display four large pictures. The students work in pairs and ask and answer about the clothes they are wearing. Monitor and correct any errors you hear. Next, direct the students to the picture of James and Julia. As a class describe what they are wearing. The students can also describe the coats the waiter is holding. Then ask *What's the problem?* and play the tape. The students quickly discuss the problem with their partner. Check with the whole class.

### KEY
The waiter tries to give James the wrong coat when he leaves the restaurant. He has given James's coat to another customer, who is leaving the restaurant.

## DISCOVERING LANGUAGE EXERCISE 9
Play the conversation again, stopping after James says *This isn't mine.* Elicit what he says and write it on the board. Continue to play the conversation and do the same with *What's **yours** like?* and ***His** is a long black one.* Then direct students to the three sentences in the exercise and ask them to work in pairs to replace the words in italics with one pronoun. Check the answers with the class.

### KEY
1 mine   2 yours   3 his

Point to *mine* and ask *What's this talking about?* Elicit *James's coat.* Then ask *Why not 'my'?* and elicit that *my* must be followed by *an object* (= my coat) and *mine* includes the object and **cannot** be followed by one (*mine* = *my coat*). It is not necessary to tell students the names of the forms (*my* = possessive adjective, *mine* = possessive pronoun) unless they specifically want to know.

### TAPESCRIPT

JAMES:   Well, that was a nice meal.
JULIA:   Lovely. I enjoy eating out.
WAITER:  Here you are, madam. Your coat, sir.
JULIA:   Thank you very much.
JAMES:   Er, this isn't mine.
WAITER:  I'm sorry, sir. What's yours like?
JULIA:   His is a long, black, leather one.
WAITER:  Oh. I can't see one like that. Not leather.
JULIA:   James, look over there. Isn't that man wearing your coat?
JAMES:   What? Yes, he is. Wait …!

### Extra practice
Divide the students into groups of four. Using the chart, they write sentences with both forms, e.g. *This is my pen. It's mine. Those are their books. They're theirs.* Then reorganise the students into different groups. They use their sentences to test each other. They read out the first part of a sentence and the others must supply the second part, e.g.
A: *This is my pen.* B/C: *It's mine.*

## EXERCISE 10
Elicit the rule for the use of possessive pronouns if you didn't do so in Exercise 9. Copy the three sentences from Exercise 10 onto the board. The students complete the gaps and compare their answers with their partner. Then check the answers with the whole group.

### KEY
1 her, hers   2 our, ours   3 theirs, their

## EXERCISE 11
Direct the students to the pictures in the Students' Book. Check that they remember *buttons, collar, belt, hood, pockets* and *zip*. Then choose a picture and refer the students to the example exchange. Get them to ask you the questions and take on the role of B. Drill the questions as necessary. Then change roles: you ask the questions and one student answers. Divide them into As and Bs. Tell the Bs to choose a coat. The As then ask the Bs questions to guess which coat it is. Make sure they change roles.

# UNIT TEN

## Development

### 📼 LISTENING AND WRITING EXERCISE 1
**Background note**

In British English, we often use the word **luggage** although it is possible to use **baggage.** In American English, **baggage** is much more common.

Direct the students to the picture of Maura and the baggage enquiry form in the Students' Book. Discuss where she is (the airport) and what they think her problem could be (she's lost her baggage). Use a picture to teach *holdall*. Next, copy the form onto the board and get the students to copy it into their notebooks. Play the tape, more than once if necessary. Students compare their answers with their partners. Then check with the whole class. Elicit the answers from the students and complete the form on the board.

**KEY**

| | |
|---|---|
| Surname: | Mattioli |
| First Name: | Maura |
| Address: | International Student Hostel, Malet Street, London WC1 3LA |
| Telephone Number: | 071 637 5883 |
| Flight Number: | BA 172 |
| Arriving from: | Milan |

Description: One big, brown, leather suitcase. About one metre long and 70 cm wide. One green, cotton or nylon holdall with a black, leather handle. It's about half the size of the suitcase.

**TAPESCRIPT**

OFFICIAL: Can I help you?
MAURA: Yes, I can't find my baggage.
O: Which flight were you on?
M: Er, BA172, from Milan.
O: Right. Er, how many bags are missing?
M: Two.
O: Can you describe them?
M: Well, there's a big suitcase – it's brown and it's made of leather.
O: How big is it?
M: Um, about a metre long by, ... I don't know, about seventy centimetres.
O: OK. And you say it's made of leather?
M: Yes.
O: What about the other suitcase?
M: Er, it isn't a suitcase, it's a holdall – it's smaller, about half the size. It's green with a black handle.
O: And is that made of leather, too?
M: Well, the handle's leather, but the bag's cotton, or nylon. I'm not sure which.
O: OK. Don't worry. I'm sure we'll find them. Now, can I take your name and address?
M: My name's Maura Mattioli – that's M-A-T-T-I-O-L-I. And I'm staying at the International Student Hostel, that's a student hostel in Malet Street – M-A-L-E-T Street, London WC1 3LA.
O: Malet Street, London WC1. Right. And can you give me a telephone number where I can contact you today or tomorrow?
M: Yes. The hostel number is 071-637 5883.
O: Right. Well, that's everything. I'll call you later today when the next flight from Milan arrives to let you know what's happening. When we find the bags, we'll send them to you immediately.
M: OK. Thank you very much.

### SPEAKING EXERCISE 2

Divide the students into As (airport officials) and Bs (passengers). Direct the As to the pictures in Exercise 2 and the Bs to the picture of their bag on page 121. Establish that the As have different bags and that the Bs have lost only one. If you wish, the As can copy the form from Exercise 1 into their notebook and fill in their partner's details as they roleplay the conversation. Monitor and make a note of any errors. Check the answer with the class and use the board to correct any errors you heard.

### READING EXERCISE 3
**Background note:**

*The Importance of Being Earnest* is a famous comedy by Oscar Wilde about mistaken identity and falling in love. Lady Bracknell lost her baby boy when the nanny left him by mistake in a handbag at a railway station in London. The baby was brought up by a stranger who called him Jack. (He pretends to be called Earnest in the story.) Eventually, at the end of the story, Jack discovers that Lady Bracknell is his mother. **Oscar Wilde** was a famous Irish writer. Many of the clever and funny things he said in conversations have become famous.

Before the students read the text, ask if they have heard of Oscar Wilde or *The Importance of Being Earnest*. Then check that students understand *perambulator* and *bassinette* from the definitions. Reassure them that they do not need to understand all the vocabulary to understand the story. Then direct the students to the six statements and the text. They read the text and decide if the statements are true or false. Check the answers with the whole class.

**KEY**

1 True   2 True   3 True   4 False   5 True   6 False

# 11 You and your body

## The human body

> **Focus**
> - Parts of the body
> - Aches and pains
> - Asking about problems
> - Talking about illness
> - Making suggestions
> - Giving advice: *Why don't you?/ You should(n't) ...*
> - Further practice: *have/has got*

### EXERCISE 1
Direct the class to the pictures in the Students' Book showing parts of the human body. If possible, draw a simple outline of the human body on the board (which students copy into their notebooks if necessary). Students label the parts they know on the pictures in the book, or on the board. Check that all the students understand the vocabulary and drill where necessary. Students now read the texts and try to complete the rest of the labels. They should check this in pairs and use dictionaries where necessary. Elicit the remaining body parts by pointing at the picture on the board and asking students for the names, or ask students to come to the board and label the diagram. Make sure you cover all the vocabulary presented on page 80. For practice, erase the names of the parts of the body from the board and point to each in turn, asking students to supply the name.

**KEY**

1. arms B, chest A, neck E, legs C, back D, waist F
2. head A, nose D, eye C, mouth E, ear B
3. feet B, toes C, ankles A
4. hips A, knees B, arms E, elbows D, shoulders C
5. heart A
6. hands C, fingers B, lungs A
7. skin A, face B

### EXERCISE 2
To demonstrate the task, read out the example statement and ask *Which parts of the body?* Elicit *neck* and *chest*. Direct the students to the exercise. They work in pairs and do the same with the other five statements. Monitor and help. Check the answers with the whole class.

**KEY**

1 waist, leg   2 fingers   3 knee   4 elbow
5 a) mouth   b) ears   c) eyes   d) lungs

### Extra practice

1. To revise the pronunciation of the vocabulary in Exercise 1, write the words in phonemic script on separate pieces of paper. Number each piece of paper and display them around the classroom. The students write the numbers in a list in their notebooks. In pairs, they move around the classroom and write down the words in their notebooks, e.g. /niː/ = knee.

2. The students stand in a circle. Begin by saying *This is my foot* and point to your foot. The student next to you continues *This is my foot and these are my toes.* The next student continues. If a student forgets one of the parts, they sit down.

3. To revise the vocabulary, write it mixed up on the board, e.g. *nglu* (lung). The students work together to decipher the words.

### EXERCISE 3
If possible, bring in pictures of the jobs in the exercise and others the students know. To demonstrate the task, ask *Which parts of the body are most important for a teacher?* Elicit a reply, e.g. *The most important part of the body for a teacher is the head because they have to think a lot.* Then direct students to the exercise. They work in groups of three and discuss which are the most important parts of the bodies for the six jobs listed and the reasons. Monitor and correct any serious errors you hear. Discuss their answers as a class. Extend the activity with other jobs (use your pictures), if you wish.

**KEY**

Possible answers:
1 a painter – eyes/hands   2 a runner – legs/lungs
3 a pilot – eyes/head   4 a drummer – arms/feet
5 a Sumo wrestler – legs/arms
6 a swimmer – arms/shoulders

### EXERCISE 4
**Note:** In American English, *have* is commonly used instead of *have got*. This occurs when talking about illness, e.g. *I have a cold*, rather than *I've got a cold*.

To introduce the language, mime 'looking unhappy'. Elicit *What's the matter?* Drill the question chorally and individually. Then mime that your leg hurts and say *My leg hurts.* Drill the exchange chorally and in open pairs. Display pictures of a finger, an arm and an ankle or write the words on the board. Get the students to use these parts of the body to practise similar exchanges. Then get the students to ask you the question again and reply. Get the students to give you some advice. If necessary, use a picture of a person sitting down and elicit *You should sit down*. Drill the response and then the complete exchange and then elicit/supply *That's a good idea*. Drill the four-line dialogue chorally and in open pairs. Next, indicate your three pictures on the board. Using these as prompts, the students practise the dialogue in closed pairs.

Direct the students to the picture in the Students' Book and discuss who the people are and what they are doing. Write the two comprehension questions from the exercise on the board. Play the tape once with books closed. The students compare their answers with their partners. Then check the answers with the whole class. Play the tape again while students read.

**KEY**

1 His arms hurt.   2 Why don't you stop for a moment? You should ask me to help you with the heavier boxes.

## DISCOVERING LANGUAGE EXERCISE 5

**Note:** Students often try to use the infinitive with *to* after *should* and *why don't you*, e.g. *You should **to** go*. Drill the correct use of the infinitive without *to*, e.g. *You should go*, as much as necessary.

Refer the students back to the conversation in Exercise 4 and their answers. Get them to read it and find two expressions for giving advice. Write the phrases on the board and highlight the form and pronunciation. Drill each form chorally and individually if necessary. Highlight the fact that *Why don't you ...?* is a question form (followed by a question mark), but *You should ...* is a statement.

**KEY**

Why don't you ...? You should ... (Both are followed by the infinitive without *to*.)

## EXERCISE 6

Direct the students to the three pictures in the Students' Book. Quickly remind them of the four-line dialogue they practised in Exercise 4. Use realia, mime and drawings on the board to teach the 'remedies' in the Students' Book. Then they work in pairs and use the pictures to practise similar dialogues. Monitor and make a note of any errors. To check their answers, get the students to roleplay their exchanges for the whole class. Finally, use the board to correct any errors you heard.

**KEY**

1  My back hurts.   – rest/stop work/lie down/put some cream on
2  My leg hurts.   – rest/sit down/go to the doctor
3  My feet hurt.   – rest/sit down/put a plaster on

## EXERCISE 7

The students will probably need a lot of practice with the pronunciation of the words ending in *ache* /eɪk/, and *cough* /kɒf/. Mime 'headache' and elicit *What's the matter?* Reply *I've got a headache*. Drill the exchange. Use mime to elicit *I've got backache/ toothache/stomachache and earache*. Make sure the students understand that the indefinite article (*a*) is used with *headache* but that the other aches do not usually have an article. Then elicit *I've got a cold/ cough*. The students practise these exchanges in open and closed pairs. Then display/draw a picture of a person on the board with his head in his hands and ask *What's wrong with him?* and elicit *He's got a headache*. Drill the exchange chorally and in open pairs. Establish that *What's wrong with him?* is the same as *What's the matter with him?*

Refer the class to pictures 1-6 in the Students' Book. Point to Picture 1 and ask *What's the matter with him?* Elicit the response and drill the exchange. The students then work in pairs and practise similar exchanges using the other pictures. Monitor and correct any errors.

**KEY**

1  a headache – lie down/take an aspirin
2  a cold – stay at home/keep warm/take an aspirin
3  coughs – take some medicine
4  toothache – go to the dentist/take an aspirin
5  earache – go to the doctor/keep warm
6  stomachache – stop eating/take some medicine

### Extra practice

1  The students work in pairs. One of them thinks of an illness, the other must guess what it is, e.g.
   A: *Have you got a headache?*
   B: *No, I haven't.*
   They continue until they guess what the matter is. Then they give their partner advice.

2  Each student thinks of an illness or a problem that they have, e.g. *I've got backache. I haven't got any friends.* They mingle and get advice from the others, e.g.
   A: *What's the matter?*
   B: *I've got backache.*
   A: *You should go to the doctor.*
   B: *That's a good idea./Maybe.*

The aim of the activity is for the students to find the 'best' advice for their problem.

## 🔊 EXERCISE 8

Copy the sentences onto the board and get the students to copy them into their notebooks. Play the first sentence. Get the students to identify the main stress and mark it on the board. Then do the same with the other sentences. Check the answers on the board with the whole group. Then play the tape again, pausing for the students to repeat.

**KEY AND TAPESCRIPT**

EXAMPLE: He's got a <u>head</u>ache.
1 She's got a <u>cold</u>.   2 They've got <u>coughs</u>.   3 She's got <u>tooth</u>ache.   4 He's got <u>ear</u>ache.   5 She's got <u>sto</u>machache.

# Accidents

> **Focus**
> - Accidents
> - Talking about events in the recent past
> - Present perfect simple: *have/has* + past participle
> - Adverb: *just*

## EXERCISE 1

Direct the students to the picture of Marco's room in the Students' Book. Explain that a friend is bringing her small children to visit him. Ask *Is the room OK?* (No) and elicit some of the problems. Make sure the students know *electric kettle*. Then indicate the table and ask *What should he do?* and elicit *He should clear/tidy the table.* Write this sentence on the board. The students work in pairs and write more sentences about what he should do. Monitor and help with the vocabulary. Then get them to read out their sentences and write them on the board. Leave the list on the board for Exercise 2.

**KEY**

He should put a fireguard in front of the fire/move the glasses/lock (close) all the cupboards/move his records and CDs/put his notes away.

## 🔊 EXERCISE 2

**Note**: This is the first time that the present perfect tense and past participles have been presented in *Look Ahead*. The present perfect is used here to express a recent action. The other uses of the present perfect are introduced later in the book, so you do not need to mention them in this lesson.

If you wish to present the new structure before doing Exercise 2, tell the students to watch what you do. Pick up a book and put it on the floor. Ask *What have I done?* Elicit *You put the book on the floor* and correct it: *You've put ...* To check the concept ask *Where is the book now?* (On the floor) *Am I putting it on the floor now?* (No) *Did I put it on the floor a long time ago?* (No) Drill the response chorally and individually. You do not need to explain the form to the students at this stage as this is highlighted in the next exercise. Open the classroom door and ask *What have I done?* Elicit *You've opened the door.* Use the same questions to check concept and drill the exchange.

Refer the students to the list on the board from Exercise 1. Explain that Marco is talking to Teresa on the phone and that they must listen and tick [✔] the things that Marco has done. Play the tape, stopping after 'bought a fireguard' and elicit what he says. Tick *fireguard* on the board. Then play the complete conversation. The students compare their answers with their partners. Play the conversation again while students read. Then check with the whole class on the board: ask *What's he done?* Elicit *He's bought a fireguard.* Drill the exchange chorally and individually. Then use the list to elicit *He's put the glasses on a higher shelf./He's locked the cupboards.* Then ask *What about his records?* and elicit *He hasn't moved his records.* Drill the response. Finally, ask *Has he bought a fireguard?* Elicit *Yes, he has.* Do the same with the other prompts. The students then practise in closed pairs.

**KEY**

He's bought a fireguard.
He's put the glasses on a higher shelf
He's locked all the cupboards.

## 🔊 EXERCISE 3

Copy the example exchange onto the board. Check that students understand *monsters* and *sweet*. Play the tape and together underline the main stresses. Establish that the students stress the 'contrast' words (e.g. <u>little</u> <u>monsters</u> and <u>sweet</u>). Then they practise the other two dialogues in pairs. To check their answers, get volunteer pairs to read them out to the whole class. Encourage peer correction. Drill the exchanges chorally if necessary.

**KEY**

1 warm, <u>freezing</u>  2 late, <u>early</u>

## DISCOVERING LANGUAGE EXERCISE 4

Refer the students back to the conversation in Exercise 2. Get them to find the first example of a statement in the present perfect: *I've bought a fireguard*. Write the sentence on the board and underline *I've bought*. Give the name of the tense and elicit how it is formed (*have/has* + past participle). Get the students to find more examples of the present perfect in the conversation, including negative statements and questions. Then direct the class to the definition of its use in their books. They read the three definitions and decide which one is correct. Discuss the answer as a class. If necessary, use the examples and the concept questions from Exercise 2 if the students are still having problems.

**KEY**

c

## EXERCISE 5

Copy the chart onto the board. Write in the infinitives and complete the column for the past simple tense as a class. Refer the students back to the conversation in Exercise 2 and get them to complete the chart with the past participles. Check the answers with the whole class and complete the chart on the board. Leave it on the board for Exercise 6.

**KEY**

bought   moved   done   put   locked   had

## EXERCISE 6

**Note**: For information on the pronunciation and spelling of *ed* endings, see *Look Ahead 1* (Unit 11). The Extra practice activity after this exercise revises the pronunciation of the *ed* ending.

Point to the chart on the board from Exercise 5. Ask *Which are regular verbs?* (*move* and *lock*) *How do we form the past participle?* (In the same way as the past simple, by adding *ed*). Establish that for regular verbs, the forms of the past simple tense and past participles are the same. It may be necessary to remind the students of the pronunciation rules for *ed*, i.e. /t/ after voiceless consonants such as /s/ and /k/; /d/ after voiced consonants such as /dʒ/, /m/ and vowels; /ɪd/ after /t/ and /d/.

### Extra practice

If your students need revision of the pronunciation of *ed* endings, draw the following grid on the board:

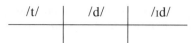

Write infinitives on the board, e.g. *play, stay, travel, hate, ask*, etc. Ensure that they all have regular past participles. The students change the infinitives into past participles and place them in the correct column according to the pronunciation of their endings.

## EXERCISE 7

Copy the chart from the exercise onto the board, without the past participles.

Elicit the past participles if possible and write them in the chart. Drill as necessary and then refer the students to the chart in their books. Direct them to the first picture in the Students' Book and ask *What's she done?* Elicit *She's fallen down the stairs*. If necessary, check that the students remember that they use *has* for third person singular and *have* for the other forms. Drill the exchange chorally and individually. Refer the students to the other pictures (with their pronouns) in the exercise. They work in pairs and ask and answer about the people in the pictures. Make sure they change roles. Monitor and correct any errors. To check the answers, get pairs to practise their exchanges for the whole class.

**KEY**

2  What's he done?    He's cut his finger.
3  What's she done?   She's hit the boy.
4  What have they done?   They've burnt the toast.
5  What's she done?   She's eaten a box of chocolates.
6  What have you done?   I've broken the chair.
7  What have you done?   We've smashed the window.

## EXERCISE 8

Copy the dialogue from the Students' Book onto the board. Ask *What has she done?* (She's washed her hair). Then ask *Which word tells you that this happened a very short time ago?* Elicit *just*. Ask *Where does 'just' go in the sentence?* Elicit their answer and highlight its position in the sentence on the board (between the auxiliary and the past participle). Refer the students back to the first picture in Exercise 7. Ask *What's she done?* Write their reply on the board, adding *just* if the students don't use it. Then they write a sentence for each of the other pictures. Check the answers with the whole class.

## EXERCISE 9

Write the verbs from the exercise on the board and establish that they are all regular. To demonstrate the task, ask a student *Have you washed your face today?* Elicit *Yes, I have./No I haven't.* Get the students to ask you. Drill the exchange if necessary. Using the verbs on the board, they interview each other.

### Extra practice

1 Prepare a list of actions that you can mime, e.g. eat a sweet, move a chair, fall down, break a fingernail, cut some paper, etc. Mime the first action and the students must guess what you've just done. They can do this as a team activity or in pairs. You can also use a tape of different sounds in the same way, e.g. doorbell ringing – students say *Someone has just arrived at the door.*

2 Divide the students into pairs. They stand face to face and look at each other for a minute. Then they turn back to back and change something about their appearance, e.g. take off a watch, change their hair. They then turn round to face their partner again. They decide what their partner has just done, e.g. *You've taken off your watch.* They then change partners and do the same again.

3 Bring in about ten pictures of people with different expressions, e.g. looking sad, happy, out of breath, etc. The students work in groups and decide why each person looks like this, e.g. *He's happy because he's just found a new job*, etc. They compare their ideas as a class.

## Emergencies

**Focus**
- Emergency procedures
- Further practice: giving advice
- Further practice: present perfect simple
- Further practice: modal *should* + infinitive

### EXERCISE 1
Write these two questions on the board: *What's just happened?* and *What's happening now?* The students look at the two pictures in the Students' Book and discuss the two questions in pairs. Elicit some of their ideas but do not confirm if they are correct.

### EXERCISE 2
Direct students to the four questions. Play the tape once. Students compare their answers to the questions and to Exercise 1 with their partners. If necessary, play the tape again. Check the answers with the whole class.

### KEY
1 She's just won a holiday for two in Italy.
2 She's not sure.
3 He thinks she should go to hospital.
4 An ambulance is going to take Rachel to hospital.

### TAPESCRIPT

RACHEL: I've done it! I've done it!
JULIA: What?
RACHEL: I've won a holiday for two, in Italy.
JULIA: That's great. Congratulations.
RACHEL: Italy! Beautiful weather. Beautiful food.
JULIA: Rachel! Look out! Rachel! Are you all right? Are you OK?
RACHEL: I don't know. I've broken my leg, I think.
JULIA: Now, don't worry, Rachel. Which leg is it?
RACHEL: This one.
JULIA: And where does it hurt?
RACHEL: There.
JULIA: Now, I won't hurt you. I'll be careful. Mmm. I can't feel anything.
RACHEL: Have I broken it?
JULIA: No, I don't think so. But I'm not sure.
TOM: What's happened?
JULIA: It's Rachel. She's hurt herself.
TOM: Has she broken anything?
JULIA: I'm not sure. I don't think so.
TOM: OK. OK. Don't move her. She should go to hospital. I'll call an ambulance.

### COMPARING CULTURES EXERCISE 3
**Background note**
In Britain the number to phone in an emergency is 999. These calls are free from private or public telephones. The number can be used to contact the police, an ambulance or the fire service.

Write *999* on the board and see if the students recognise what it is. Then direct them to the questions, the information about British emergency services and Tom's business card in the Students' Book. They read the text and then answer the questions. Check the answers with the whole class.

### KEY
1 999
2 the telephone operator
3 the service he wanted (ambulance) and the telephone number of MAP (071 636 2091)
4 the emergency service operator for ambulances
5 the address of MAP (42 Kingsway, London WC2 4BB) and that someone has fallen and possibly broken a leg

UNIT ELEVEN

### EXERCISE 4
Students read the instructions to the exercise. They work in pairs and discuss what happens in their countries and if they have ever called the emergency services.

# Body language

> **Focus**
> • Body language

### COMPARING CULTURES EXERCISE 1
To introduce the subject, discuss as a class how people communicate, e.g. by speaking, using facial expressions and gestures, etc. Establish that what is normal in one culture may not be in another, e.g. discuss if it's usual in the students' countries to shake hands when they meet a friend or to kiss them. Then direct the class to the six pictures in the Students' Book. Ask *Does everybody look happy?* (No). Then direct them to the empty thought bubbles and the list of 'thoughts'. Point to the first picture and elicit which thought is appropriate for the picture. Students work in pairs and match the other pictures and thoughts. Check the answers as a class but do not discuss what happens in their countries until the next exercise.

**KEY**

1 F   2 B   3 D   4 C   5 E   6 A

### EXERCISE 2
Direct the students to the statements in the Students' Book. In a multilingual class students should work with others from a different country. To demonstrate the task, discuss the first statement as a class. Then they discuss the other five statements in their pairs. As a class, discuss what happens in their countries and encourage them to explain why they use certain body language. Then refer them back to the first statement in the exercise and establish how true it is for their countries. Get them to read the example sentence. They then work individually or with a student from the same country and write true statements about their countries.

### Extra practice
Students write advice for foreigners visiting their countries for the first time. The advice should centre on social manners and etiquette, and it should be introduced by *You should never/always ...*

## Development

### 🔲 LISTENING EXERCISE 1
**Background note**
The **London Contemporary Dance School** was formed in 1967 as the Contemporary Dance Group. Since then, it has had a decisive impact on Britain's modern dance scene. It is now one of Britain's major dance education centres and is also an important venue for performances.

Direct the students to the picture of Mary Evelyn in the Students' Book. Discuss where Mary is and what they think her job is. If necessary, revise the vocabulary for parts of the body. Play the introduction to the tape and confirm that she is a dance teacher. Then tell the students that they must make a list of the parts of the body that Mary mentions. Tell them that they will hear one part of the body that they may not know. They should try to identify it and understand it from the context. Play the tape, stopping after 'arms'. Elicit what she says and write *arms* on the board. Then play the complete tape. Students compare their lists in pairs. Then check the answers with the whole class and write the parts of the body on the board. Point out *wrist* if necessary.

**KEY**

arms   legs   head   hand   wrist   shoulder
(*Wrist* is the unknown part of the body.)

**TAPESCRIPT**

MARY EVELYN
I've always loved to watch dancing. I find it fascinating because it's something which crosses all barriers. It's often called the language of dance. It's a way of communicating emotion or feelings, stories, without having to use words.
  Strength is very, very important to the dancer, and stamina. They have a great deal of work to do to make the body mobile. That's to make all the, the arms, the legs, the head move freely and to have control over the different parts of the body. Isolation in dance is very important. It is crucial that the dancer learns to use all the different parts of the body in separation from each other so that, for instance, while the whole of the rest of the body was still, they could move just a hand from the wrist, or just the head, just a shoulder. Each part of the body must be mobile on its own.

I've always loved the human body and the way it works, and this is something which I'm still discovering. The endless possibilities for the body, for all the parts of the body to work in isolation from each other or together. This is a study which I imagine will take me all my life.

## EXERCISE 2

Direct the students to the questions in the Students' Book. Make sure they understand all the vocabulary. Then play the tape again. Check the answers with the whole class.

**KEY**

1 b  2 b  3 a  4 b

## READING EXERCISE 3

Direct the class to the comprehension questions and the information about the evening school of the London Contemporary Dance School. The students read the texts and answer the questions. If you wish, set a time limit to encourage the students to scan the texts for the necessary information. Get them to compare their answers with their partners. Check the answers with the class.

**KEY**

1 a, c  2 £4.20  3 £49

## SPEAKING EXERCISE 4

Divide the students into As and Bs. Direct the As (the receptionist) to the information about the evening school. The Bs (client) look at the information about what they want to study on page 122. Monitor and make sure they understand their information. Tell the Bs to make notes about the information that Student A gives them. As they roleplay their conversations, monitor and make a note of any errors. When they have finished, the Bs use the information and their notes from the roleplay to check if the As have given them the correct information. If you wish, they can then change roles: the As want to find out about Level 1 Contemporary Dance next autumn. Finally, use the board to correct any errors you heard.

## READING AND WRITING EXERCISE 5

**Background note**

The information about Viviana Durante is true. **Swan Lake** is the name of a famous ballet with music by the Russian composer Tchaikovsky. It was written in 1876 and was first performed in Russia.

Direct the students to the information about Viviana Durante. Teach *soloist* and make sure they understand *Swan Lake*. They read the text. Then direct them to the biographical notes. Establish that this is extra information about Viviana and that they must write a paragraph about her using all the information. Write the first sentence on the board as a class. Monitor and help. The students can compare texts and make any changes to their own.

**KEY**

(This is a model answer. Variations are possible.) Viviana Durante works as a principal dancer for the Royal Ballet Company in London. She is small and strong with a long neck and pale skin. She has got dark hair and eyes. She is Italian and was born in Rome in 1968. She came to Britain as a child in 1978. She could not speak English and she missed her family a lot, but she was already a very good dancer. In 1984 she joined the Royal Ballet. A few years later a soloist in *Swan Lake* hurt herself in the second act and Viviana had to take her part. Soon after that, in 1989, she became a principal dancer.

# 12 People's lives

## Achievements

**Focus**

- Individual achievements
- Describing people and jobs
- Talking about past experiences
- Adverbs: *ever, never*
- Further practice: present perfect simple, superlative adjectives

### EXERCISE 1

**Note:** In this unit, the students are introduced to two uses of the present perfect (for experience and for duration). Each use needs to be presented separately. The students may find the form and concepts difficult as they are probably expressed in a different way in their L1.

Direct the class to the three pictures in the Students' Book. Explain that the three people are famous. In groups of three, the students discuss why they think the people are famous. Get quick feedback from the whole class but do not confirm their answers yet. They then read the texts to find out if their ideas were right. Check the answers with the whole class.

# UNIT TWELVE

**KEY**

Sigeru Miyamoto is famous because he created the most famous video game in the world. (Super Mario Brothers)
Pat Kerr is famous because she raised almost a million pounds to set up an orphanage in Bangladesh.
Ocsi Tabak is famous because he is one of Europe's last human cannonballs.

## EXERCISE 2

Refer the students to the questions in the Students' Book. They read the texts again and answer the questions. Encourage them to check their answers with their partner. Check the answers with the class.

**KEY**

1. a) Pat Kerr   b) Ocsi Tabak   c) Sigeru Miyamoto
2. It's a video game.
3. She works in an orphanage in Bangladesh.
4. He became a human cannonball when he was twelve years old.

## EXERCISE 3

Write the adjectives on the board in random order and draw three columns, like this:

| PERSON | JOB | PERSON OR JOB |
|--------|-----|----------------|
| brave  |     |                |

Ask *Do you use 'brave' for a person, a job or both?* Elicit the students' answer and write *brave* under person. The students then work in pairs and write the adjectives in the columns in the same way. If they do not have dictionaries, monitor and help with the vocabulary they do not know and encourage them to ask other students. Then point to each column and elicit their answers. Drill the adjectives as necessary.

Refer the students back to the three people in the texts. Get them to read the example sentence in the Students' Book. In pairs, they use the adjectives to talk about the people and their jobs. Monitor and correct any errors.

### Extra practice

Bring in pictures of people doing other jobs. The students work in groups of three and use the adjectives from Exercise 3 to discuss the jobs and the kind of people who do them. They make notes. Then they regroup and compare their adjectives.

## DISCOVERING LANGUAGE EXERCISE 4

**Note**: The past participle *been* is often pronounced with the weak vowel /ɪ/, like this /bɪn/. It can be pronounced /biːn/ but this is likely to sound emphatic.

Direct students back to the texts in Exercise 1. Get them to find sentences with *ever* and *never*. Elicit the sentences and then write one with each example on the board. In pairs, they discuss the three questions in Exercise 4. Check the answers with the whole class. Using the sentences on the board, revise how the present perfect simple is formed. Highlight the use of *ever* and *never* in questions and their position in the sentences. Refer them to the other four examples in the exercise to check their rules and identify the irregular past participles *known* and *seen*. Highlight the fact that we use neither of the adverbs in positive statements.

**KEY**

1. present perfect simple
2. The sentence with *never* is a statement. *Ever* is used in a question.
3. They both come before the past participle: *ever* comes after the subject pronoun and in front of the past participle, *never* comes between the auxiliary verb and the past participle.

If you wish, do the following activity as a concept check and for very controlled practice of the structure. (Equally, this could be used for presentation purposes before tackling Exercise 4.) Bring in four pictures: a recognisable place abroad or in your country that some of the students have visited, an unusual food, an unusual drink and an unusual sport. Display your first picture and ask, e.g. *Have you ever been to Paris?* Elicit from some students *Yes, I have.* To check the concept ask *Are you there now?* (No), *Did you go in the past?* (Yes), *Do I know when?* (No). Then ask the question again and drill *Yes, I have* and *No, I haven't*. Get the students to ask you the question, reply and drill the exchange. Then do the same with the other pictures, making sure to check concept and drill each time. The students work in closed pairs and ask and answer about the four pictures. Then point to a student in the class and ask *Has he ever been to Paris?* Elicit *Yes, he has* and drill the exchange. Then do the same with another student to elicit *No, she hasn't*. Drill both exchanges in open pairs. Then the students work with a different student and interview them about their first partner, e.g. A: *Has Pablo eaten snails?* B: *No, he hasn't*. Finally, say to a student *Tell me about Pablo* and elicit *He's been to Paris. He hasn't eaten snails*. If necessary, elicit or give the form *He's never eaten snails*. Drill the positive and negative forms. Get some students to tell you about themselves to elicit the first person singular form.

## EXERCISE 5

Copy the sentences onto the board and get the students to copy them into their notebooks. Play the example sentence. Together mark the main stresses on the board. Then play the other sentences, stopping for the students to mark the stress in the sentences in their notebooks. Check the answers with the whole class on the board. Then play the tape again, pausing to allow the students to repeat.

### KEY AND TAPESCRIPT

Example: Have you <u>e</u>ver been to the c<u>i</u>rcus?
1  Have they <u>e</u>ver had a comp<u>u</u>ter?
2  Has he <u>e</u>ver travelled by pl<u>a</u>ne?
3  I've n<u>e</u>ver seen that stunt.
4  They've n<u>e</u>ver had comp<u>u</u>ter games.
5  He's n<u>e</u>ver been abr<u>oa</u>d.

### Extra practice

Draw this grid on the board:

|       | GREECE | A LION | A CAR | PRAWNS | BY BOAT |
|-------|--------|--------|-------|--------|---------|
| Clare | ✗      | ✓      | ✓     | ✗      | ✓       |
| Max   | ✓      | ✓      | ✗     | ✓      | ✗       |
| Ruth  | ✓      | ✗      | ✗     | ✓      | ✗       |
| Chris | ✗      | ✗      | ✓     | ✗      | ✓       |

The students work in groups and make sentences about the people, e.g. *Clare's seen a lion at the zoo, she's driven a car and she's travelled by boat, but she's never been to Greece and she's never eaten prawns.* If your students need the practice, they could do a preliminary question-and-answer phase, using *ever*, e.g. *Has Clare ever been to Greece?*

## EXERCISE 6

Copy the first two or three rows of the questionnaire onto the board and complete it for yourself. Say to the students *I've never been to ...* and elicit *Why do you want to go there?* (If necessary point to *reason* on the board to elicit the question form). Then give a reply. Practise similar exchanges with the other prompts. Then point out *Something to do, A sport to try* and *A person to meet* and make sure students know the past participles of the verbs. Get them to copy the questionnaire from the exercise into their notebooks. They complete it with things that they have never done that they want to do. They then interview their partner. To check their answers, have a class discussion about some of the things the students want to do.

## EXERCISE 7

Direct the students back to your questionnaire on the board. To demonstrate the task, point to the first prompt and elicit a sentence about yourself. Write it on the board, e.g. *(Your name) has never been to ... She wants to go there because ...* The students work with the same partner as in Exercise 6. They swap questionnaires (or ask and answer again) and write sentences about their partner using the sentence on the board (or the one in the book) as a model. Monitor and help. To check answers, the pairs swap texts and read about themselves.

### Extra practice

Divide the class into two teams. Each team has a list of ten different irregular infinitives, e.g. *be, go, eat, drink, meet, see, buy, have, put, lose, cut, do, hit, fall, burn, break, hurt, win, speak, come.* The first team begins by saying the infinitive, the second team replies with the past simple form and the first team finishes with the past participle. Then the second team chooses another infinitive. Award a point for each correct past simple form or past participle.

## EXERCISE 8

The aim of this exercise is to contrast the present perfect with the past simple. Use the same pictures that you used for Exercise 4 to elicit the present perfect. Display the picture of the place and ask *Have you ever been to Paris?* Elicit *Yes, I have.* Ask *When did you go?* and elicit *I went in ...* To check the concept, ask *In the first question, do we know if the person has been to Paris?* (No) *Is it a general or specific question about the past* (General). *Do we know if the person has been to Paris in the second question?* (Yes). *Is it a general or specific question about the past?* (Specific. We want to know when.) Draw a timeline on the board to show that the present perfect is used for an unspecified time in the past and the past simple is used with a specific time.

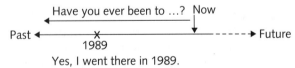

Yes, I went there in 1989.

Drill the four-line exchange chorally and individually. Do the same with the other three pictures, checking the concept each time. The students then work in closed pairs and ask and answer about the four pictures. Monitor and correct any errors you hear.

Direct students' attention to the dialogue in Exercise 8. Get the students to read the dialogue and discuss the first question in pairs. Check the answer with the whole class.

# UNIT TWELVE

**KEY**

The present perfect simple tense is used in the first three lines. The past simple is used at the end to tell the story.

Students complete the chart to show the structure of the second question. Drill the question in the chart. The students then interview each other about their most embarrassing experience. They can interview three or four different students to give them more practice. If you wish, you can discuss the exercise as a class.

**KEY**

| QUESTION WORD | VERB *BE* | ARTICLE | SUPERLATIVE ADJECTIVE | NOUN |
|---|---|---|---|---|
| What | 's | the | most embarrassing | experience |

(that)

| NOUN/ PRONOUN | *HAS/ HAVE* | | PAST PARTICLE |
|---|---|---|---|
| you | have | ever | had? |

### EXERCISE 9

Copy the prompts in the Students' Book onto the board. Refer the students back to the conversation in Exercise 8. Point to the first prompt and the conversation to elicit a similar dialogue. Drill each line chorally and individually. Make sure the students understand that they must replace the superlative adjective with the one in the prompt. They then work in pairs and practise similar conversations using the prompts. Monitor and correct any errors you hear. To check their answers, point to the prompts and indicate pairs to roleplay the conversation for the whole class.

### Extra practice

1 This activity gives follow-on practice from your contrast of the present perfect and past simple tenses. Write the headings *place, food, drink, sport* on the board. Each student writes a sentence for each heading, e.g. *I've been to ...*, etc. They then mingle and find other students who have done these things and talk about their experiences.

2 The students think of five people they are close to amongst their families or friends. They write a sentence about each person, describing something interesting they have done in their lives. They tell their partner about these people's experiences.

3 Tell the students to think of a favourite place. It can be a room, a place outside or a town. Write the beginnings of these sentences on the board:
*I've never ... there.*
*I've ...*
*I didn't ...*
*I've ... many times.*
*I wouldn't like to ... there.*
The students complete these sentences about their place and write them (and others, if possible) in their notebooks. They then tell another student about their place using their notes. They work with several different partners.

## Changes

**Focus**
- Life changes
- Periods of time

- Talking about situations that continue into the present
- Expressing regret
- Apologising

- Adverbs: *for, since*
- Further practice: present perfect simple

### EXERCISE 1

Direct the students to the picture of Alan and Rosie. Discuss what they think is happening and how they are feeling. Then ask students to read the statements and write 1–5 in a list on the board. Explain that some of the statements are true and some are false. Play the conversation with books closed. Students compare their answers in pairs. Check the answers with the whole class.

**KEY**

1 True  2 True  3 False  4 False  5 False

### EXERCISE 2

**Note**: This is the first time that the present perfect tense used to express duration has been presented in *Look Ahead.* You may wish to introduce the language before doing Exercise 2 or to do further presentation/consolidation after Exercises 3 and 4. The second stage of these notes, after the key, provides further presentation work.

Refer the students to the conversation in the Students' Book. Write 1–3 on the board and indicate the gaps in the conversation. Play the tape for the students to complete the conversation. They compare their answers with their partners. Then check the answers with the class.

**KEY**

1 How long   2 for three years   3 since 1990

Write these notes on the board, using a picture if possible to introduce Susan.

Name:             Susan Marks
Marital status:   Married (3 years)
Address:          13 Greenbank Walk, Barnsley (2/6/92)
Job:              Hairdresser (5 years)
Company:          Champu (3/9/91)

Point to the biography on the board and ask *Is she married?* Elicit *Yes, she is*. Then ask *How long has she been married?* and elicit *Three years*. Provide the full sentence *She's been married for three years* and write it on the board. To check the concept, ask *Is she married now?* (Yes), *When did she get married?* (Three years ago). Draw this timeline on the board to show that the action took place in the past but the result continues in the present.

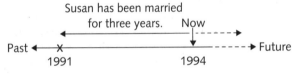

She got married in 1991.

Then ask *How long has she been married?* and drill the response. Point to *marital status* and elicit the question from the students. Drill the whole four-line exchange chorally and individually. Then indicate her address and ask *Where does she live?* and *How long has she lived there?* Elicit *She's lived there since 2nd June 1992*. Use the questions and timeline to check the concept and drill the exchange. The difference between *for* and *since* is highlighted in Exercise 4. Use the other two prompts to elicit similar four-line exchanges. The students then practise these four exchanges about Susan in closed pairs. Then get the students to ask you about where you live and your job, e.g. s: *Where do you live?*
T: *I live in .....*
s: *How long have you lived there?*
T: *I've lived there for ...*
Drill each exchange. The students then work in closed pairs and interview each other.

## DISCOVERING LANGUAGE EXERCISE 3

Direct the students to the exercise. They discuss the questions with their partners, referring to the conversation. Then check the answers with the whole class, insisting on full sentences to highlight the structure. If necessary, use the timeline from the Exercise 2 notes on the board. Ask students to supply the two adverbs used in answering the question *How long?* + present perfect tense, and elicit *for* and *since*.

**KEY**

1 Yes, he is.
2 He's worked there for three years.
3 He moved to Brighton in 1990.
4 Yes, he is.
5 He's lived there since 1990.

### EXERCISE 4

Copy the four sentences onto the board and underline *for* and *since*. In pairs, students discuss when we use them. Write these two prompts on the board:
?_____ + a period of time
e.g. _____
?_____ + a point in time
e.g. _____
Discuss as a class which one refers to *for* and which one refers to *since*. Complete the prompts on the board with the correct form and write the examples from the exercise under each prompt.

**KEY**

*for* + a period of time, e.g. *for nine months, for a year*.
*since* + a point in time, e.g. *since 1992, since last November*.

### EXERCISE 5

Write 1 – 6 in a list on the board and direct the students to the sentences in Exercise 5. They complete the sentences with *for* or *since*. Encourage them to compare their answers with their partners. Then check the answers on the board, writing the time expressions next to the adverbs.

**KEY**

1 for   2 since   3 since   4 for   5 since   6 for

### EXERCISE 6

Draw two columns on the board and get the students to copy them into their notebooks:

Direct the students to the expressions in the exercise. Ask *Do we use 'for' or 'since' with 'a long time'?* Elicit *for* and write *a long time* in the correct column on the board. The students work in pairs and write the time expressions in the correct column. Check the answers with the whole class and write them on the board. Leave the chart on the board for the next exercise.

**KEY**

| FOR | SINCE |
|---|---|
| a long time | I was a child |
| months | I was a teenager |
| ages | last summer |
| years | the beginning of the year |
|  | I started school |

**Extra practice**
Prepare a list of twenty expressions that take *for* or *since*, e.g. *ten years ago, last summer, six minutes, two seconds*. Include those from Exercise 6. Divide the class into teams. Read out an expression. The first team to shout out the correct answer (*for* or *since*) gets a point. If they shout out the wrong answer, they lose a point. Some teams may finish with minus scores!

## EXERCISE 7
Refer the students back to the chart in Exercise 6. Point to the first expression and make a true sentence about yourself, using a negative form of the present perfect, e.g. *I haven't seen my uncle for a long time*. Then do the same with another time expression in a positive sentence. Establish that the sentences are true and refer students to the model in their books. The students then work in pairs and take it in turns to make true sentences about themselves using the nine expressions in Exercise 6.

**Extra practice**
As an extension to Exercise 7, get each student to write six true statements about themselves using the present simple tense, e.g. *I live in Bogotá, I have got two dogs, I play football*. They work in groups and read out their first statement. The others have to find out how long they have done these things, e.g.
A: *I have got two dogs.*
B/C: *How long have you had two dogs?*
A: *For six years.*

## EXERCISE 8
Write the verbs in the Students' Book on the board and check that the students remember their past participles. To demonstrate the task, ask a student *How long have you had that coat?* Elicit *I've had it for ... years*. Cross off *have* on the board. The students then interview each other in pairs using the verbs. Monitor and make a note of any errors. To check the answers, get the students to practise their exchanges for the whole class. Finally, use the board to correct any errors you heard.

**Extra practice**
Bring in a picture of a large family or group of people. Display it on the board and name all the people in the family. It's fun if the family or group is famous, e.g. the British royal family or an acting or singing family. Write the names of the people in a list on the board and get the students to copy the list into their notebooks. Then give each student a cue card with the name of one of the people and a piece of information about him/her, like this: *Anne/Tim married/1993*. The students mingle and tell each other about their person, e.g. *Anne has been married to Tim since 1993*. They write full sentences in their notebooks. Check as a class and write the sentences on the board.

## EXERCISE 9
Direct the class to the picture in the Students' Book. Check that students know who Julia and Tom are and what their working relationship is (Tom is Julia's boss). Direct students to the questions in the exercise. The students listen to the tape with their books closed. They compare their answers with their partner. If necessary, play the tape again and then check the answers with the whole class.

**KEY**

1. She's decided to leave MAP Advertising.
2. Yes, she has.
3. She's worked there for nearly five years.
4. She'd like to do something different. She wants to travel, to learn to ski. She wants to live abroad and learn a new language.
5. Tom is sorry, but he is sympathetic.

**TAPESCRIPT**

TOM: Yes?
JULIA: Can I talk to you for a moment, Tom?
T: Of course, Julia. Sit down. What is it?
J: I've decided to leave.
T: Leave?
J: Yes. I've decided to leave MAP Advertising.
T: Oh, no. Is it because we're moving out of London?
J: Well, yes. But there are other reasons.
T: I know. You've never liked working here and you've found another job.
J: No. I've enjoyed working here. And I've learnt a lot. But ...
T: But what?

J: Well, I haven't had time for other things. I've worked here for four and a half years, nearly five, and I'd like to do something different.
T: You <u>have</u> found another job.
J: No, I haven't. Really.
T: Well, what do you mean, something different?
J: I want to travel. You know, I've never been to the United States.
T: Haven't you?
J: No. And I want to learn to ski. I want to live abroad and learn a new language. There are lots of things that I haven't done.
T: Well – what can I say? – I'm really sorry. But I understand.
J: Thank you, Tom.

## EXERCISE 10

Write *I'm really sorry* on the board. Play the tape and discuss which words Tom stresses. Then write the other sentences for expressing regret on the board. Play each one, stopping for the students to repeat. Make sure they place the main stress on the adverb in each phrase.

#### KEY AND TAPESCRIPT

I'm <u>rea</u>lly <u>sor</u>ry.   I'm <u>so</u> <u>sor</u>ry.   I'm <u>ve</u>ry <u>sor</u>ry.
I'm <u>ter</u>ribly sorry   I'm <u>aw</u>fully <u>sor</u>ry.

## COMPARING CULTURES EXERCISE 11

Tell the students that British people say *Sorry* a lot and not just when they want to apologise for something. Discuss when else the students think the British say *Sorry*. Then direct them to the uses and pictures in the Students' Book. Get them to read the uses. Check that they understand *interrupt* and *bump into*, demonstrating both if necessary. Then point to the first picture and ask *Which use is it?* Elicit the answer (C). They work in pairs to match the other pictures and uses. Check the answers with the whole class. Do not discuss what happens in their countries as this is the aim of the next exercise.

#### KEY

1 C    2 A    3 E    4 D    5 B

## EXERCISE 12

Refer the students back to the five pictures in Exercise 11. In a multinational class students work with others from different countries. In groups of three, they compare what they say in the same situations in their countries and if they use *Sorry* in other situations. Discuss as a class. Discuss also (in L1 if necessary) if they feel that the British are very polite because they use *Sorry* so much.

# Development

## SPEAKING EXERCISE 1

Bring in a picture of an old person and elicit how old the students think the person is. Then discuss what they mean by 'old'. Write the question *Why do some people live longer than others?* on the board, along with the list of possible factors from the Students' Book. The students discuss different reasons. Make sure they make notes. Then elicit their ideas and write them on the board for the next exercise.

## READING EXERCISE 2

Direct the students to the picture of Charlotte Hughes and the text in the Students' Book. Ask *How old do you think she is?* After a few guesses, ask them to read the first sentence of the article to find out. Then refer the students back to their list of reasons for long life on the board. Tell them to read the article quickly and tick the reasons from the list that she mentions. They add any other reasons to their list. Check answers around the class, and discuss how similar Charlotte's ideas are to theirs.

#### KEY

Healthy eating and a strong moral code.

## EXERCISE 3
### Background notes

A **phonograph** is one of the earliest types of record player. A **nursing home** is usually a private establishment where people live who cannot look after themselves (especially old people). They are looked after by nurses. It is common in Britain and the United States for older people to live in a nursing home when they are too old or ill to take care of themselves, rather than living with their families.

Direct the class to the comprehension questions about Charlotte Hughes in the Students' Book. The students read the article again, more carefully this time, and answer the questions. Tell them not to worry about unfamiliar vocabulary as that will be dealt with in Exercise 4. Encourage them to compare their answers with their partners. Check the answers with the whole class.

#### KEY

1 She was born in 1877. (Her age depends on the year in which you are using this book.)
2 She's seen the introduction of the phonograph, the fax machine, test-tube babies, different means of transport and a decline in the standard of people's values.

3   She lives in a nursing home.
4   She was thirteen.
5   She was a teacher.
6   She was sixty-three.
7   He was a captain in the army.
8   She sends them a greetings telegram on their 100th birthday.

## EXERCISE 4
Copy the definitions onto the board and direct the students back to the article. To demonstrate the task, tell the students to find a word for a type of officer in the army. Elicit the answer and write *a captain* next to the definition on the board. The students then do the same with the other vocabulary. They compare their answers with their partners. Then check the answers with the whole class and write the words on the board.

### KEY

1 a captain    2 a horse-drawn carriage    3 a phonograph
4 prime minister    5 a nursing home

## WRITING EXERCISE 5
Direct the students back to the article in Exercise 2 and discuss the subject of each paragraph. Highlight the main tenses that are used to talk about each subject and write them on the board:
Biography = past simple (Paragraph 1)
Changes = present perfect simple (Paragraph 2)
Reasons for a long life = present perfect simple (Paragraph 3)

Then tell the students to think of an elderly person that they know and explain that they are going to write three paragraphs about them. They may want to interview the person about their life before they write the text. They can do the writing in class or at home. If possible, get them to find a photograph of the person and display their writing for other students to read.

## LISTENING EXERCISE 6
**Background note**
A **full driving licence** means that you are fully qualified to drive all types of cars (though not vehicles over a certain size), and small motorbikes.

Remind the students of Alan and his plans from page 90. Ask *What do you think he had to do to get the job?* Elicit *fill in a form, send in his curriculum vitae, go to an interview*. Brainstorm the types of information that the students include on CVs in their countries. Then direct them to Alan's curriculum vitae in the Students' Book. Ask *Is it complete?* (No). Check that they understand the headings, particularly 'availability' and teach 'to give one month's notice'. Then the students listen to the tape and complete the CV with the missing information. They compare their answers with their partners. Play the tape again and then check the answers with the whole class.

### KEY

Hope Secondary School, Manchester    1981–1986
Queen Elizabeth Hospital, Birmingham    1987–1990
5 O levels in Maths (Grade A), Biology (Grade A), English (Grade C), French (Grade C), Chemistry (Grade C) in 1986.
Seaview Home, Brighton    1990–1992
Brighton General Hospital    1992–now/present
Leisure Interests: all kinds of music, plays the saxophone, loves animals, reads wildlife magazines, photography (especially animals and birds)
Travel: in Europe
Driving licence: full driving licence
Health: very good
Availability: must give one month's notice to Brighton General Hospital

### TAPESCRIPT

INTERVIEWER: So you went to secondary school in Manchester. When was that?
ALAN: 1981. I stayed there for five years and left in 1986, just after I took my O level exams.
I:   What subjects did you study at O level?
A:   I did Maths, and Biology, English, French.
I:   Just a minute. OK.
A:   And Chemistry.
I:   Right. What grades did you get?
A:   Oh, er, I got grade A for Maths and Biology, and, yes, grade C for the others.
I:   And then you went to study nursing at Queen Elizabeth Hospital, Birmingham. Did you start immediately?
A:   No, the following year, 1987. It was a three-year course.
I:   When you completed your nursing course, your first job was at Seaview Home. What were your responsibilities?
A:   General care for the old people – it's an old people's home. It wasn't really what I wanted to do, though, so I left after two years, in 1992 when I got a job at Brighton General. I've been at the hospital since then, but I've told you about my responsibilities there.
I:   Yes, we've covered that. And are you free to go overseas at any time?
A:   Yes, I'm available, well, almost immediately. I do have to give a month's notice at the hospital, of course.
I:   A month. Have you travelled before, Mr Timpson?

A: Yes, I have, but only in Europe. I've got a motorbike.
I: So you've got a full driving licence?
A: Yes, and I've taken my motorbike to Europe a number of times.
I: OK. And what are your other main interests?
A: I enjoy all kinds of music – and I play the saxophone. I love animals, so I read a lot of wildlife magazines, and, I'm also taking classes in photography. If I go to Africa, I'd like to spend some time taking photographs of animals and birds – in my free time, of course.
I: Fine. Now, all volunteers have a medical examination before they go, of course, but in general, how's your health?
A: Oh, very good. I've never missed a day's work.

## WRITING EXERCISE 7
Get the students to draw a blank outline of the CV from Exercise 6 into their notebooks. They use this outline to write a CV for themselves.

## SPEAKING EXERCISE 8
The students draw another blank outline of the CV in their notebooks. Divide the students into As (the interviewer) and Bs (the interviewee). If necessary, elicit the questions they will ask, e.g. *Where did you go to school? Where have you worked?* Drill the questions and write them on the board. The As interview the Bs and complete the blank CV in their notebooks with information about their partner. Then they change roles and the Bs interview the As and complete a CV for them. Monitor and make a note of any errors you hear. To check their answers, the students swap CVs and compare what they have written about their partner with their partner's own CV. They discuss any differences and the interviewers correct any errors on their CVs. Finally, use the board to correct errors you heard.

### Extra practice
If your class are interested in jobs, bring in some job advertisements in English or some pictures of jobs. These can be anything – doctor, miner, prime minister etc. Explain that they are looking for a job to do in the summer. They decide which job they would like to apply for – it doesn't matter if they have no experience as they can use their imagination! Using the same questions as in Exercise 8, they work in pairs and interview each other.

# Progress check 4

## Vocabulary

### EXERCISE 1
1 plastic   2 glass   3 wool   4 leather   5 metal
6 paper

### EXERCISE 2

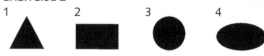

### EXERCISE 3
1 belt   2 hood   3 collar   4 pocket   5 sleeve
6 button   7 zip

### EXERCISE 4

| A | B | C |
|---|---|---|
| head | arm | leg |
| nose | chest | foot |
| mouth | waist | toe |
| brain | elbow | knee |
| face | heart | ankle |
|  | lung |  |
|  | shoulder |  |
|  | finger |  |

### EXERCISE 5
toothache, stomachache, cold, cough, earache

### EXERCISE 6
1 interesting   2 frightening   3 clever   4 bored
5 ordinary   6 sensitive   7 favourite   8 useful

## Grammar and functions

### EXERCISE 7
1 anywhere   2 Everyone/Everybody
3 somewhere   4 No one/Nobody   5 anything
6 nothing   7 someone/somebody

### EXERCISE 8
1 What colour are they?   2 How long is it?
3 How wide is it?   4 How much does it weigh?
5 What's it made of?   6 What are they like?
7 Whose is it?   8 What's the matter with her?
9 Have you (ever) been to China?

UNIT THIRTEEN

### EXERCISE 9
1 mine, My   2 your, yours   3 their, theirs
4 hers, her   5 mine, Their   6 your, Ours

### EXERCISE 10
became, bought, cut, done, eaten, fallen, felt, flown, had, hit, learnt, listened, locked, lost, made, met, moved, put, seen, tidied, tried, washed

### EXERCISE 11
2 She's just climbed a mountain.
3 We have just played tennis.
4 You have just painted a picture.
5 They have just cleaned the windows.
6 I've just broken/smashed the mirror.

### EXERCISE 12
1 since   2 for   3 for   4 for   5 since   6 since

## Common errors

### EXERCISE 13
1 Can you give me *some* information about train times, please?
2 She's got *a* terrible headache.
3 He's a doctor and it's a very hard *job*. (Or ... *it's very hard work*.)
4 Please tidy all the cupboard*s*.
5 It's *the* most expensive holiday we've ever had.
6 I'm trying to lose weight, but I still *love chocolate*.

### EXERCISE 14
1 t   2 w   3 t   4 h   5 h

# 13 Things going wrong

## Damage and loss

### Focus
- Accidents and disasters
- Reporting what someone said
- Further practice: talking about past experiences
- Present perfect/past simple contrast
- Reported statements
- Adverb: *ago*

### 🔊 EXERCISE 1
To introduce the topic, direct the students to the photograph in the Students' Book. Discuss where they think the place is and what's happening. Teach *flood*, *storm* and *disaster*. They may want to know *typhoon*, *tornado*, *hurricane*, *volcanic eruption* and *earthquake*. Then write the two questions in the Students' Book on the board. Check that students know where Venice is. Play the tape with books closed. Students compare their answers in pairs. Then play the tape again with students reading, and check the answers with the class.

**KEY**

1 He was in a flood two years ago in Venice.
2 Because the ground floor of his house was flooded.

### DISCOVERING LANGUAGE EXERCISE 2
The aim of this exercise is to revise the use of the present perfect tense contrasted with the past simple and to present *ago*. Use your pictures of the place, food, etc. from Unit 12 to revise the two uses, if necessary. Elicit an exchange like this:
T: *Hiromi, have you been to Paris?*
S: *Yes, I have.*
T: *When did you go?*
S: *I went in 1991.*
Students can practise this and other exchanges based on the pictures if necessary.

Play the conversation from Exercise 1 again for students to shadow. Then direct them to the questions in Exercise 2. They discuss them with their partner. Check the answers with the whole class. Draw the timeline from Unit 12 on the board to remind the students of the differences between the present perfect and past simple.

To check the students understand *ago*, repeat the exchange from the beginning of this exercise, adding *So that was three years ago*. Ask *Can you use 'ago' to talk about the present?* (No), *Can you use 'ago' with days, months, years?* (Yes), *What about with 'yesterday'?* (No) *Why not?* (It's for periods of time, like *for* rather than specific times/days.). Drill *Hiromi went to Paris three years ago*. Practise similar exchanges using the other pictures from Unit 12 chorally and in closed pairs.

**KEY**

1 The present perfect is used in the first question because Becky is asking a general question about the past and she doesn't know if Marco has been in a flood or not. She uses the past simple in the other two questions because she's asking for information about a specific time in the past.
2 (The answer will vary from class to class.)
3 The past simple.

## EXERCISE 3

To demonstrate the task, tell the class a true sentence about yourself using *three years ago*. They write five true sentences about themselves in their notebooks. Monitor and help. To check their answers, get some of the students to read out their sentences to the whole class.

## EXERCISE 4

Direct the class to the pictures in the Students' Book. Discuss what they can see in each picture and check they know *break-in*. Write the dialogue prompts on the board. To demonstrate the task ask a student *Have you ever been in a flood?* Elicit *Yes, I have*. If the student says *No, I haven't* ask *Do you know someone who has been in a flood?* and elicit a reply. Then ask *When was that?* and elicit a reply. Drill each line of the exchange chorally and individually. The students then work in pairs and practise similar conversations, using the prompts and the pictures. They can work with several different students. Monitor and correct any errors you hear. For feedback, discuss the experiences as a class.

### Extra practice

Prepare a cue card for each student. You can use these prompts: sleep in a cave? ride in a police car? meet a famous person? visit Disneyland? win a competition? faint? eat frogs? find any money? see a ghost? ride an elephant? be on TV? give a speech? First, the students write a full question on their cue card, e.g. *Have you ever slept in a cave?* Check that they know the past participles of the verbs. Then they mingle and ask their questions to find students who have done the activity on their cue card, e.g.
A: *Have you ever slept in a cave?*
B: *Yes, I have.*
A: *Why/When did you sleep in a cave?* etc.
For feedback, they tell the whole class who has done these things. If you have a large class, they can do the activity in smaller groups.

## 📼 EXERCISE 5

Direct the students to the comprehension questions and pictures in the Students' Book. Play the conversation. The students compare their answers with their partners. If necessary, play the tape again. Check the answers with the whole class.

### KEY

1 She's been at the police station.
2 Because she has lost her briefcase and she wanted to report it to the police.
3 Her cheque book, papers for work, her appointment book.
4 When she went shopping and wanted to buy something.
5 3

### TAPESCRIPT

TOM: Rita? Are James and Julia there? We have a meeting at two-thirty and it's ...
JULIA: Sorry I'm late, Tom.
T: It's all right, Rita. Where have you been?
J: At the police station.
T: Where?!
J: At the police station. I've lost my briefcase. Or perhaps someone's taken it. I don't know.
T: Oh, no. What happened? Sit down. Was there anything important in it?
J: Important! My cheque book, all the papers I need for work, my appointment book ...
T: Oh, that's terrible. But how did you lose your briefcase?
J: Well, as you know, I was with a client all morning and we had lunch together. After I had lunch, I went shopping. And when I wanted to buy something, I couldn't find my cheque book. Then I remembered that it was in my briefcase. And my briefcase was in my car.
T: So you went back to your car.
J: I went back to my car. No briefcase.
T: And then you went to the police?
J: Not immediately. Before I went to the police station, I called the client's office. No luck. They said the briefcase wasn't there.
T: Excuse me. Yes? Yes, there is. Julia Marsh. Really? I'll tell her. It was very kind of you to call. Bye. That was the manager of the Europa restaurant. Just after lunch today he found a black leather briefcase under a table. When he opened the case, he found a lot of papers. He said they had the name MAP on them. And he found a cheque book with the name Marsh on it. J Marsh. J for Julia?
J: Ah.

## EXERCISE 6

Play the conversation again, stopping after 'They said the briefcase wasn't there'. Get students to repeat the sentence and write it on the board. Establish who *they* refers to (the people in the client's office) and ask *What did the people in the client's office actually say to Julia?* Elicit 'The briefcase isn't here'. Do the same with the second sentence. Write the sentences on the board, like this:

1 Direct speech: They said, 'The briefcase isn't here'.
  Reported speech: They said the briefcase wasn't there.

UNIT THIRTEEN

2 Direct speech: He said, 'The papers have the name MAP on them.'
Reported speech: He said the papers had the name MAP on them.

Leave these sentences on the board until you do Exercise 8.

## EXERCISE 7
As a class, build up a picture of the events of Julia's day, e.g. *She had a meeting with a client in the morning and then they had lunch.* Then direct the students to the prompts in the Students' Book and make sure they haven't forgotten anything that she did. Divide the class into As (Tom) and Bs (Julia). Elicit some of the questions that Tom asked, e.g. *Where have you been? What's the matter? What happened?* The students then work in pairs and recreate the conversation. Monitor and correct any errors.

## DISCOVERING LANGUAGE EXERCISE 8
The students read the examples and discuss the questions. They work in pairs. Then check the answers with the whole class. Use the two examples on the board from Exercise 6 to highlight the main changes, e.g.
They said, 'The briefcase isn't here.' Present simple tense → *here.*
They said that the briefcase wasn't there. Past simple tense → *there.*

### KEY
1 It changes to the past simple tense.
2 *that*
3 It changes to *there.*
4 The pronoun *Your* changes to *my.*

## EXERCISE 9
Get the students to read out what Julia says and write the text on the board. Then point to the first sentence on the board and ask *What did she say?* Elicit *She said that she was sorry but she couldn't find her cheque book.* Drill the sentence. The students work in pairs and report the whole quote in the same way. Make sure they do the exercise orally. Then they report the conversation to you and you write it on the board. As a class highlight the verbs, pronouns and adverbs that change in reported speech.

### KEY
Julia said that <u>she</u> <u>was</u> sorry, but <u>she</u> <u>couldn't</u> find <u>her</u> cheque book. It <u>wasn't</u> in <u>her</u> bag. <u>She</u> said that <u>she</u> <u>kept</u> it in <u>her</u> briefcase, and <u>she</u> <u>thought</u> that that <u>was</u> in the car.

## DISCOVERING LANGUAGE EXERCISE 10
Write the first pair of reported speech sentences on the board. Ask *What is the difference between the two sentences?* and establish that they mean the same but that the form is different. Establish that it is impossible to use *say* + personal pronoun (*He say me*) in English. Then write *they had the MAP name on them* on the board and get the students to supply the beginning of the sentence using *They said* and *They told.* Write the two sentences on the board.

### KEY
The difference in construction is: *to say* (*that*) + verb clause (no personal pronoun after *say*); *to tell* + personal object pronoun + (*that*) + verb clause.

## EXERCISE 11
Explain that James phoned Tom because he was late too. Display a picture of a garage and ask *Where did he say he was?* and elicit *He said (that) he was at a garage.* Drill the sentence. Then ask *What did he tell Tom?* and elicit *He told Tom (that) he was at a garage.* Drill both sentences as necessary and write them on the board. Then direct the class to the four sentences in the Students' Book. They work in pairs and report the sentences. If you wish, Student A can report the sentence using *say* and Student B then reports it using *tell.* Make sure they each practise both structures. To check the answers, get the students to dictate the sentences to you. Highlight all tense and pronoun changes.

### KEY
1 James said (that) there was a problem with his car.
   James told Tom (that) there was a problem with his car.
2 James said (that) the brakes didn't work.
   James told Tom (that) the brakes didn't work.
3 James said (that) he couldn't drive it.
   James told Tom (that) he couldn't drive it.
4 James said (that) he needed a taxi.
   James told Tom (that) he needed a taxi.

### Extra practice
1 Prepare some present simple sentences in direct speech on cue cards, like this:
*I like living here. They can't speak French. The weather isn't very good.*
The students work in groups of three. A and B are on the telephone and C is asking what A is saying. If possible, each group should sit in a row with Student B in the middle. Each student has five statements. The conversation works like this:
A: *I like living here.*

C: *What did she say?*
B: *She said she liked living there.*
When A has said their five statements, they move one place to the left and change roles.

2 You can use the same statements as in the previous activity for a team game. Divide the class into teams. Read out the first statement to Team A. They report it back to you. If it is correct, give them a point. If it's incorrect, say the statement to the next team and so on. The students can also write their own statements using the present simple to test each other.

## Asking for help

> **Focus**
> - Emergency and counselling services
> - Problems and solutions
> - Reporting what someone asked
> - Reassuring and calming someone
> - Reported questions
> - *Ask + if/what/how*, etc.
> - Further practice: reported speech

### COMPARING CULTURES EXERCISE 1
**Note**: In Exercise 1 a conditional structure is used: *If* + present simple + present simple, or the zero conditional. It is not necessary to highlight its use unless the students have specific questions as it is quite straight forward. The main aims of this exercise are to lead into the topic of 'asking for help' and to check vocabulary.

If possible, bring in pictures of the different people and emergency services that are mentioned in the exercise. Display them, or write the names of the services, on the board and check that the students know them. Ask *Why do you sometimes contact these people?* Elicit some situations. Direct students to the prompts in the exercise. Point at the first one and ask *What do you do if you have a fire?* Elicit *If you have a fire, you call the fire brigade.* Then get students to match the problems with the places or people in the same way. They discuss the exercise in pairs. To check the answers, point to each prompt and get the students to say a full sentence.

#### KEY
2 If you have a break-in, you call the police.
3 If you lose your wallet, you go to the police/the Lost Property Office.
4 If you are ill, you go to a doctor/you call a doctor.
5 If you have an accident, you call the ambulance service/the police.
6 If you have a legal problem, you go to a solicitor.
7 If you have an emotional problem, you go to a friend.

### EXERCISE 2
**Background notes**
In Britain **Help the Aged** collects money and helps old people. **Shelter** does the same for people who have no homes. The **Samaritans** is an organisation which helps people who are experiencing serious problems and who have no one to share their problems with. The Samaritans usually talk to people on the phone rather than in person and the service is free. **ChildLine** is a telephone helpline for children to call when they are frightened or have problems they cannot discuss with people they know. **MIND** gives advice and practical help to people who are mentally ill. They also help their families. **Weight Watchers** helps people who want to lose weight. **Relate** helps people who have problems with their personal relationships.

If possible, bring in leaflets about different organisations in your country or Britain. Alternatively, write the names of some British organisations on the board. Explain that they are organisations in Britain which help people and that these kinds of organisations are common in Britain. The students work in groups of three. They discuss the kinds of problems or people they think these organisations help and if they have similar organisations in their countries. Then discuss as a class.

### EXERCISE 3
Discuss with the class if it is usual for students in their countries to go to a university or college away from their home town. Explain that most students in Britain go to a university in a different place and that sometimes they have problems. Write the heading *Problems* on the board. Get the students to work in pairs and make a list of the possible problems that students away from home could have. Monitor and help with vocabulary. Then discuss their answers as a class and write the problems on the board under the heading. The students copy the list into their notebooks. Leave the list on the board for the next exercise.

### EXERCISE 4
Direct the students to the picture of Jan Murray in the Students' Book. Explain that she is a 'student counsellor' and check that the students understand what she does in her job (she tries to helps students

UNIT THIRTEEN

solve their problems). Direct them to the list in their notebooks from Exercise 3. They read the text and tick the problems that she mentions on their lists. They add any other problems that are not on their lists. The students compare their list of problems in pairs. To check their answers, get the students to read out their lists. On the board tick the ones they mention, erase any that they don't mention and add any other reasons that are not on the original list.

**KEY**

They are worried about their studies and their exams. They want help with financial or legal problems, usually connected with renting flats and houses. They may want to talk about a medical problem but not with their doctor. They are often lonely and miss their families and friends. One student needed the name of a childcare centre.

## DISCOVERING LANGUAGE EXERCISE 5

Direct the students back to the text in Exercise 4 and ask them to find the six reported questions. Elicit the six direct questions and write them on the board. Then get them to discuss the questions in pairs. Monitor and help. Check the answers with the whole class.

**KEY**

When is your office open? What sort of problems do the students have? Do you know a good child care centre? What's the matter? Do other students feel the same? Where can I go to meet people?

1 In direct questions, the subject and verb are inverted so that the verb comes before the subject. In reported questions normal statement order is used, i.e. the verb comes after the subject.
2 *If* is used to report *yes/no* questions, not ones that begin with a question word.

For further consolidation, draw this chart on the board and complete it with information about yourself:

| Name?    |     |
|----------|-----|
| Address? |     |
| Pets?    | dog |

Point to the first prompt and get students to ask you *What's your name?* Reply and then elicit the other questions in the same way: *Where do you live? Have you got any pets?* Then ask another student *What did they ask me?* and point to *name* on the board. Elicit *They asked you what your name was*. Repeat the indirect question as a model and drill it chorally and individually. Then point to *address* and say to a student *What did they ask me?* Elicit *They asked you where you lived/what your address was*. Again drill the response chorally and individually. Do the same with the *pets* and elicit *They asked me if I had any pets*. Then get the students to repeat the direct and indirect questions and write them on the board, like this:

| What's your name?      | They asked you what your name was.      |
| Where do you live?     | They asked you where you lived.         |
| Do you have any pets?  | They asked my if I had any pets.        |

Highlight the differences in word order, the tense change and the use of *if*. Get the students to copy all the questions into their notebooks.

## EXERCISE 6

Direct the students to the exercise. They work in pairs and change the direct questions into reported questions. Do the first one together as a example. Make sure they do the exercise orally first, then allow them to write if they want to. To check the answers, get them to tell you each reported question and write it on the board. Drill each one. Establish that the tense and pronoun changes are the same as in reported statements, and that no question mark is used.

**KEY**

1 John asked her how he could get a room at the university.
2 Bob and Kate asked her if the medical centre was open in the holidays.
3 Marion asked her if she could talk to her about something personal.
4 Sam asked her when the office was open in the evening.

## EXERCISE 7

The aim of the exercise is to give the students practise in writing direct and reported questions. It is an information-gap exercise. First, check that the students understand *ladder* and *identification*. Divide the students into As and Bs. The As look at the policeman's report in the exercise. They read the report and then write the conversation between the policeman, Mr Jones and the neighbour. The first line is done for them as an example in their books. In the meantime, the Bs turn to page 122. They read the conversation and complete the report. It is important that the As and Bs do not read each other's texts. When they have finished, they work in pairs (an A and a B). They swap texts. The As check the Bs' report against the one on page 99 and the Bs check the As' conversation on page 122. They correct any errors they find. If you wish to check their answers orally, get the As to read out the conversation line by line. The Bs report each line.

### Extra practice

1 This is a variation of the 'telephone' activity that you used for the reported statements. Change the sentences into questions, e.g. *Do you like living here? Can't they speak French? What's the weather like today?* Write the questions on separate cards, one set of cards for each group. The students work in groups of three. They place the cards face down in a pile on the desk. Explain that they are all questions. The first student (A) picks up a card and asks the question. C says *What did he/she ask?* and B turns the question into a reported question, e.g. *She asked if I liked living there.* This could also be done as a game, with one student at a time picking up cards and saying the questions, the other students making reported questions in turn. If a question is correct, the student reporting it keeps the card. If it is incorrect, the card is placed at the bottom of the pile and the game continues with the next card.

2 Use the same cue cards as in the first activity. Write the reported questions on separate cue cards. Each student should have a direct question and an indirect question. Make sure they do not have the same pair. They mingle and read out their direct question to another student until a student replies with the indirect form.

3 Divide the students into pairs to do a running dictation. One is the scribe and the other is the runner. Explain that they must report a conversation to their partner, who writes it down in indirect speech as a report. The report will include reported questions and statements. Display the conversation (sample below) on the board. Make sure the scribes are facing away from the board. The runners read as much as they can remember, run to their partner and report the conversation. The scribe writes it down, e.g. *The police officer asked the man what his name was. He said it was Smith.* When the students have finished, get them to read the report to you. Write it on the board, including any mistakes. Encourage peer correction. If you wish to make it competitive, tell the class to count a mark for every mistake they made. The pair with the highest score loses!

SAMPLE CONVERSATION
POLICE OFFICER: What's your name?
MAN: It's John Smith.
POLICE OFFICER: Where do you live?
SMITH: I live in Wimbledon, London.
POLICE OFFICER: And what do you do?
SMITH: I'm a bank manager.
POLICE OFFICER: Are you married?
SMITH: Yes, I am.
POLICE OFFICER: Have you got any children?
SMITH: Yes, I have got two daughters.
POLICE OFFICER: Thank you, Mr Smith.

### EXERCISE 8

Direct the class to the picture in the Students' Book. Discuss what they think Lucy's problem is. Write the two comprehension questions on the board. Play the tape. Students listen with books closed, then compare their answers in pairs. Then check the answers with the whole class.

#### KEY

1 She's upset because she's lost one of her earrings. (Her father gave them to her and they are very expensive.)
2 She can help her look for it.

### EXERCISE 9

Ask the class to read the functions from the conversation in Exercise 8. Check that the students understand *reassure*. Ask students to find the sentence which corresponds with the first function. The students then work in pairs and match the other functions and sentences in the same way. Elicit their answers and write them on the board. Establish that *Don't worry* is used to reassure someone. Leave the list of functions on the board for Exercise 11.

#### KEY

1 I've lost one of my earrings.
2 Dad gave them to me and they're really expensive.
3 What's the matter?
4 Don't worry. It'll be all right. Now, why don't you tell me where you've been …
5 Calm down. I'll help you look for it.

### EXERCISE 10

Copy the sentences onto the board and get the students to copy them into their notebooks. Play the first phrase and elicit which words are stressed. Mark them on the board. Then play the tape, stopping after each phrase for the students to mark the stress. Check the answers with the whole class on the board. Then play the tape again, pausing for the students to repeat.

**KEY AND TAPESCRIPT**

(Stressed words are underlined.)
<u>Calm</u> <u>down</u>! It's O<u>K</u>. It'll be <u>all</u> <u>right</u>. <u>Don't</u> <u>worry</u>! Everything's <u>fine</u>.

## EXERCISE 11

Refer students to the pictures in the Students' Book and discuss what they think the problem is in each situation. Then direct the students back to the list of functions on the board from Exercise 9. In pairs they write a conversation for each picture following the model from Exercise 8. Monitor and help.

## EXERCISE 12

The students act out their conversations from Exercise 11 for the whole class. If you have a large class, they can act them out in groups of six or eight.

## ENGLISH AROUND YOU

Focus students' attention on the cartoon. Explain that *Have a nice day!* is often used in shops and restaurants in the USA when someone is leaving. Ensure that students understand the irony here: the customer is clearly not going to have a nice day as he is about to walk into an incoming customer.

# Development

## SPEAKING EXERCISE 1
**Background notes**
Christine Bahr is a real person.
  **Firefighter** is the term now used to talk about men or women who work in the fire brigade. It often replaces **fireman,** which refers to men rather than both sexes.

Direct the students to the picture of Christine Bahr and the two questions in the Students' Book. They discuss the questions in groups of three. Get quick feedback but do not confirm their answers yet.

## READING EXERCISE 2

Write the three comprehension questions in the exercise on the board and direct the students to the text about Christine. They read the text and then discuss the answers to the questions in pairs. Check the answers with the whole class.

**KEY**

1 She's a firefighter.   2 No.   3 Twenty-four hours.

## EXERCISE 3

Explain that students are going to find out about an incident that really happened to Christine. Use a visual or verbal explanation to check that they understand *hydrant*. Direct the students to the questions and the text. After they have read the text, students check their answers with their partners. Then check the answers with the whole class. Discuss Question 5 but do not confirm their answers as that is the aim of Exercise 4.

**KEY**

1  No, it didn't.
2  Christine Bahr.
3  They tested some hydrants on the streets.
4  They turned on the television to watch a football game.

## 🎧 LISTENING EXERCISE 4

Direct students to the matching exercise in the Students' Book. Say to the class *What's the name of an inter-city road?* and get them to identify it (Highway 101). Do the same with the other local places that are listed in the exercise. Explain that the students are going to find out what happened to Christine. Play the tape for the students to check their answers. The students discuss what they think happened with their partners. Then check the answer with the whole class.

**KEY**

Matching: 1 b   2 c   3 d   4 a
Exercise 3: Question 5, Christine went out to a really big fire in Berkeley.

**TAPESCRIPT**

CHRISTINE BAHR
We got on Highway 101 with our lights and sirens going. Once we crossed the Bay Bridge and were heading towards Berkeley, I looked up and I could see the flames on the ridges and I was, I was, shocked. When we turned the corner we saw a thirty-foot jet of gas shoot out at us – a broken gas line.

## 🎧 EXERCISE 5

Copy the events onto the board and establish that they are not in the correct order. Play the tape, stopping after 'we made entry into the house'. Elicit that this is the first event and write *1* next to it on the board. Then play the whole tape. Check the answers with the whole class on the board.

**KEY**

1 They entered the house.
2 They climbed up a narrow staircase.
3 They went into a child's room.
4 The room filled with smoke.
5 They started to go down the staircase.
6 Christine saw some photographs of the family.

**TAPESCRIPT**

CHRISTINE BAHR

While we were on Broadway Terrace, we were asked to fight an attic fire in one of the homes. After we made entry into the house we climbed up a narrow staircase into a small child's room and I only had a second to look around me before the room filled with smoke and it was too hot to stand up. So we backed out down the staircase. And as we were coming down the stairs, I saw photographs hanging on the wall and I felt at that point that these people were going to lose their home and I thought that if I could take the pictures they would at least have something. So I snatched them off the wall and I grabbed a towel and I wrapped them in a towel, and I hunched over them so that they wouldn't get wet, and I put them down in a neighbour's yard. It was unbelievable to see so much burning at once and, um, it was like someone had dropped a bomb on Oakland.

### EXERCISE 6
**Background note**

In American English, the word **yard** is used in the same way as **garden** in British English.

Direct the class to the questions. Get the students to read the questions and check they understand *yard*. Play the tape again. Encourage them to check their answers with their partner. Then check the answers with the class.

**KEY**

1 d   2 b   3 c

### WRITING EXERCISE 7

First discuss as a class what you should and shouldn't do if a fire starts in the school. Then direct the students to the fire instructions in the Students' Book and check they understand all the symbols. Using their ideas from the discussion and the symbols, they work in pairs to write a list of things they should and shouldn't do in a fire. Monitor and help. To check their answers, draw on the board the following grid:

| IN A FIRE YOU | |
|---|---|
| SHOULD | SHOULDN'T |
|  |  |

Elicit their sentences and write them on the board under the headings.

### EXERCISE 8

Tell the students to imagine there is a fire in their home and they can save one thing that is really important to them. In groups of four, they tell each other the thing they want to save and why. Compare their answers as a class. Then direct them to the example paragraph. Using the paragraph as a model, they write a similar paragraph about their chosen object and the reasons for saving it. Make sure they begin with *The most important thing to me is my ...*, and not *I would like to save my ...* As they write, monitor and help.

# 14 Celebrations

## Good times

**Focus**
- Celebrations
- Congratulations

- Wishing someone well
- Congratulating someone

- Adverbs: *yet, already*
- Further practice: present perfect simple

### EXERCISE 1
**Background notes**

In Britain, it is traditional to send cards to mark important times in someone's life. On these cards there are often symbols. A **horseshoe** is a symbol of good luck, especially when moving to a new home. Some homes have a horseshoe over the front door. A **key** is used when someone reaches the age of eighteen. They are legally independent of their parents and have the 'key' to leave home. In Britain, the age of majority used to be twenty-one, but this was lowered to eighteen in 1970. **Bells** are used for a wedding day, symbolising the church. **Rings** are often also used for weddings. A **stork** is a large white bird with a long beak, neck and legs. In former times, young children were told that new

113

## UNIT FOURTEEN

babies were brought by a stork. They are still used as a symbol of new birth.

**Notes**:
1 In the message for the new home card, the word *moving* has two meanings: the action of moving house from one house to another and as an adjective meaning an emotional experience.
2 It is unusual to use the verb *marry* without an object, e.g. *They married yesterday*. It is more common to use *get married*, e.g. *They got married yesterday*.

To introduce the topic, bring in a greetings card in an envelope and tell the class that it arrived in the post this morning. Encourage them to guess what is inside the envelope – let them feel it to establish that it is some kind of card. Then brainstorm the type of card it could be and write the names of the five types of card from the exercise in the corner of the board: birthday, moving house, birth of new baby, congratulations, wedding. Leave the list on the board. Open your card and show it to the class to see if they guessed correctly.

If possible, bring in some English greetings cards or direct the students to the cards and the sentences in the Students' Book. To demonstrate the task, point at the first sentence and ask *Which card goes with this sentence?* Elicit *Card E*. The students then work in pairs and match the other sentences and cards. Check the answers with the whole class. Drill the sentences if necessary and check that they understand *get married*. If necessary, revise the use of the present perfect with *just* from Unit 11.

**KEY**

1 A  2 C  3 B  4 E  5 D

### EXERCISE 2
Direct the students to the messages inside the cards. Ask *Which message goes with Card A?* Elicit *This greeting comes to wish you both ...* (Message 4). The students then work in pairs and do the same with the other messages and the cards. Check the answers as a class. Make sure that they understand *Congratulations* and *to celebrate an anniversary*. Point out that *Congratulations* is followed by the preposition *on* + noun or gerund, and that *anniversary* in English is not a synonym for *birthday* (in Message 3 it refers to wedding anniversary).

**KEY**

1 D  2 B  3 A  4 E  5 C

### EXERCISE 3
Direct the class to the statements by people in the Students' Book. The students read them quickly. Discuss as a class what they think has happened to the person in each case, e.g. *Number 1 has got married*. Teach *honeymoon*. Ask *Which card did they receive?* Elicit *Card A*. They then read the other texts and choose a card for each situation. Encourage them to compare their answers with their partner.

**KEY**

1 A  2 C  3 B  4 D  5 E

### DISCOVERING LANGUAGE EXERCISE 4
Refer the class to the five statements in Exercise 3. Get them to read the first one and find out what the person has done/has not done e.g. *She hasn't travelled much yet*. Elicit the answers and write them on the board. The students then work in pairs and do the same with the other statements. Check the answers with the whole class. Get the class to read the five statements about *yet* and *already*. Then direct them to the sentences on the board and discuss if the first statement is true or false. They work in pairs and discuss the other statements. Check the answers with the whole class. Use the sentences on the board to highlight the use and position of the two adverbs.

**KEY**

1 True.
2 False. *Yet* is used in questions and negative statements. *Already* is used in affirmative statements.
3 False. *Yet* comes at the end of a question or sentence.
4 True.
5 True.

To consolidate *yet* and *already*, display a picture or draw two people (Clare and Robert) on the board and show the students your greetings cards. Copy this list onto the board:

| CARDS TO SEND | | |
|---|---|---|
| Birthday | Susan | ✔ |
| Exam | Mark | ✗ |
| Wedding | Joyce and Peter | ✗ |
| New Baby | Ray and Barbara | ✔ |

Explain that Robert must send all these people a card and Clare is checking to find out if he has sent them all. Say to the class *What does Clare ask Robert?* and point to *birthday – Susan*. Elicit *Have you sent Susan a birthday card yet?* To check the concept, ask *Is Clare asking about the past or future?* (Past) *Does she know exactly when in the past?* (No) *Does she know if Robert has done it yet ?* (No). Get the students to repeat the question again, then point to the tick [✔] and elicit *Yes, I have.* Drill the exchange chorally and individually. Then elicit similar exchanges using the other prompts on the board. The students practise the exchanges in open and closed pairs. Next, point to *birthday – Susan* and say *Make a sentence about Robert.* Elicit *Robert has already sent Susan a birthday card.* To check the concept, ask *Has Susan received a birthday card from Robert yet?* (Yes) Drill the sentence chorally and individually. Then point to *exam – Mark* and elicit *Robert hasn't sent Mark a card yet.* To check the concept ask *Has Mark received a card from Robert?* (No). Drill the sentence chorally and individually. Elicit similar sentences using the other prompts on the list on the board.

### Extra practice
Prepare/find some pictures of everyday activities, e.g. washing up, cutting the grass, and stick them onto card. On the other side of the card, put a large tick [✔] or cross [✘]. Use them to do a chain drill or a mingling activity. The student with the picture asks a question, e.g. *Have you done the washing up yet?* The other student looks at the back of the card and replies either *Yes, I have* or *No, I haven't.*

### EXERCISE 5
**Background note**
In Britain, precious metals and stones are used to symbolise wedding anniversaries, e.g. twenty-five years = silver wedding, forty years = ruby wedding, fifty years = golden wedding.

Direct the students to the announcements in the Students' Book. Ask *In Number 1, has Sue gone to Australia yet?* Elicit the full sentence *Sue hasn't gone to Australia yet* and write it on the board. The students then work in pairs to write sentences about the other announcements using *yet* or *already*. Monitor and help. If some students finish early, get them to compare their sentences with another pair. Check the answers as a class and write the sentences on the board.

#### KEY
2 Robert has already passed his exams.
3 John hasn't played in the match yet.
4 Cyril and Ivy haven't had their ruby wedding anniversary yet./They have already been married for forty years.
5 Pat and Mike haven't got married yet.
6 Ronald has already retired/had his retirement party.
7 Tom has already passed his (driving) test.

### Extra practice
1 Display a large picture/wallchart and write some true/false statements connected with it on the board, e.g. *They've just bought a newspaper. He's already been to the post office. They haven't gone into the restaurant yet.* The students look at the wallchart and decide if the sentences are true or false. This activity checks their understanding of the adverbs. Alternatively, display the wall chart and get the students to write sentences about the people on it using *just*, *yet* and *already*.

2 If your students are learning English in an English-speaking country, prepare a questionnaire based on the local environment, e.g. the places they have/haven't visited, local food they have/haven't tried, like this:

|   | 1 | 2 | 3 | 4 |
|---|---|---|---|---|
| 1 Oxford? | | | | |
| 2 fish and chips? | | | | |
| 3 the musical *Cats?* | | | | |
| 4 a London bus? | | | | |

They work in groups of four and find out who has or hasn't done these things, e.g.
A: *Have you been to Oxford yet, Carlo?*
B: *No, I haven't.*
A: *Have you eaten fish and chips yet?*
B: *Yes, I have.*

### COMPARING CULTURES EXERCISE 6
Refer the students to the cards in Exercise 1 and the announcements. Get them to find a picture of a key. Explain that it is a 'symbol' and discuss what they think it means and if they use the same symbol in their country/countries. Then they discuss the exercise in small groups (if possible, of different nationalities). Monitor and correct any errors you hear. Check their answers as a class.

#### KEY
1 a) a horseshoe   b) a key   c) hearts   d) bells, rings
   e) a stork

### EXERCISE 7
**Background note**
In Britain, greetings cards are big business. Cards are sent on many occasions, including Christmas, Easter, Mother's Day and Father's Day, engagement, marriage, thanking someone for dinner or a party, Valentine's Day (14th February), retirement, new job, passing a test or examination, and sympathy on the death of a relative.

UNIT FOURTEEN

If possible, bring in examples of different kinds of cards from England or your country. Write the names of the kinds of cards on the board. Then the students work in small groups and list which of the cards they send in their countries, who they send them to and who they receive them from. Monitor and make a note of any errors. Then discuss as a class and use the board to correct any errors.

### 📼 EXERCISE 8

Copy the expressions onto the board. Play the first one. Together underline the syllables that are stressed. Then play the tape, pausing for the students to mark the main stresses in the other expressions. Check their answers as a class and mark the stresses on the board. Then play the tape again for the students to repeat the expressions.

**KEY AND TAPESCRIPT**

(Stressed syllables are underlined.)
Congra<u>tu</u>lations!   Happy <u>Birth</u>day!   Well <u>done</u>!
Good <u>luck</u>!   Have a <u>wonder</u>ful <u>time</u>!

**Extra practice**
Prepare cue cards for each student with statements like these on them:
*I've passed my driving test. I've got a new job. I've got my driving test tomorrow. I've got a job interview tomorrow. It was my birthday yesterday. I'm starting my new job tomorrow.*
Students mingle and read out their statement to another student, who must reply with an appropriate expression from Exercise 8.

### EXERCISE 9

To introduce the exercise, tell the class about a happy event which has recently happened to you. Elicit an appropriate response, e.g.
T: *I've just passed my driving test.*
S: *Congratulations!*
Divide the class into pairs. They ask and tell each other about a recent happy event in their lives. Then direct them to the form in the Students' Book. They write an announcement on the form about their partner. Monitor and help. Then they swap announcements and check that the facts are correct. For feedback, get them to read their announcements out. Drill for correct pronunciation and highlight the use of the prepositions after *Congratulations*, *Best wishes* and *Well done*.

### EXERCISE 10

This writing task can be done as homework or in a later lesson. The students write a letter responding to their partner's announcement. Then they 'post' it to their partner. If the events actually took place, they can also supply some photographs.

**Extra practice**
As a follow-up to Exercises 9 and 10, give each of the students one of your greetings cards (avoid sensitive topics such as death). They decide who they are going to send the card to and then write a short message inside. They 'post' the card to the student. If you are worried that some students will not receive a card, prepare a few extra in advance to post to them.

## Leaving

> **Focus**
> - Parties
> - Speeches and toasts
>
> - Toasting someone
> - Thanking someone
> - Further practice: wishing someone well
>
> - Further practice: present perfect, *yet, already*

### EXERCISE 1

Remind the class of Julia and ask *What has she decided to do?* (To leave MAP Advertising). Explain that James and Rita are planning her leaving party. As a class, brainstorm the things to do when you organise a leaving party, e.g. invite people, make food, buy a present. Make sure that students understand *move furniture*. Then divide the class into As (Rita) and Bs (James). Direct the As to their list of tasks in Exercise 1 and the Bs to their list on page 122. Establish that they must find out if the other person has done their tasks yet. Get two students to read out the example exchange. The students then work in their pairs and ask and answer about the different tasks. Monitor and make a note of any errors. To check their answers, write the headings *Done* and *Not done* on the board. Point to *Done* and elicit what they have done and then do the same for *Not done*. Finally, use the board to correct any errors you heard.

**KEY**

Rita has already ordered some food. She hasn't borrowed any cassettes or bought Julia's present yet. James has already bought the drinks and written a card for Julia. He hasn't moved the furniture or asked Sally to answer the phones yet.

## EXERCISE 2
**Background note**
In this exercise Tom Hall '**toasts**' Julia. A **toast** is a message of congratulations, proposal of success, etc. marked by people raising their glasses and drinking together.

Direct the class to the three pictures of Julia's leaving party in the Students' Book. Elicit what is happening in each picture. Explain that the pictures are not in the correct order. Play the tape for the students to put the pictures in the correct order. They compare answers with their partner and then check with the whole class. Then direct them to the three sentences. In pairs, they match the pictures and the sentences. Check that they understand *toast*. Check the answers with the whole class.

**KEY**

The order is: Picture B (Sentence 3), Picture C (Sentence 1), Picture A (Sentence 2)

**TAPESCRIPT**

TOM: Quiet. Quiet, please. Thank you. Next week we'll be in our new offices in the country. But one person will not be there: Julia. Julia has done a lot for MAP Advertising. She has been here for five years and I've enjoyed working with her very much. But she has decided to leave. I haven't tried to persuade her to stay because I know she wants to try something new. Julia, come here, please. This is from all the staff and myself. It comes with our thanks and our best wishes for the future.
JULIA: Thank you everybody. Thank you very much.
TOM: Now, here's to Julia, and her new life.
ALL: To Julia!

## EXERCISE 3
Direct students to the four questions in the Students' Book. Get the students to discuss their answers in pairs. Then copy the toast onto the board. Play Tom's speech again for the students to check their answers to the questions and complete the toast. Check their answers as a class.

**KEY**

1 Five years.   2 Yes, very much.
3 To try something new.   4 No, he hasn't.
Toast: here's to, To

## COMPARING CULTURES EXERCISE 4
Write these two questions on the board:
1 When do people in Britain toast someone?

2 What do they say?
Get the students to read the text in the Students' Book. They discuss the questions with their partner. Then check as a class. Next, divide the class into groups, of different nationalities in a multinational class. They discuss the questions in relation to what happens in their country/countries.

## EXERCISE 5
Explain that after a toast in Britain, it is usual for the person to give a short reply. Direct the class to Julia's notes for her speech and the beginning of what she says. Students work in pairs and use the notes to reconstruct Julia's speech. Then nominate As and Bs in each pair. Still in their pairs, they stand up and the As make the speech quietly to the Bs. The Bs can help if the As have a problem. Then they change roles and the Bs give the speech to the As. Give positive feedback as making a speech in English is quite difficult for students at this level.

**KEY**

(Model answer only; other versions are possible.)
Friends and colleagues, I'd like to thank you all for this wonderful party and your lovely present. This is a sad day for me. I've been at MAP Advertising for five years, and it's like my second home. My colleagues are now good friends. I'd like to give special thanks to Tom for his help and support. I've learnt a lot from him. But it's also a happy day because I'm going to find a new job, visit new places and make new friends. MAP is going to move to new offices, and I'm going to start a new life. So best wishes to MAP for the move to the country and to everyone here. Thank you all for everything. And now let's drink a toast to MAP!

## EXERCISE 6
Tell the students that it is the end of term and they are going to make a speech thanking you (their teacher). In pairs, they make notes and then practise the speech. Monitor and help. Next, regroup the students so that they are working in different pairs. They give the speech to their partner, who acts as the teacher. Make sure they both give a speech. Monitor and make a note of any errors. If they enjoy doing the activity, they can change partners and give their speech to another 'teacher'.

## EXERCISE 7
Direct the class to Julia's letter and the questions in the Students' Book. They work individually and then compare their answers with their partner. Check the answers with the class.

# UNIT FOURTEEN

**KEY**

1 It's a thank you letter. Julia is writing to thank her colleagues at MAP for her leaving card and present.
2 They gave her a book on Charlie Parker and some CDs of jazz and blues music.
3 1 c)  2 a)  3 b)  4 e)  5 d)

## EXERCISE 8
### Background notes

In English several different endings of letters are possible: **Love** is used by women when writing to friends or relatives and by men when writing to relatives or very close friends. **Best wishes** is used in informal letters to friends or acquaintances to whom the writer is not particularly close. **Yours faithfully** is used to end formal letters when you don't know the name of the person you are writing to and the letter begins **Dear Sir/Madam**. **Yours sincerely** is used in formal letters when you know the name of the person you are writing to and the letter begins **Dear Mr/Ms ...**, or **Dear + name**.

Direct the students to the beginnings and endings of the letters. Ask *How do you finish Letter 1?* Elicit the answer (c, Yours sincerely). The students then do the same with the other examples. They compare their answers with their partner and then check with the whole class. Compare what people write in Britain with what the students write in their countries.

**KEY**

1 c  2 a  3 d  4 b
Julia ended her letter 'Best wishes' because she knows the people at MAP quite well, but they are not particularly close friends.

## EXERCISE 9

Refer the students back to Julia's letter in Exercise 7 and remind them of the order of paragraphs in the letter. If necessary, write the order on the board to provide a model for the students. Get them to think of a present they have received recently and who sent it. Check they have all thought of something. If they cannot think of anything, bring in some pictures of different presents stuck onto card, with the name of the person who gave it on the back of the card, e.g. mother, best friend, colleague. As they write the letter, monitor and help. They then swap their letter with their partner, who checks it for any grammatical errors. If they have a photograph of the present or have used one of your pictures, they can display the picture and the letter on the noticeboard for the other students to read.

# Development

## READING EXERCISE 1

Direct the students to the picture of the wedding ceremony and the text in the Students' Book. Use the picture to teach *wedding ceremony*. Then get the students to read the text. In pairs, they name the people in the picture and complete the sentences. Check with the whole class.

**KEY**

Picture: 1 registrar  2 groom  3 bride  4/5 witnesses
Sentences: 1 religious, civil  2 sixteenth  3 five, two witnesses

## EXERCISE 2

Ask students to find and underline the sentences in the text using *get married* and *marry*. They read out the sentences and you write them on the board. Students discuss the differences. Check the answers with the class.

**KEY**

*Get married* is intransitive (it doesn't have a direct object); two people get married; one person gets married *to* another.
*Marry* can be used as a transitive or intransitive verb with the same meaning as *get married* but this is unusual. It can also be used as a transitive verb with a different meaning: *The registrar marries two people.*

## SPEAKING AND WRITING EXERCISE 3

Direct the students to the picture of the wedding ceremony. Discuss where they think the people are from and what they especially notice about them. Then write the prompts from the exercise on the board. The students work in groups (if possible, of different nationalities) and discuss the prompts in relation to wedding ceremonies in their country/countries and in Britain. Monitor and correct any errors you hear. Then discuss as a class.

Next, they write sentences about wedding ceremonies in their countries. If you have a mixed nationality class, they can display their writing without the name of their country. The others read the text and try to guess which country it is.

## LISTENING EXERCISE 4
### Background notes

Norman Stevens is a real person. In the **registry** (or **register office**, there are lots of letters on the wall from people he has married, thanking him for all his help. **Kensington and Chelsea** is a borough in

West London. Parts of it are very rich and fashionable but it also has a poorer area in the north.

Direct students to the questions. Play the tape. The students compare their answers in pairs. Then check the answers with the whole class. If you wish, play the tape again, asking students what problems Norman has experienced in his time as a registrar. Discuss the answers.

**KEY**

1  23 years   2  about 10,000 couples   3  22

**TAPESCRIPT**

NORMAN STEVENS

I have been a registrar for twenty-three years. I'm not sure exactly how many couples I've married in those years, but it's probably around ten thousand. The most weddings I've ever done in one day was actually twenty-two. I have never actually forgotten the words completely, but I have sometimes started the first declaration a second time, or started the second declaration first. Even though I personally have married about ten thousand couples, what I have to remind myself all the time is that for them it's their first time, and for them it's a very special day.

## WRITING EXERCISE 5

Direct the class to Penny's invitation. Copy Sarah's reply onto the board. The students work in pairs to fill in the missing words. Elicit their answers and write them on the board. Highlight the use of *look forward to* + gerund and *would love to* + infinitive. Drill the forms if necessary.

**KEY**

1  you and Joe are getting married
2  Thank you
3  to come (to your wedding)
4  on February 15th
5  Best wishes

## EXERCISE 6

Tell the students to imagine that they are going to have a party to celebrate something. Make sure they have all thought of some event to celebrate. Then direct them to the instructions in the exercise. If your students find writing difficult, copy Penny's invitation onto the board, underlining what they must replace, e.g. *Joe and I are getting married!* The *ceremony* is at *Kensington and Chelsea registry office* at *10 a.m.* on *February 15th*, etc. Monitor and help. When they have finished, they 'post' their invitation to another student who then writes a reply and sends it back.

# 15 In the future

## Predictions

> **Focus**
> - Means of prediction
> - Weather and weather forecasts
>
> - Predicting
> - Predicting with differing degrees of certainty
> - Expressing hopes for the future
> - Giving reactions: *I hope/think so. I hope not./I don't think so.*
>
> - *Will* + infinitive for prediction
> - Adverbs of degrees of certainty: *perhaps, probably, definitely, certainly*
> - Irregular comparative and superlative adjective: *less, least*
> - Further practice: superlative adjectives

### EXERCISE 1

To introduce the topic, bring in a horoscope and weather forecast from a newspaper. Ask the class *How can we find out about the future?* Use your examples to prompt discussion and write the students' ideas on the board. Then direct the students to the pictures in the Students' Book and compare their ideas on the board with the ones in the book. Add any new ones to the board and drill each one chorally and individually. Leave the list on the board for Exercise 2. Then ask *Are weather forecasts accurate?* and elicit a genuine response, e.g. *I think so.* To check the concept of accuracy ask *Are weather forecasts 100% certain?* (No) *So they're not completely accurate?* (No). Ask the students about the accuracy of some of the other ways of predicting the future to elicit *I don't think so./Of course not!/I don't know./It depends.* Then get two students to read out the example exchange. The students work in pairs and discuss the different ways of predicting the future.

### COMPARING CULTURES EXERCISE 2

Refer the students to the ways of predicting the future on the board and to the three questions in the Students' Book. They work in small groups (if possible, of different nationalities) to discuss the questions. Monitor and make a note of any errors. Get feedback as a class and add any other ways of

# UNIT FIFTEEN

predicting the future to the list on the board. Finally, use the board to correct any errors.

## 🎧 EXERCISE 3

You may need to revise the use of *will* + infinitive for making predictions. Draw a large outline map of your country on the board and add some weather symbols which are appropriate for your climate, e.g. a sun to show 'sunny', '30°C', etc. Point to the first symbol and ask *What will the weather be like tomorrow?* Elicit *It'll be sunny.* To check the concept, ask *Are you completely sure?* (No) *Is it possible to be completely sure?* (No) *Why do you use 'will' for the future?* (Because you are making a prediction about the future.) Drill *It'll be sunny* chorally and individually. Then display a symbol for 'rain' and elicit *It won't rain tomorrow.* Drill the sentence. Then point to the symbol for 'sunny' and say *Ask me the question.* Elicit *Will it be sunny tomorrow?* and give the answer *Yes, it will.* Drill the exchange chorally and individually. The students then work in pairs to practise similar exchanges using the map and the symbols. Monitor and correct any errors you hear. To elicit full sentences, ask *What do you think the weather will be like tomorrow?* Elicit a positive opinion, e.g. *I think it'll be sunny* and a negative opinion, e.g. *I don't think it'll rain.* Drill the two sentences. Point out the fact that the negative opinion is formed by the use of *don't think* rather than *I think it won't ....*

If possible, bring in a picture of a girl aged about sixteen. Show the students the picture and ask *Do you think she is sure about her future?* (No). Then direct students to the sentences in the Students' Book. Explain that someone is interviewing the girl about her plans. Play the tape until 'are there?' Together complete the first sentence on the board. Then play the complete interview. Students compare their answers with their partner. If necessary, play the tape again and then check the answers with the whole class. If your students find the pronunciation of *will* + infinitive and adverbs difficult, drill each sentence on the board. Leave the sentences on the board for the next exercise. Then discuss the last question in the exercise as a class.

### KEY

1 won't  2 will  3 will  4 will  5 won't  6 will
Adverbs: *certainly* and *definitely*

### TAPESCRIPT

INTERVIEWER: Excuse me. I'm doing a survey. Can I ask you a few questions?
GIRL: OK. What do you want to know?
I: Well, first of all ... how old are you?
G: Sixteen. Sixteen and a half.
I: Right. When you leave school, will you get a job, do you think?
G: Probably not. There aren't many jobs around, are there?
I: OK. Do you think you'll get your own home, away from your parents?
G: Oh, yes, I'm sure I will, in the next few years. I'll find the money somehow and move in with friends.
I: Will you think about moving away from the area? Somewhere where there are more jobs?
G: Yes, it's possible.
I: What about marriage and children? Do you think you'll get married in the next five years, say?
G: Probably, but I certainly don't want children yet. I'm too young.
I: OK. One more question. Would you like to travel?
G: I'd like to, but I don't think I will. I can't speak foreign languages, and anyway, you certainly need money for that. Maybe later.
I: Thanks very much.

To check the concepts of the adverbs, draw this scale on the board:

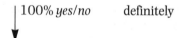

Ask *Will the girl leave home?* (Yes) *Are you sure?* (Yes) *Which words can you add to show that you are very sure?* Elicit *definitely* and *certainly*, and then the complete sentence *She will definitely leave home.* Drill the sentence and write *definitely* and *certainly* next to *100% yes/no* on the board. Establish that these adverbs come after *will.* Then ask *Will she have children immediately?* and elicit *She definitely won't have children immediately.* Establish that the adverb comes before *won't.* Then use the other information to elicit sentences with *probably* and *perhaps.* Write the adverbs on the scale in their order of probability. If necessary, use your weather visuals for further practice.

### DISCOVERING LANGUAGE EXERCISE 4

Refer the class back to the sentences in Exercise 3. In pairs, they look at the sentences and discuss the questions in Exercise 4. Then check the answers with the whole class and highlight the positions of the adverbs on the board.

### KEY

1 *Will* is used here to refer to what we **believe** about the future.
2 *Probably, certainly, definitely* come **before** *won't* but

**after** *will*. *Perhaps* comes at the beginning of the sentence.

## EXERCISE 5
Write prompts on the board which are appropriate for your students, e.g. *travel abroad/move house/have children/change job/study another language/learn another sport/get married/get a pet/live in another place/lose your hair*. Then point to the first prompt and ask a student *Do you think you will travel abroad?* (Add a time phrase, e.g. *in the next year*, if you wish.) Elicit an answer, then get students to ask you the question. Drill the exchange chorally and individually. Next, direct the class to the example exchange in the Students' Book. Highlight the difference between *I think so* and *I hope so* (*I hope so* is more of a wish than a plan and is less definite). The students then work in pairs to interview each other about their futures. Make sure they make notes. Monitor and correct any errors you hear. Students use their notes to write sentences about their partner. Then they swap sentences with their partner who checks for grammatical and factual errors.

### Extra practice
If your students get on well, collect in the sentences that they wrote about each other in Exercise 5. Read them out without the names, e.g. *He will probably go to university to study engineering*. The students work in groups and decide who the sentences refer to. Alternatively, write sentences about each student on separate cue cards (without their names). Give each student one or two cards. They mingle and find out who their statement refers to by asking questions, e.g.
A: *Matthias, will you go to university to study engineering?*
B: *No, I won't./Probably.*

## EXERCISE 6
Display some pictures to teach/revise the adjectives to describe weather. Then ask *Which is the sunniest country in (Europe)?* (Use your continent here.) Elicit the answer. To check the idea of the superlative, ask *Is it sunnier than ...?* (giving two or three other countries). Then drill the exchange chorally and individually. Do the same with the other adjectives.

Next, ask the class *What do you think is the sunniest place in the world?* Elicit their answers and write one or two on the board. Then do the same with the other adjectives. Point out that the superlative form of *little* is *the least*. They may also need to be reminded of the comparative form *less*. Then direct the class to the weather facts in the Students' Book. They work in pairs to complete the chart using the information in the text. Check the answers with the whole class. Finally, compare the answers with their guesses on the board.

### KEY

| The lowest temperatures | Antarctica |
| The most sun | Yuma, Arizona, USA |
| The least sun | South Pole |
| The most rain | Tutunendo, Colombia |
| The least rain | Arica, Chile |
| The strongest winds | Antarctica |
| The most fog | Newfoundland, Canada |

### Extra practice
To provide practice of superlative adjectives, write a questionnaire like this on the board:

| WHO HAS GOT | NAME |
| --- | --- |
| the biggest family? | |
| the oldest grandparent? | |
| the warmest hand? | |
| the sweetest smile? | |
| the strongest handshake? | |

The students mingle and interview each other. (If your students are sensitive about shaking hands, then change the prompts.)

## EXERCISE 7
Copy the chart onto the board. Refer the students back to the text in Exercise 6. They work in pairs and find the nouns to match the adjectives. Check the answers as a class.

### KEY

| ADJECTIVE | NOUN |
| --- | --- |
| sunny | sun |
| rainy (wet) | rain |
| windy | wind(s) |
| cloudy | cloud(s) |

## EXERCISE 8
### Background note
The **British Meteorological Office** (or **Met Office**) collects information on the weather in Britain and gives weather forecasts to the public.

Direct the students to the weather symbols and explain that these are used in British newspapers and on TV. Point to the first symbol and ask *What is that for?* Check that students understand *sunny*

UNIT FIFTEEN

*intervals, thunderstorms, above/below zero*. The students work in pairs to match the symbols and their meanings. Check the answers with the whole class.

**KEY**

A 6  B 7  C 3  D 10  E 1  F 5  G 8  H 2  I 4  J 9

## EXERCISE 9

Direct the class to the weather forecast and map in the Students' Book. Get the students to read the first statement and point out the words in italics. Ask *Is the first part true or false?* (False – they will be low). The students then work in pairs and do the same with all the other words in italics. Make sure they correct the false ones. Check the answers with the whole class by asking them to read out the weather forecast with changes where necessary.

**KEY**

(Corrections are in italics.)
Temperatures will be generally *low* in Scotland and the north of England, but will be *above zero* in the rest of the country. There will be *snow* in Scotland, moving into northern England later in the afternoon. Wales and the South West will be cloudy with sunny intervals and with winds of up to *twenty* miles an hour. The rest of England will be *cloudy*. In Northern Ireland, temperatures will be just above zero. There will be rain and some *thunderstorms* in inland areas.

# Problem solving

**Focus**
- Problems and solutions
- Stating consequences
- First conditional: *If ...*

## 🎧 EXERCISE 1

Direct the class to the picture of Julia. Remind them of Julia and what she has decided to do (to leave MAP Advertising). Ask *Does she look happy?* (No). Encourage the students to speculate why she is unhappy. Then write the two comprehension questions on the board. Check that students understand *advice* and *options*. The students listen to the conversation with their books closed. They compare their answers with their partner and then check as a class. Play the tape again; students have their books open and shadow the conversation.

**KEY**

1 She doesn't know what to do about her future.
2 She can stay at MAP or go to Germany.

## DISCOVERING LANGUAGE EXERCISE 2

Copy the sentences onto the board and ask the students to discuss the questions in pairs. Then check as a class and highlight the order of the tenses on the board. Point out the use of the comma after the first clause when the sentence begins with *if*.

**KEY**

1 the present simple tense
2 *will* + infinitive without *to*

To consolidate the concept of the first conditional, tell the class that you haven't decided what to do this evening and that you have two choices depending on the weather. Show the class a picture of someone sitting in the garden (or choose/draw pictures which are suitable to your climate and the time of year) and ask *What will I do if it's sunny?* Elicit *You'll sit in your garden if it's sunny*. To check the concept, ask *Am I certain that it will be sunny?* (No) *Is it possible that it will be sunny?* (Yes). Drill the sentence chorally and individually. Then get the students to ask you the questions about this evening. Elicit *What'll you do if it's sunny?* Drill the question, concentrating on the pronunciation of the contraction *what'll* /wɒtl/. Then display a picture of the cinema and ask *What'll I do if it rains this evening?* Elicit *You'll go to the cinema if it rains*. Use the questions to check the concept and drill both exchanges chorally and individually. Get each student to think of one thing that they will do if it's fine this evening and one thing if it rains. They interview each other in closed pairs. Make sure they change partners several times.

## EXERCISE 3

Refer the students back to the conversation in Exercise 1. Ask *What are the advantages if Julia stays at MAP?* Elicit the first advantage: *If Julia stays at MAP, she won't have to find another job*. The students then work together and discuss the other advantages and disadvantages to Julia's options. Monitor and correct any errors you hear. Check their answers as a class and if necessary drill the conditional forms. Draw this grid on the board:

|         | ADVANTAGES | DISADVANTAGES |
|---------|------------|---------------|
| MAP     |            |               |
| Germany |            |               |

## EXERCISE 4

Direct the class to Julia's list of options in the Students' Book, but get them to cover up the advantages and disadvantages. To demonstrate the task, get them to brainstorm the advantages and disadvantages of staying at MAP. Then let them read what she has written. They then work in pairs and do the same for her other options. Monitor and make a note of any errors. Check their answers as a class and write any extra advantages or disadvantages on the board (you can expand the grid from Exercise 3). Finally, use the board to correct any errors you heard.

## EXERCISE 5

The students work with the same partners as in Exercise 4. Get them to read the example text in the Students' Book. Using Julia's notes in the Students' Book and their ideas on the board, they write about the options. Monitor and help. To check their answers, get volunteer pairs to read out their paragraphs. Encourage peer correction.

## 📼 EXERCISE 6

Copy the sentences onto the board. Play the first clause in the first sentence and mark the intonation at the end with an arrow. Then do the same with the second part of the sentence. Play the other sentences, for the students to mark the intonation patterns. They compare their answers in pairs. Then check the answers with the whole class and mark the patterns on the board. Discuss the rule for the intonation patterns. Then play the sentences again, pausing for the students to repeat.

### KEY AND TAPESCRIPT

1 If she goes to Germany, she'll miss her friends.
2 She'll miss her friends if she goes to Germany.
3 If she stays at MAP, she'll have to leave London.
4 She'll have to leave London if she stays at MAP.

### Extra practice

1 Think of the beginning of a conditional sentence which could apply to all your students, e.g. *If I pass my exams.../If I go out tonight...* Write the beginning of the sentence on the board and get each student to complete it with a true fact about themselves. Make sure they write their sentence. They then mingle and read out their sentences to each other. Each student must find the student who has the most similar sentence to theirs.

2 Prepare a cue card for each student with either the beginning or the end of a conditional sentence. This is fun if the sentences can be true about your students, e.g. *If Pilar passes her exam,/she'll go to university./I'll watch TV tonight/if I can't go out*. The students mingle and read out their half of the sentence. They must find the other half.

3 Read out a conditional sentence to the whole class, e.g. *If I have the time, I'll go on holiday.* Prompt a student to continue, e.g. *If I go on holiday, I'll go to France.* Then the next student continues with *If I go to France*, etc. They can also do this in groups of about eight. The group that keeps going the longest wins the game.

4 If you have access to a film or series of slides, show part of the film and then pause it. The students make predictions about what will happen, e.g. *If he knocks on the door, the dog will bark.*

## EXERCISE 7

Direct the class to the pictures and the texts of the five problems in the Students' Book. Get them to read the first problem and then discuss together how they can solve it. If necessary, draw a diagram on the board to show the answer and use it to elicit the example conditional sentence. Check that the students understand *rope*, *ditch* and *plank*. The students then work in pairs and try to solve the other problems. Check answers with the class. Encourage students to draw diagrams on the board in order to help them explain how to solve the problems. They should use the first conditional to explain, as in the example.

### KEY

1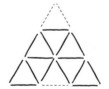

2

3 She ties the rope around the tree on the land, and then carries the other end of the rope on a walk round the lake. As she passes the halfway mark, the rope starts to wrap around the tree on the island. When she reaches her starting point, she ties the other end of the rope to the tree on the land and pulls herself across on the rope.

4

5 If she takes the mouse across the river first, she will leave the cat and the cheese together. She then goes back and collects the cheese. She takes the cheese across and collects the mouse. She takes the mouse back to the other side, leaves it there and collects the cat. She takes the cat across and leaves it with the cheese. Finally, she goes back to collect the mouse.

### EXERCISE 8
To introduce the exercise, tell the class about a real or imaginary problem that you have, e.g. Six people are coming for a meal tonight and you haven't got much time to prepare it. Elicit advice, using structures the students have learnt, e.g. *You can go to the supermarket; you'll find some ready-made meals.* Discuss the options, e.g. *If I buy ready-made meals, my friends will think I'm lazy.* Then tell each student to think of a problem in their lives. Explain that it can be real or imaginary. They then tell their partner about their problem: their partner gives them advice and they discuss the options together. Make sure they change roles. Monitor and make a note of any errors you hear. If you wish to extend the activity, they can mingle and get advice from all the students in the class. For feedback, they tell the whole class who gave them the best advice. Finally, use the board to correct any errors you heard.

### EXERCISE 9
Direct the students to the picture of Julia and James and the comprehension questions in the Students' Book. Play the tape once. The students compare their answers in pairs. Play the conversation again and then check the answers with the class.

#### KEY
1 She doesn't know. She thinks she'll go to Germany.
2 He hopes he'll still be in advertising.
3 She's not sure. She'll get married if she meets the right man.

#### TAPESCRIPT
JULIA: Well, this is it.
JAMES: This is it.
JU: My last day at MAP Advertising.
JA: What are you going to do? Have you decided yet?
JU: Not really. I think I'll go to Germany – and look for a job there.
JA: You don't sound very happy, Julia.
JU: I know. It's just that, well, I hope I'm doing the right thing.
JA: Oh, you'll be OK.
JU: I hope so.
JA: You can always stay at MAP. It's not too late.
JU: No, I'm not going to do that. What about you, James? Where will you be five years from now?
JA: What a question! I'll be married and I'll have two children.
JU: Really?
JA: Of course not. I don't know where I'll be five years from now. I hope I'll still be in advertising. I like it. Will you get married, Julia?
JU: Perhaps. If I meet the right man, I'll get married. But I don't know.

### ENGLISH AROUND YOU
Focus students' attention on the cartoon and the caption. Explain that the first conditional is often used to present two options for people to do, e.g. *I'll get the car if you bring the suitcases down.* Ensure that students understand the joke: it is hardly a fair allocation of responsibilities for the man washing up.

## Development

### SPEAKING EXERCISE 1
Copy the British saying about the weather onto the board and explain that it is an old proverb. Direct the students to the picture of the shepherd in the Students' Book and elicit what his job is. In pairs the students discuss what they think the saying means, using dictionaries if necessary. Get quick feedback. Then the students read the explanation to see if their guesses were correct. Get them to write down as many sayings about the weather as they can in their language(s). If you have a monolingual group, discuss in English what they mean. If you have a multilingual class, the students discuss what they mean with a student of a different nationality.

### READING EXERCISE 2
To introduce the topic, ask the class if they watch the weather forecast on TV and why, e.g. to decide what clothes to wear, to find out if they should go away at the weekend. Discuss what they think of the weather forecast and the presenters in their country/countries. During the discussion, check that the students understand *script* and *radar.* Direct the students to the statements. Explain that some of the statements are false. Then refer the class to the article in the Students' Book. They read the article and correct the statements. They compare their

answers with their partners. Then check as a class and correct the statements on the board.

**KEY**

1 True.   2 False. They are professional meteorologists.
3 False. They are broadcast live.   4 True.
5 True.   6 True.
7 False. Seventy per cent of television viewers cannot remember what they saw on the weather forecast.

## 📼 LISTENING EXERCISE 3

Copy the list of areas onto the board. Tell the class that they are going to listen to a television weather forecast. Write *Moscow* on the board and ask students which part of the world it is in. Elicit the correct answer (Eastern Europe), and ask students to complete the rest of the exercise in pairs. Check their answers with the whole class.

**KEY**

a) 3   b) 4   c) 1   d) 2

## 📼 EXERCISE 4

Tell the class that they are going to listen to a television weather forecast. Ask them to choose one city from Exercise 3, and to listen to the parts of the forecast that refer to that area and make notes. Play the tape, more than once if necessary. They compare their answers in pairs. Then check the answers with the whole class.

**KEY**

| | |
|---|---|
| MOSCOW | a) good but cool |
| | b) fine |
| BEIRUT | a) dry, sunshine |
| | b) fine |
| BRUSSELS | a) wet and windy, quite cold |
| | b) wet and windy, and a bit cool |
| ROME | a) quite dry, sunshine |
| | b) fine |

**TAPESCRIPT**

And now over to Terry Price for the weather forecast.

Well, a mixed picture over the next few days. Today in Britain, very wet and windy – in northern Europe. You can see from the satellite picture that the highest temperatures, as they so often are, are in the southern parts of Europe, where it's also quite dry, particularly the eastern parts of the Mediterranean. The forecast suggests that it's going to be quite cold over northwestern parts of Europe for the rest of the day, even some snow on the Scandinavian mountains.

So that's today's chart, with showery conditions in many parts of northern Europe but the best of the sunshine in the south and throughout the Mediterranean and in the Canary Isles as well. And pretty good but cool in the eastern parts of Europe too.

Now let's look at tomorrow's chart. Very much the same in the south except that the rain is starting to push down into the northern parts of the Mediterranean there. Elsewhere, staying fine in eastern Europe and fine in central and eastern parts of the Mediterranean as well. But still wet and windy in many northwestern parts of Europe, including southern parts of Scandinavia, and a bit cool too.

## WRITING EXERCISE 5

The students can do this exercise for homework. If your students like making displays, they can draw a weather map to illustrate their weather forecast.

## READING AND SPEAKING EXERCISE 6
### Background note

**Bill Foggitt** is a real person who comes from Yorkshire, a county in the north of England.

Direct the class to the drawing of the animals and insects in the Students' Book. Use the drawings to teach *fly*, *spider* and *web*. Then tell the class about Bill Foggitt and explain that he has a different way of forecasting the weather, using the insects and animals in the picture. See if the students can guess what his methods are. Then draw the outline of the key grid on the board.

Direct the class to the article and the four sentences. They read the article. In pairs, they decide which sentences are true for Mr Foggitt and which are true for The Met. Office. Check their answers as a class and tick the appropriate box on the board.

**KEY**

|  | MR FOGGITT | THE MET. OFFICE |
|---|---|---|
| Sentence 1 | ✓ | |
| Sentence 2 | | ✓ |
| Sentence 3 | | ✓ |
| Sentence 4 | ✓ | |

# Progress check 5

## Vocabulary

**EXERCISE 1**
1 c  2 b  3 e  4 f  5 a  6 d

**EXERCISE 2**
1 rainy and windy  2 cloudy  3 snow  4 fog
5 sunny  6 hottest

**EXERCISE 3**
1 get engaged  2 get married  3 registrar
4 wedding  5 reception  6 bride  7 husband
8 honeymoon

## Grammar and functions

**EXERCISE 4**
1 Have you ever had a break-in?
2 When was it?
3 How did it happen?/What happened?

**EXERCISE 5**
1 He told me (that) there was something wrong with his leg.
2 She said (that) she couldn't find Tom.
3 He said (that) my tickets weren't there.
4 She told me (that) she didn't enjoy jazz.
5 She asked me what they wanted.
6 He asked me if I could wait for him.
7 She asked me how much the red sweater was.

**EXERCISE 6**
a) A past event: Well done! Congratulations!
b) A future event: Good luck! Have a wonderful time!
c) A present event: Happy anniversary! Happy Birthday!

**EXERCISE 7**
1 Perhaps my sister will come too.
2 She probably won't want to come.
3 We'll definitely have some coffee.
4 Perhaps we'll go for a walk.
5 We'll probably eat in a restaurant.
6 Perhaps my parents won't leave until the next day.

**EXERCISE 8**
1 Will your parents bring their dog? I hope not.
2 Will your sister's boyfriend come too? I don't think so.
3 Will they come by car? I think so.
4 Will they sleep at your house? I hope so.
5 Will you tell them about your job offer? I think so.
6 Will you ask their advice? I don't think so.

**EXERCISE 9**
1 I'll continue to work at the hospital if I stay in Brighton.
2 If I stay in Brighton, I won't be able to travel.
3 If I leave Brighton, I'll visit new places.
4 I'll make new friends if I leave Brighton.
5 If I leave Brighton, I won't have job security.

## Common errors

**EXERCISE 10**
1 She has already found a job.
2 I haven't eaten anything yet.
3 Have you ever been to Brazil?
4 The sun shines most of the time.
5 We probably won't sell our flat.

**EXERCISE 11**
1 Congratulations on your new job!
2 Can I talk to you about my problems?
3 I'd like to thank you for this lovely present.
4 It will rain in the south of Scotland.
5 We'll be able to sleep late tomorrow.
6 My salary depends on my exam results.

**EXERCISE 12**
1 She told me that she couldn't come./She said to me that she couldn't come.
2 He asked me what I wanted.
3 I left school three months ago.
4 Do you believe in horoscopes?
5 It will snow in Scandinavia.

**EXERCISE 13**
1 brakes  2 equipment  3 independence
4 marriage  5 loneliness

# Language Awareness Worksheets

## Introduction

This section of the Teacher's Book contains six worksheets with facing answer keys. These worksheets are designed to draw attention to the complexities of some of the key language areas presented in the Students' Book and to encourage teachers to explore the broader parameters of language use. Although pre-intermediate students expect to be presented with relatively straight-forward rules, patterns and contexts of use, we as teachers need a much wider knowledge and awareness, particularly to allow informed responses to questions and problems that may arise in class. The worksheets are *not* intended for use directly by pre-intermediate students.

Each worksheet is divided into three sections. The first section asks you to reflect on what we expect pre-intermediate students to know about each language area (and what they will in fact have been taught by the end of *Look Ahead 2*). The second considers aspects of the language area which students will not be taught until later in the *Look Ahead* course at levels 3 and 4. The final section highlights some common errors or inappropriacies of use and invites you to add problems that are particular to your own students.

## Who are the worksheets for?

### 1 INDIVIDUAL TEACHERS WORKING ALONE

Although it is always helpful to discuss language points with other teachers, it is possible to work through the tasks on your own. You can then compare your answers with the key on the facing page, or you may wish to turn to grammar books to research certain areas more deeply.

### 2 TEACHER TRAINEES WORKING WITH A TEACHER TRAINER

The worksheets can be photocopied and can therefore be used freely as input or follow-up self-study materials for seminars and courses. Ways of working with the materials are described more fully under 3 below, but one possible procedure is to do the tasks in pairs or small groups and follow this up with a feedback and discussion session led by the trainer.

### 3 GROUPS OF TEACHERS WHO MEET TO SHARE THEIR EXPERIENCE AND IDEAS

Teachers working in the same institution or geographical area often meet regularly to discuss issues relating to their teaching. Meetings such as these are particularly useful to teachers who are relatively new to the profession and who can be helped by the greater experience of their colleagues. However, more experienced teachers will also find it helpful to remind themselves of the complexities of language forms and usage.

You can work through a complete worksheet in a self-development session, or select one or two sections from a worksheet. There are a number of possible ways of preparing for sessions. You can – individually – read and think about either the worksheets themselves or the general focus beforehand, and list questions that they raise in your mind. You can read the relevant section of the Grammar Reference section in *Look Ahead* Students' Book 2, to remind yourself of what we teach pre-intermediate students. You can also think about and note down problems that, in your experience, pre-intermediate students have with the particular language area, and awkward questions that they tend to ask.

Following the session, you may wish to explore the area further in grammar books that are available to you. You may even wish to adapt the worksheet for use in class with advanced level students. It is also valuable, in your private reading, to watch for contextualised examples of language patterns and to reflect on how they exemplify – or bend – the rules and guidelines focused on in the worksheets.

# WORKSHEET 1

# The present simple and present progressive

..........................................................................................................

## What do we teach our pre-intermediate students about the present tenses?

**1** Match the uses of the present tenses on the left with the example sentences on the right.

1  arrangements for the future
2  present routines/habits
3  present situations without a time limit
4  situations/events at the time of speaking
5  temporary present situations
6  present thoughts/feelings
7  conditions for future events

a) She lives in Bristol.
b) He catches the train to work.
c) They're staying with my sister.
d) They're sitting in the garden.
e) She thinks so.
f) I'll come if it doesn't snow.
g) We're writing reports tomorrow.

**2** Look again at sentences a) – g) above. What problems might students have with the spelling and pronunciation of each verb form?

..........................................................................................................

## What will students need to learn at more advanced levels?

**3** Look at these examples and describe other uses of the two present tenses.

PRESENT SIMPLE
a) Queen offers to pay income tax
b) The earth spins on its axis.
c) Clint Eastwood plays a caring father.
d) The school term starts next week.
e) 'And now you put it in the oven...Good.'
f) 'Then the man points a gun at the shop assistant and tells him to...'

PRESENT PROGRESSIVE
g) They're always playing music late at night.

**4** Study these pairs of sentences and explain the differences in meaning.

a) 1 Tony works in France.
   2 Tony is working in France.
b) 1 If we go walking, I'll need strong shoes.
   2 If we're going walking, I'll need strong shoes.

c) 1 Fiona wins again!
   2 Fiona is winning again!
d) 1 She always brings us cakes.
   2 She's always bringing us cakes.

**5** The present tenses are often used with adverbs and adverbial phrases. Read the two sentences below. In which position in the sentences are the expressions on the right commonly used?

a) She goes to the hairdresser's.   occasionally
   ↑    ↑   ↑              ↑         twice a week
   1    2   3              4

b) He is meeting a friend.   now
   ↑  ↑↑       ↑       ↑     next Monday
   1  2 3      4       5

..........................................................................................................

## What mistakes do students often make?

**6** Explain the mistakes in these sentences. What problems do your students often have?

a) He's runing for the bus, but he miss it most days.
b) 'What's the weather like today?' 'It snows a lot.'
c) She always is late to class.
d) Do they show the Scotland/Ireland match now on television?

# WORKSHEET 1

# Key

**1** 1g) (but c could also refer to the future; it depends on the context) 2b) 3a) 4d) 5c) 6e) 7f)

**2** Pre-intermediate students often have problems with the spelling of those present participles that do not simply add -*ing* to the infinitive form (e.g. *hit – hitting, write – writing*) and with those third person singular present simple forms that require more than the addition of *s* (e.g. *catch – catches, do – does, cry – cries*). Possible pronunciation problems include the third person endings /s/ (*thinks*), /z/ (*lives*) and /ɪz/ (*catches*), and the pronunciation of /ɪŋ/ (-*ing*), especially after *y* (*staying*).

**3** The present simple is commonly used:
  a) in newspaper headlines.
  b) to express general truths about the world.
  c) in reviews of films, books etc.
  d) to refer to future events that can be checked against fixed schedules and are therefore considered to be definite.
  e) with the subject *you* for instructions or methods of doing things.
  f) to add drama to stories and jokes, usually in colloquial English, and to simultaneous commentaries.

The present progressive is commonly used:
  g) with *always* to describe repeated events which you have an attitude towards (especially one of irritation or surprise).

**4** a) 1 This describes a situation with no particular time limit.
     2 In this sentence the situation is seen as temporary.
   b) 1 In this conditional sentence a walk is no more than a possibility.
     2 In this sentence, a walk has been suggested or arranged.
   c) 1 The use of the dramatic present simple shows that the winning has been completed: Fiona has won.
     2 In this sentence, Fiona is ahead but has not won yet. The action continues after the comment.
   d) 1 This is a statement of fact about a habit.
     2 In this sentence, the speaker is adding attitude to the fact; in this case the attitude is probably surprised appreciation, but intonation or more context will make the attitude clear.

**5** The adverbs and adverbials can be added in the following positions:
  a) *occasionally* [routine] – positions 1, 2 and 4.
     *twice a week* [routine; specified frequency] – positions 1 and 4 (less commonly, 3).
  b) *now* [present situation] – positions 1, 3 and 5.
     *next Monday* [arrangement for the future] – positions 1 and 5.

**6** a) These are mistakes in form: the form of the present participle (*running*); the form of the present simple third person singular (*misses*).
   b) The wrong tense is used in the response. The question refers to the situation now, and the answer should be: *It is snowing a lot*.
   c) The adverb is in the wrong position. The correct version is: *She is always late to class*. Frequency adverbs precede most verbs, but follow the verb *to be*, auxiliaries and modals.
   d) This is almost certainly a wrong choice of tense. The present progressive should be used if the question refers to the time of speaking: *Are they showing the Scotland/Ireland match now on television?* The sentence is only correct if the speaker is asking about a new habit of showing all Scotland/Ireland matches on television.

# WORKSHEET 2

# Stative verbs

## What do we teach our pre-intermediate students about stative verbs?

**1** Look at the two groups of sentences, a) and b)
1 Which group of sentences contains stative verbs?
2 What sort of verbs does the other group of sentences contain?

a) I'm going now.
   Our team is playing very badly.
   They're moving house at the moment.
   I'm looking for the cat.

b) They know me well.
   She understands the problem.
   He prefers golf to basketball.
   I hate fast food.

**2** What are the characteristics of stative verbs? Think about form and meaning.

## What will students need to learn at more advanced levels?

**3** Group the common stative verbs below into four basic categories:
a) feelings/desires *adore*    c) senses
b) thoughts/beliefs            d) being/having

adore be believe belong detest dislike doubt exist hate have hear know like love own possess prefer realise remember see sound smell suppose understand want wish

**4** Some verbs which are normally only used in simple forms can also have progressive forms, usually with different meanings. Compare these pairs of sentences. How does the verb change in meaning in each case?

a) 1 It's a tree.
   2 He's being a tree.
b) 1 The children love this museum.
   2 Look! The children are loving it.
c) 1 What do you think?
   2 What are you thinking?
d) 1 I hope we'll see the sea.
   2 I'm hoping we'll see the sea.
e) 1 I've got problems.
   2 I'm having problems.
f) 1 My foot hurts.
   2 My foot's hurting.

**5** The verbs below can also have both stative meanings, expressed with simple forms, and dynamic meanings, expressed with progressive forms. Write pairs of sentences with the present simple and present progressive forms of each verb. Explain the differences in meaning.

a) weigh   b) measure   c) taste   d) smell
e) feel    f) appear    g) look

**6** Which modal verb is commonly used with verbs of the senses (e.g. *taste, see, feel*) when they are used as stative verbs?

## What mistakes do students often make?

**7** Explain the mistakes in these sentences. Which sentences are wrong in any context? What problems do your students often have?

a) He's having a headache.
b) I'm hating grammar exercises.
c) What are you meaning?
d) How much is the bag weighing?

# WORKSHEET 2

# Key

**1** 1  *Know, understand, prefer, hate* in group b) are examples of stative verbs.
2  *Go, play, move, look for* in group a) are examples of dynamic verbs, used in progressive and simple forms, which refer to actions, events or processes.

**2** Stative verbs are normally not used in progressive forms. They refer to states or situations that are not usually within our control.

**3** a) adore, detest, dislike, hate, like, love, prefer, want, wish
b) believe, doubt, know, realise, remember, suppose, understand
c) hear, see, sound, smell
d) be, belong, exist, have, own, possess

**4** a) The progressive form in sentence 2 indicates that the situation is dynamic and temporary. He is pretending, perhaps in a play; he is normally, of course, *not* a tree.
b) The progressive form in sentence 2 emphasises the temporary nature of the children's reaction, which the speaker feels could change.
c) Question 1 means *What is your opinion?* Question 2 is asking for a person's thoughts at the present moment, a different sense of the same verb.
d) The use of the progressive form in sentence 2 suggests a more tentative hope; the speaker is prepared for disappointment.
e) The second sentence may suggest that the problems are more temporary, but it also suggests a series of different problems rather than the same problems which are continuing for some time.
f) When a normally stative verb refers to a bodily sensation, there is usually no difference in meaning or implication between the progressive and simple forms.

**5** a) Stative use: e.g. *How much does this parcel weigh?* (= What is its weight?) *It weighs 6 kilos.*
Dynamic use: e.g. *I am just weighing this parcel.* (= I am putting it on the scales to find out its weight.)
b) Stative use: e.g. *The table measures a metre by two metres.* (= These are its measurements.)
Dynamic use: e.g. *She's measuring the table.* (= She is using a tape measure to discover its measurements.)
c) Stative use: e.g. *This soup tastes delicious.* (= Its taste is delicious.)
Dynamic use: e.g. *I'm tasting the soup.* (= I'm trying it to find out how it tastes.)
d) Stative use: e.g. *These dustbins smell awful.* (= Their smell is awful.)
Dynamic use: e.g. *We're smelling the different teas.* (= We're testing the smell of each one.)
e) Stative use: e.g. *She feels sick,* (referring to a bodily sensation) *It feels smooth,* (referring to texture)
Dynamic use: e.g. *She's feeling the cloth.* (= She's touching it.) Note that *She's feeling sick.* means the same as *She feels sick.*
f) Stative use: e.g. *The plane appears to be in the air.* (= It seems to be in the air.)
Dynamic use: e.g. *The plane is appearing above the trees.* (= It is coming into sight.)
g) Stative use: e.g. *He looks ill.* (= He appears to be ill.)
Dynamic use: e.g. *He's looking at me.* (= His eyes are on me.)

**6** We often use *can* with sense verbs when they are used as stative verbs: e.g. *I can see you! We could hear a noise.*

**7** a) This is a correct sentence with a sense which is probably not intended. It suggests that the headache is not genuine but a pretence. *He's got a headache.*, on the other hand, indicates a genuine headache, a situation that the person cannot control.
b) This is a correct sentence only if it refers to a temporary situation. *I hate grammar exercises.* would express a general feeling.
c) The use of a progressive form is wrong. The question should be: *What do you mean?*
d) This is wrong. The stative form is: *How much does the bag weigh?*

# WORKSHEET 3

# Verb structures

## What do we teach our pre-intermediate students about verb structures?

**1** Classify the verbs and verb phrases below into three groups:
a) those followed by an infinitive with *to*
b) those followed by an infinitive without *to*
c) those followed by an *-ing* form (a gerund or a present participle)

agree   can't stand   decide   dislike   enjoy   finish   hope   learn   let's   offer   practise   prefer   promise   want   would like   would prefer

**2** Look again at the verbs and verb phrases in Exercise 1.
1 Which verb belongs to two of the three groups? Can you think of other verbs that can take an *-ing* form or an infinitive?
2 Which of the verbs and verb phrases above cannot be followed by a noun or noun phrase instead of a verb structure?

**3** Some verbs which are normally only followed by an *-ing* form or a noun phrase can, in certain contexts, be followed by an infinitive with *to*. What does *to* mean in these sentences?
a) He stopped to look at my work.
b) I practised to improve my performance.

## What will students need to learn at more advanced levels?

**4** Look at these pairs of sentences. Each verb can be followed by an infinitive or an *-ing* form. In which pairs is there a significant difference in meaning between the sentences?
a) 1 I started to work.
   2 I started working.
b) 1 We tried to talk to her.
   2 We tried talking to her.
c) 1 Can you remember to phone him?
   2 Can you remember phoning him?
d) 1 We regret to announce new job cuts.
   2 We regret announcing new job cuts.
e) 1 I hate to see you like this.
   2 I hate seeing you like this.
f) 1 They'll continue to fight.
   2 They'll continue fighting.

**5** What other common verb structures are there? Complete these sentences. Then match each verb structure with one or more of the patterns below.
a) She agreed...   c) You taught...   e) We gave...
b) I allowed...    d) He said...      f) They told...

1 verb + indirect object + *to* infinitive
2 verb + (*that*) clause
3 verb + indirect object + (*that*) clause
4 verb + indirect object + direct object

## What mistakes do students often make?

**6** Explain the mistakes in these sentences. What problems do your students often have?
a) Let's to go now.
b) Don't worry. I'll remember writing to you.
c) She stopped to work and made a cup of tea.
d) They taught to build walls.

© Longman Group UK Ltd. 1994

## WORKSHEET 3

# Key

**1** a) agree   decide   hope   learn   offer   prefer   promise   want   would like   would prefer
   b) let's
   c) can't stand   dislike   enjoy   finish   practise   prefer

**2** 1 prefer. Some other verbs that can take an *-ing* form *or* an infinitive are: *like, love, begin.* (See exercise 3 below.)

   2 rarely: agree   decide
     never: hope   let's

**3** In the examples, *to* is used to express purpose and means '*in order to*'.

**4** a) No difference.
   b) There is a significant difference.
     1 We wanted to talk to her so we made an effort to do this, but we probably did not manage to talk to her. e.g. *We tried to talk to her but we couldn't because she was busy.*
     2 We certainly talked to her in an attempt to achieve what we wanted. e.g. *We tried talking to her but we couldn't convince her that we were right.*
   c) There is a significant difference.
     1 Will you please remember (in the future), that you need to phone him?
     2 Can you remember (now) if you have already phoned him?
   d) A significant difference is usually intended.
     1 This is a special use of 'regret', with certain verbs. We are sorry about the new job cuts that we are now having to announce.
     2 We are sorry that we announced new job cuts. We wish we hadn't announced them /had to announce them.
   e) No significant difference.
   f) No difference.

**5** a) Pattern 2
   b) Patterns 1 and 4
   c) Patterns 1, 3 and 4
   d) Pattern 2 [also Pattern 3, with the addition of the preposition *to*: *He said to me that...*]
   e) Pattern 4
   f) Patterns 1, 3 and 4

**6** a) *Let's* should be followed by an infinitive without *to*: *Let's go now*.
   b) The construction *remember + -ing* is possible, but not correct in this sentence. The correct version is: *Don't worry. I'll remember to write to you.*
   c) This sentence is grammatically correct but does not make sense. It should read: *She stopped working and made a cup of tea.*
   d) In this case, *teach* must be followed by an (indirect) object (a noun phrase or a pronoun) and then an infinitive with *to*: *They taught us to build walls.*

© Longman Group UK Ltd. 1994

# WORKSHEET 4

# Modal verbs

## What do we teach our pre-intermediate students about modal verbs?

**1** Look at the examples of modal verbs below. What are the characteristics of modal verbs? Think about their forms and why we use them.
a) I could come.
b) You shouldn't smoke.
c) Would he enjoy it?

b) 1 Can you help us?
   2 Could you help us?
c) 1 Shall we go home now?
   2 Should we go home now?
d) 1 I'll like the results.
   2 I'd like the results.

**2** What are the differences in meaning expressed by the modal verbs in each of these pairs of sentences?
a) 1 I can't play chess at all.
   2 I couldn't play chess at all.

**3** How do students know the time reference of modal verbs? Experiment with different contexts for the sentences below. Do the sentences refer to the past, present or future?
a) Shall I book some tickets?
b) I could write stories.

## What will students need to learn at more advanced levels?

**4** What generalisations can we make about functional uses to help students?

a) CERTAINTY
Which two of the speakers (A-D) below are reasonably certain about their information? Which two speakers are not sure?
A: He should be at work.
B: He could be at work.
C: He'll be at work.
D: He can't be at work.

b) ADVICE/PERMISSION/PROHIBITION
Which modals (*can, could, will, would, shall, should* and their negative forms) can complete the sentence on the right to express:
1 advice?
2 permission?           You ..... go out tonight.
3 prohibition?

c) OFFERS/REQUESTS
Which modals (*can, could, will, would, shall, should*) can complete the offer of help (1)? Which can complete the request for help (2)?
1 ..... I help you?
2 ..... you help me?

**5** Explain the differences in meaning between these pairs of sentences.
a) 1 They should go to Brazil.
   2 They should be in Brazil soon.
b) 1 OK, I'll speak to him.
   2 I'll kill him!
c) 1 You will see her tomorrow, I'm sure.
   2 You will see her, even when I ask you not to!
d) 1 I would go out more if I were you.
   2 I would go out more in those days.

## What mistakes do students often make?

**6** Explain the mistakes in these spoken sentences. What problems do your students often have?
a) We can't to do this exercise.
b) I shall not be there.
c) Will I carry those books for you?
d) It is better that you don't leave this mess here.

# WORKSHEET 4

# Key

This worksheet explores those modal verbs which are first introduced in *Look Ahead* levels 1 and 2.

**1** FORM
Modal verbs are auxiliaries and are followed by an infinitive without *to*. There is no third person *s* in the affirmative form. Questions are formed by inversion of the subject and verb. Negatives are formed with *not*. All modal verbs have negative short forms, and some also have short forms in the affirmative; there is no single rule to help students to know if they can abbreviate a modal in spoken or informal English.

USE
Some modal verbs have straightforward dictionary meanings (e.g. *can/could = be able to*). On many occasions, though, modal verbs are used to express attitudes: to people (e.g. through degrees of formality); to information (e.g. through degrees of certainty); and to intentions (e.g. through degrees of decisiveness).

**2** a) *can't* for present lack of ability; *couldn't* for past lack of ability.
b) *can* for an informal request; *could* for a more polite request.
c) *shall* for a suggestion; *should* to refer to what it is advisable or responsible to do.
d) *will like* to express predicted future pleasure; *would like* for a present wish.

**3** Modal verbs depend heavily on context for time reference.
a) *Shall I book some tickets now/tomorrow?* (The offer or suggestion is made at the time of speaking, but the action to which it refers can take place in the present or future). The time reference here is determined by the time adverb.
b) *I could write stories when I was a child.* (past ability); *I could write stories after work if I had more time.* (hypothetical present situation); *I could write stories when I finish my course.* (future possibility). The time reference in these examples is provided by the subordinate clause which contextualises the main clause.

**4** a) Speakers C and D are reasonably certain; speakers A and B are not sure (and speaker B is even less sure than speaker A). Note that the speakers could either be speculating about the present or referring to the future.
b) 1 advice: *could, should, shouldn't*, and (with appropriate intonation) *can*.
2 permission: *can, could* (..., *I suppose*.), and *shall*. In modern English the use of *shall/shan't* for permission/prohibition is a written literary usage rather than a spoken one.
3 prohibition: *can't, won't, shan't*.
c) 1 *can, could, shall*
2 *can, could, will, would*.

**5** a) 1 *should* is used to say what is advisable.
2 *should* is used to deduce what is probably true.
b) 1 *'ll* for a promise.
2 *'ll* for a threat.
c) 1 *will* is used for a definite prediction about the future.
2 will is used to express annoyance at a habit.
d) 1 *would* is used to say what is advisable.
2 *would* refers to a past habit.

**6** a) A mistake in form: a modal verb should be followed by an infinitive without *to*.
b) A mistake in register: in conversational English, the short form *shan't* (or *won't*) is used.
c) An inappropriate choice of modal. The correct modal here is *shall*, not *will*.
d) An awkward circumlocution to avoid using a modal verb. *You shouldn't leave this mess here.* would sound much more natural.

# WORKSHEET 5

# Tag questions

## What do we teach our pre-intermediate students about tag questions?

**1** Look at these examples and explain how tag questions are formed.
a) You don't like this room, do you?
b) Breakfast starts at eight, doesn't it?
c) We can't stay there, can we?
d) Stella's English, isn't she?

**2** Does the speaker expect the answer 'yes' or 'no' to each of the questions above?

**3** Read these tag questions aloud. How sure is the speaker that Stella is English in each case? How does the intonation pattern affect the function of the question?
a) Stella's English, isn't she?
b) Stella's English, isn't she?
c) Stella isn't English, is she?
d) Stella isn't English, is she?

## What will students need to learn at more advanced levels?

**4** Look at some other examples. What amendments do you need to make to the explanations you gave in Exercise 1 for the structure of tag questions?
a) He's working now, is he?
b) I'm late, aren't I?
c) There won't be any free seats, will there?
d) Nobody here knows you, do they?
e) Help yourself, won't you?

**5** Now read these questions aloud. Explain how the different structural and intonation patterns affect the function of each question.
a) Do you understand?
b) You understand, do you?
c) Try to understand, will you?
d) Try to understand, won't you?

## What mistakes do students often make?

**6** Explain the mistakes in these sentences. What problems do your students often have?
a) Those are foreign, isn't it?
b) You didn't enjoy it, didn't you?
c) We haven't got tickets, don't we?
d) A: I'm not late, am I?
   B: That's right.

…

# Key

**1** Tag questions, which are used to check or confirm information, are formed with a statement followed by a question tag. A negative statement is followed by an affirmative question tag. An affirmative statement is usually followed by a negative question tag. The verb form in the question tag is an appropriate auxiliary, modal, or form of the verb *to be*, in the same person and tense as the verb form in the statement. The pronoun in the tag corresponds to the subject of the statement part.

**2** When the verb in the statement is affirmative, we expect the answer *yes*. When it is negative, we expect the answer *no*. We expect the following answers to the example questions:
   a) No (I don't).   c) No (we can't).
   b) Yes (it does).   d) Yes (she is).

**3** a) The speaker is not sure that Stella is English.
   b) The speaker is fairly sure that she is English, and is just checking the information.
   c) The speaker is not sure that Stella is not English.
   d) The speaker is fairly sure that Stella is not English and is just checking information.

**4** a) Tag questions can be affirmative in both parts. (It is very rare for both parts to have negative verb forms.)
   b) *Aren't* is used instead of *am not* in a question tag when the subject is *I*.
   c) If *there* is the subject of the statement part, it is not replaced by a pronoun but is repeated in the tag.
   d) If *nobody* is the subject of the statement part, the pronoun *they* and a plural verb form are used in the tag.
   e) A question tag using *will/won't* [also *can/can't/could/would*] can also follow an imperative form.

**5** a) This is an open question; I do not know whether you understand or not.
   b) This may be an open question, but it is more likely that I am surprised, sceptical, irritated or worried by the fact that you claim to understand.
   c) An imperative form can be followed by a question tag to make a request or order. Tone of voice is extremely important in differentiating between the two functions, but rising intonation is more likely to signal a request or tentative command. In this case, I want you to try to understand, so I am asking you to make an effort.
We can also vary the directness of request by our choice of tag:
   Direct      *Close the door, will you?*
   Less direct *Close the door, could/would you?*
   d) Falling intonation and the negative question tag, *won't*, are more likely to indicate a command or a rather abrupt request.

**6** a) *Isn't it?* sometimes occurs as an all-purpose tag in dialects of English, but it is not acceptable in standard British English. The correct form of the question tag here is: *aren't they?*.
   b) The use of two negative verb forms in a tag question is very occasionally used to show anger or aggression but is so rare that students of any level are best advised to avoid the construction. In this case, the negative question tag should be replaced with *did you?*
   c) The question tag should be affirmative, and the use of the auxiliary *do* is incorrect. The tag should be *have we?*, since *have* (in the correct form) is the auxiliary which is used with *have got*.
   d) B's answer is unhelpful in that it does not tell A whether he/she is or is not late. The correct answer is probably: *No, you aren't* (*late*). It would also be possible for B to show anger by giving the reply that A is not expecting: *Yes, you are* (*late*).

# WORKSHEET 6

# Reported speech

## What do we teach our pre-intermediate students about reported speech?

**1** Match these common reporting verbs with the structures that can follow them. Write a sentence to exemplify each structure.

REPORTING VERBS   REPORTING STRUCTURES
say
tell
ask

a) ...*someone to* + infinitive
b) ...*someone* (*that*) + clause
c) ...(*that*) + clause
d) ...(*someone*) *if* + clause
e) ...*to someone* (*that*) + clause
f) ...(*someone*) *when\where* etc. + clause

**2** Look at these pairs of sentences. What changes do we make to speech when we use a past tense verb to report it?

a) 1 'I don't want to go.'
   2 He said he didn't want to go.
b) 1 'Can you help me?'
   2 She asked me to help her.
c) 1 'Why is the party here?'
   2 She asked why the party was there.
d) 1 'Does Penny need any money?'
   2 He asked if Penny needed any money.
e) 1 'Don't leave tomorrow!'
   2 She told him not to leave the next day.
f) 1 'I usually come home early.'
   2 He told us that he usually went home early.

## What will students need to learn at more advanced levels?

**3** Think of other verbs that can be used for reporting. Find a reporting verb in Box B with a similar meaning to a verb in Box A.

| A | B |
|---|---|
| say  answer<br>promise  stress<br>think  tell (...that)<br>ask (...to)  tell (...to)<br>ask (...if) | request  inform<br>swear  emphasise<br>state  reply  believe<br>inquire  order |

In which pairs of verbs are the reporting structures the same? In which pairs are they different?

**4** Look at these pairs of sentences. What amendments do you need to make to the guidelines you formulated in Exercise 2?

a) 1 'I don't enjoy golf.'
   2 He said he doesn't enjoy golf.
b) 1 'Could you help me?'
   2 He asked if I could help him.
c) 1 'I can't travel with you.'
   2 I said I couldn't travel with you.
d) 1 'Is the game here tomorrow?'
   2 They asked whether the game was here tomorrow.
e) 1 'There's nobody here. Why's that?'
   2 She asked why there wasn't anybody there.

## What mistakes do students often make?

**5** Explain the mistakes in these sentences. What problems do your students often have?

1 You said me it was her birthday!
2 We asked what did it cost.
3 I told them to not bring presents.
4 They asked was there a meeting.

## WORKSHEET 6

# Key

We are concerned here, as in the Students' Book, with the use of past tense reporting verbs to report direct speech containing present tense verbs.

**1** Say:   c)/e)  *He said (to me)(that) she was in the States.*

    Tell:    a)  *She told us to leave.*
              b)  *She told us (that) she wanted to leave.*
              d)/f)  *She told us if/when she wanted to leave.*

    Ask:    a)  *They asked him to sit down.*
             d)/f)  *They asked (him) if/where he wanted to go.*

**2** When speech is reported using a past tense reporting verb, the following changes are common in the reported clause:
  a) Present tense verbs become past tense forms [*don't want* → *didn't want*]. Pronouns change [*I* → *he*] with a change of perspective.
  b) The structure of a request usually changes [*Can...help?* → *asked someone to* + infinitive], although you could also report the request as: *She asked (me) if I could help her.*
  c) The word order of a reported question is the word order of a statement [*Why* + verb + subject → *why* + subject + verb]. Adverbs and adverbial phrases of place change [*here* → *there*].
  d) *If* introduces a reported question when there is no question word.
  e) The stucture of a command changes [*(Don't) leave!* → *told someone (not) to* + infinitive]. Adverbs/adverbial phrases of time change [*tomorrow* → *the next day*].
  f) Certain verbs may change [e.g. *come* (if the original speaker was at home) → *went* (if the reporter is speaking from another place)].

**3** SAME STRUCTURE
say/state (to someone) that...
answer/reply that...
stress/emphasise (to someone) that...
think/believe that...
tell/inform someone that...
tell/order someone to...

DIFFERENT STRUCTURE
ask someone to.../request that...

DIFFERENT STRUCTURE WITH INDIRECT OBJECT
promise (someone that).../swear (to someone) that...
ask (someone if).../inquire (of someone) if...

**4** a) There is no tense change in the reported clause if the speaker wants to emphasise that what was said is still true at the time of reporting.
  b) *Could, might, would, ought to* and *had better* do not usually change. Other modals change to their past tense form (e.g. *will* → *would*).
  c) The subject pronoun does not change if the speaker reports his/her own speech. Object pronouns may not change, depending on the viewpoint.
  d) Adverbials of time and place do not change if they have the same meaning to the audiences of the original speaker and to the audiences of the reporter. In this case, the reporter is speaking in the same place and on the same day as the original speaker. You can use *whether* or *whether or not* to report a question when there are other possibilities.
  e) It is common to paraphrase when reporting speech because the exact words are less important than the meaning of the whole, and because longer speeches sound clumsy if they are reported word for word: e.g. *She said there was nobody there and she asked why that was.* sounds over-long and awkward.

**5** 1  *Said* cannot be followed by an object without *to*. In this case, the pronoun *me* is best deleted: *You said it was her birthday!*
    2  A reported question does not retain the interrogative verb form or word order. The correct report is: *We asked what it cost.*
    3  In a reported command, *not* normally precedes *to* + infinitive: *I told them not to bring presents.*
    4  Reported questions start with *if* when there is no other question word. Interrogative word order is not used in the reported clause: *They asked if there was a meeting.*

© LONGMAN GROUP UK Ltd. 1994

# Workbook Answer Key and Tapescript

## Unit one

### LANGUAGE FOCUS

**1**  1  Does Emma live alone?
   No, she doesn't. She lives with her parents.
   2  Does she work in a shop?
   No, she doesn't. She's a student.
   3  What does she like doing on weekdays?
   She likes swimming and walking.
   4  How does she usually spend Saturdays?
   She usually meets her friends.
   5  Does she get up early on Sundays?
   No, she doesn't. She sleeps until twelve.

**2**  1  's speaking   2  's seeing   3  is she going out
   4  are having   5  isn't doing   6  inviting

**3**  1  X What does this word mean?
   3  X I don't understand you.
   5  X He is wearing jeans today.
   6  X Do you know the time, please?

**4**  1  dangerous   2  exciting   3  relaxing
   4  frightening   5  expensive

**5**  1  works   2  love   3  don't notice   4  spend
   5  has   6  wants   7  am enjoying
   8  don't want

**6**  I *occasionally* go to clubs, but I listen to music at home *almost every evening*.

   I play in a band *three times a week*. And I *often* listen to local bands.

   How *often* do you hear a really good band?

   I probably hear a good one *once or twice a year*.

### SKILLS FOCUS

**1**  MIKE: Hello. International Friends Club. Can I help you?
   SUZANNE: Oh, hello. I saw your advertisement in the paper today and I thought I'd phone to find out a bit more.
   M: Yes, certainly, well we're a sort of social and cultural activity club for people from different countries. It's quite a new club – we have approximately fifty members at the moment, but we're growing all the time.
   S: Right. That sounds interesting. I'm Canadian actually, and I came to London about three months ago, so I'm looking for ways to meet some new people. Er, what kinds of activities do you organise?
   M: Well, we have a range – cultural, sports, social and language activities.
   S: Could you tell me something about the language activities?
   M: Yes, every day except Thursday we have a language evening, where people can come and practise their languages – you know, over a drink or a bite to eat. We have different languages on different evenings. Monday – Spanish; Tuesday – Italian; Wednesday – German; and Friday – French. On Thursday we usually arrange a meal in a restaurant for anyone who wants to come.
   S: Well, that sounds great. I really need to practise my French and German.
   M: OK. Well, if you can just give me your name and address, I'll send you the form and some more details. If you join now you can have the first month free.
   S: Oh yeah. How much is it to join?
   M: £25 a month, 6 months for £140, or a year for £265.
   S: Ah, I think I'd better join just for a month at first to try it. Can I pay by cheque?
   M: Yes, of course. Just make it out to the International Friends Club. Or you can pay by credit card.
   S: No, I haven't got a credit card.
   M: OK. Now your name is …?
   S: Suzanne Beauchamp
   M: Can you spell that?
   S: Yeah – Suzanne is S U Z A N N E and Beauchamp is B E A U C H A M P.
   M: And your address?
   S: 53 Jermyn Road. That's J E R M Y N – Bristol.
   M: And your phone number?
   S: Er, 548 9770
   M: 548 9770. Fine. And could I just ask you your age and occupation for our records?
   S: Sure. I'm nineteen and I'm a student.
   M: Right. I'll put the form in the post today.
   S: Thanks very much. Goodbye.
   M: Goodbye.

**1**  (Approximately) 50   2  Italian   3  French   4  £140
   5  £265

**2**  Name: Suzanne Beauchamp
   Address: 53 Jermyn Road, Bristol.
   Telephone: 548 9770

Age: 19   Occupation: Student
Nationality: Canadian

Which languages are you interested in?
French, German
Membership for: 1 month
Payment: Cheque

## HELP YOURSELF

**1**  1 A  2 J  3 B  4 I  5 G  6 C  7 D  8 H  9 F
10 E

**2**  1 Shall I clean the board?
2 What's for homework?
3 Can I help you?
4 Which page are we on?
5 What does 'trolley' mean?
6 I'm sorry I'm late.
7 Can I leave the room, please?
8 Excuse me. I can't hear the cassette.
9 How do you spell 'actually'?
10 How do you say 'Blumenkohl' in English?

# Unit two

## LANGUAGE FOCUS

**1**  1 spent  2 chose  3 taught  4 didn't hear
5 woke up  6 ran  7 caught  8 arrived
9 left  10 landed  11 didn't matter  12 needed

**2**  1 Which exam did you take yesterday?
2 How old was Jack when he learnt to drive?
3 Where did Emma stay in Greece?
4 Why did you go to Spain?

**3**  1 easy  2 excited  3 great  4 awful

**4**  1 could swim/couldn't swim
2 could play the piano  3 couldn't speak Russian
4 could drive  5 could use

**5**  1 'm going to go fishing  2 's going to hire
3 's going to learn  4 's going to sleep
5 're going to have

**6**  DENIS: That sounds good! What are you playing?
ROB: Oh, just something my brother taught me.
DENIS: Great. I didn't know you could play the guitar so well.
ROB: I learnt when I was a child. How well can you play?
DENIS: Not very well. But I enjoy listening.

## SKILLS FOCUS

**1**  1 – 3  2 – 3  3 – 1  4 – 1  5 – 2+3  6 – 2
7 – 1+2  8 – 3  9 – 1  10 – 3

**2** Before I started, I received a pack of books and cassettes and the address of my personal teacher.

During the course, I sent work to my teacher and she corrected it and talked to me about it on the telephone.

Once a month I went to a seminar where I met other students.

After six months I could speak Italian fluently!

## SOUND CHECK

### The sounds /b/ and /p/

**1**  /b/ /b/ /b/  bag  bus  beard  bicycle

**2**  a) a big book  b) a baby boy  c) the best bank

**3**  /p/ /p/ /p/  pound  penny  party  pepper

**4**  a) a Polish passport  b) a packet of postcards
c) Pass the potatoes!

**5**  a) pea  b) pack  c) birth  d) boring

a) be – pea  b) back – pack  c) birth – Perth
d) boring – pouring

### The sounds /f/, /v/ and /w/

**1**  /f/ /f/ /f/  fee  fax  foot  family

**2**  a) fine food  b) a funny film  c) Find the file!

**3**  /v/ /v/ /v/  verb  very  violin  volleyball

**4**  a) a violent video  b) vegetable vocabulary
c) Visit my village!

**5**  /w/ /w/ /w/  way  wet  want  wash

**6**  a) warm and windy  b) the working week
c) Wait by the wall!

**7**  a) fight  b) view  c) wet  d) well  e) ferry
f) vent

a) fight – white  b) few – view  c) vet – wet
d) fell – well  e) ferry – very  f) vent – went

### The sounds /l/ and /r/

**1**  /l/ /l/ /l/  lamp  lost  left  lesson

**2**  a) a lovely lunch  b) a long list
c) I love learning languages.

**3**  /r/ /r/ /r/  rope  rent  radio  routine

**4**  a) a rock record  b) a room near reception
c) She's running and riding.

**5**  a) read  b) lock  c) lent  d) present

a) lead – read  b) lock – rock  c) lent – rent
d) pleasant – present

# Unit three

## LANGUAGE FOCUS

**1**
| -ier | -er | more ..... |
|---|---|---|
| prettier | cheaper | more dramatic |
| funnier | older | more difficult |
| dirtier | faster | more comfortable |
| sunnier | safer | more relaxing |
| noisier | | |
| easier | | |

**2** 1 healthier  2 cheaper  3 noisier
4 more difficult  5 more exciting  6 better

**3** 1 Yes, but I prefer travelling by plane. It's faster.
2 Yes, but I prefer playing basketball. It's more exciting.
3 Yes, but I prefer watching videos. It's cheaper.
4 Yes, but I prefer listening to classical music. It's more relaxing.
5 Yes, but I prefer swimming in the river. It's warmer.
6 Yes, but I prefer walking on the beach. It's safer.
7 Yes, but I prefer running. It's more energetic.
8 Yes, but I prefer staying with friends. It's more enjoyable.

**4** 1 I won't talk to her now. I'll see her this afternoon.
2 I won't sign them today. I'll sign them tomorrow.
3 I won't finish it today. I'll finish it tomorrow.
4 I won't check them this morning. I'll check them this afternoon.
5 I won't have lunch now. I'll have it later.

**5** **Across**
1 change  4 park  6 leave  7 hotel  8 hot
9 bus  10 cheques  11 tour  12 miss
**Down**
1 call  2 give  3 travellers'  4 pilot  5 takes
7 home  9 boat  10 car

**6** 1 b  2 a  3 b  4 a  5 b  6 c  7 c

## SKILLS FOCUS

**1** Attention all passengers. Platform change – this is a platform change. The train now standing at Platform 9 is the 10.48 train calling at all stations to Cardiff. Please note. The train on Platform 9 is not the 10.52 to Bristol. It's the 10.48 calling at all stations to Cardiff. The 10.52 to Bristol will now leave from Platform 7.

Train announcement. The 11.20 to Bath from Platform 8 will be subject to a fifteen minute delay. I repeat, there will be a fifteen minute delay to the Bath train on Platform 8. It will now leave at 11.35, not 11.20.

The 11.28 train to Swansea has been cancelled. We apologise to customers but due to signal problems the 11.28 to Swansea from Platform 15 has been cancelled.

The 11.32 to Cheltenham is now standing at Platform 13. Please note, there will be no restaurant car on this train. I repeat there will be no restaurant car on the 11.32 to Cheltenham now standing at Platform 13.

## SKILLS FOCUS

**1**
| TIME | DESTINATION | PLATFORM | COMMENTS |
|---|---|---|---|
| 10.52 | Bristol | 7 | Platform change |
| 10.48 | Cardiff | 9 | Platform change |
| 11.20 | Bath | 8 | 15 minutes delay |
| 11.28 | Swansea | 15 | Cancelled |
| 11.32 | Cheltenham | 13 | No restaurant car |

**2** Possible answer:
Dear Mr Leyton,
   I am writing to complain about my journey from Leeds to Manchester last week.
   First of all, the train was 20 minutes late. Then there were no seats, so I had to stand for the whole journey.
   In addition, there was no restaurant car, only a snack bar.
   In the end, I arrived in Manchester late for my meeting.
   So I would like a refund of the train fare.
      Yours sincerely,

## HELP YOURSELF

**2** 3 ? (question mark)  4 ' ' (inverted commas)
5 ' (apostrophe)  6 . (full stop) ! (exclamation mark)  7 : (colon)  8 ; (semi-colon)  9 , (comma)
a) names   b) possessives

**3** 1 Is there any milk?
2 I need these things: some stamps, some envelopes and some writing paper.
3 'What a beautiful dress!' he said.
4 It's John's car. I saw him in it yesterday.
5 They're not just rich; they're really rich.

# Unit four

## LANGUAGE FOCUS

**1** 1 too narrow   wide enough
2 too small   large enough
3 too fat   thin enough
4 too cold   warm/hot enough

**2**
| shorter | (the) shortest |
|---|---|
| funnier | (the) funniest |
| more frightening | (the) most frightening |
| more expensive | (the) most expensive |
| longer | (the) longest |

3  2  most expensive
   3  most frightening   funniest
   4  shorter   longest

4  1  1 jackets   2 low
   2  3 skirts   4 loose   5 high
   3  6 trousers   7 shirts

5  1  beautiful big white   2 ugly brown
   3  wonderful red silk   4 interesting black and white

6  1  What size are you?
   2  What colour would you like?
   3  Can I try it on?   4 Is it OK?
   5  Shall I get you a smaller size?   6 How much is it?

## SKILLS FOCUS
1  1 F  2 F  3 F  4 T  5 F  6 T  7 F  8 F

## SOUND/SPELLING LINKS

### The sounds /aʊ/ and /aʊə/
1  /aʊ/  /aʊ/  /aʊ/   out   count   about

2  a) We had a flat in a large h<u>ou</u>se.
   b) The flat was on the gr<u>ou</u>nd floor.
   c) We f<u>ou</u>nd it very noisy.

3  a) H<u>ow</u> are you, John?   b) Do you like this t<u>ow</u>n?
   c) It is very cr<u>ow</u>ded on Saturdays.

4  /aʊə/  /aʊə/  /aʊə/   tower   power   our   sour

5  a) That fl<u>ower</u> is a rose.   b) I'll be there in an h<u>our</u>.
   c) We need some fl<u>our</u> and some eggs.

6  a) The computer costs a thousand pounds without tax.
   b) I'm going down to buy it now.
   c) It's a two hour trip.   d) I'll have a shower first.

### The sounds /əʊ/ and /əʊə/
1  /əʊ/  /əʊ/  /əʊ/   low   slow   shallow

2  a) Sh<u>ow</u> me a polite teenager!
   b) I kn<u>ow</u> what you mean.
   c) And Jim's my <u>ow</u>n child.

3  /əʊə/  /əʊə/  /əʊə/   lower   shallower   mower

4  a) We're going bowling tomorrow.
   b) The train is slower because there's a lot of snow on the line.
   c) The temperature is below zero.

# Unit five

## LANGUAGE FOCUS
1  1 can't cook   2 can have   3 can't stay
   4 can't play   5 can't hang   6 can make
   7 can't make

2  1 Can I have   2 can have   3 can I work
   4 No, you can't.   5 Can they park
   6 No, they can't.   7 can park

3  1 Does Jim have to go home?
   2 Does Melanie have to work today?
   3 Do I have to eat this fish?
   4 Do we have to watch this film?

4  1 don't have to   2 don't have to   3 have to
   4 don't have to   5 have to

5  1 had to drive   2 Did Sue have to take
   3 didn't have to get up   4 had to stop/give up
   5 Did you have to have   6 had to invite

6  A: Can I help you?
   C: Yes. Can you look at my earrings?
   A: What's wrong with them?
   C: They're broken.
   A: OK. Leave them here and I'll see if someone can repair them.

## SKILLS FOCUS
1  REPORTER: Two young coastguards escaped unhurt yesterday after driving their Land Rover backwards over a cliff edge and falling on to rocks thirty metres below. Mr Steve Garrison, who is twenty-one, and Mr Julian Richards, who is twenty-three, walked away from their crushed Land Rover at two a.m. on Sunday morning and were rescued by a Marine helicopter whose pilots saw the car lights pointing to the sky. The two men, back at their homes yesterday, said they had driven to the cliff top because they thought they had seen a boat in distress at sea. It was, however, a false alarm and Mr Richards was trying to turn the Land Rover around when the accident happened.
   JULIAN: I felt one wheel slip and then the car started to roll back. I knew nothing more until I was in the sea and swimming. The Land Rover fell to the edge of the sea, but I was thrown out through one of the doors. I swam back a few metres and found Steve standing on the rocks. I couldn't believe we were both still alive!
   R: Mr Garrison said he couldn't remember anything about what had happened, and the helicopter pilot who rescued them said they had been incredibly lucky to survive. The two men plan to go back to their coastguarding jobs this weekend.
   And now the weather…

1  1 b   2 b   3 a

2  a) 5   b) 3   c) 1   d) 4   e) 6   f) 2

## HELP YOURSELF
1  A sympathetic   B uninterested   C happy

D unhappy   E angry   F interested

**2** 1 A: It's next week.    4 A: It's next week.
     B: Oh, is it?            B: Oh, is it?
   2 A: It's next week.    5 A: It's next week.
     B: Oh, is it?            B: Oh, is it?
   3 A: It's next week.    6 A: It's next week.
     B: Oh, is it?            B: Oh, is it?

   1 A   2 C   3 B   4 E   5 D   6 F

**3** 1 A: Well, my sister's a police officer.
     B: Really?
   2 A: Have you got time to go to the shops for me?
     B: No.
   3 A: Do you think Della is going to be at the party?
     B: Maybe.
   4 A: Would you like to go for a coffee?
     B: Yes.
   5 A: I'm moving offices today.
     B: Oh.

   1 d   2 e   3 a   4 b   5 c

**4** 1 ⌣   2 ⌢   3 ⌣   4 ⌢   5 ⌢

**5** 1 A: Shall we go out tonight?
     B: Mm.
   2 A: I'm studying in the library this morning.
     B: Mm.
   3 A: We can watch some videos after school.
     B: Mm!
   4 A: Do you want a game of tennis?
     B: Mm-mm.
   5 A: Guns and Roses are giving a concert.
     B: Mm?

   1 a   2 c   3 b   4 e   5 d

# Unit six

## LANGUAGE FOCUS

**1** 1 Don't stay in a hotel. Stay with Suzanne
   2 Don't write to her. Phone her
   3 Don't go by car. Go by plane
   4 Don't buy any skis. Borrow some
   5 Don't go for a week. Go for two weeks

**2** Phone call
   3 Dial the number.   4 Speak.
   Instant coffee
   2 Put the coffee in the cup.
   3 Pour the water into the cup.   4 Stir.
   Photograph
   2 Take the lens cap off.
   3 Look through the viewfinder.   4 Press the button.
   Travellers' cheques
   2 Sign the cheques.   3 Give them to the cashier.
   4 Take the money.

**3** 1 is for keeping tea and coffee
   2 is for boiling water   3 is for storing books
   4 is for heating soups and snacks
   5 are for putting bags

**4** 1 turn the light on
   2 turn the heating off/down
   3 turn the tap off
   4 turn the radio up
   5 turn the light off

**5** 1 d   2 a   3 g   4 b   5 c   6 e   7 f

**6** 1 Take out / put in / press   2 Get on / hold
   3 Put in / press   4 Get in / press

**7** 1 What's this machine for?   2 Can I try it?
   3 How do I turn it on?   4 Then what do I do?
   5 How much is it?   6 I'll have one, please.

## SKILLS FOCUS

**1** 1 3 + 12   2 2   3 3 6
   4 9 + 071 or 081 + telephone number
   5 9 + 010 + 33 + Paris code + tel. no.
   6 9 + 010 + 39 + city code + tel. no.

**2** Possible answer:
   Please could you come and turn down the central heating in my room – it's too hot and I can't sleep at night. I tried to turn the knob but it was very stiff and I couldn't move it.
   Thank you.

## SOUND CHECK

### The sounds /d/ and /t/

**1** /d/ /d/ /d/   deep   date   disco   dollar

**2** a) double doors   b) a difficult dance
   c) Decide on a dish!

**3** /t/ /t/ /t/   tall   tent   toast   tomato

**4** a) ten tickets   b) Turkish tourists   c) It's time for tea.

**5** a) do   b) town   c) dime   d) dune

   a) do – too   b) down – town   c) dime – time
   d) dune – tune

### The sounds /ð/, /θ/, /d/ and /t/

**1** /ð/ /ð/ /ð/   these   that   there
   /θ/ /θ/ /θ/   think   thanks   thirty

   /d/ /d/ /d/   dark   die   document
   /t/ /t/ /t/   tights   till   television

**2** a) that theatre on Tuesday
   b) Those things on the desks are telephones.
   c) They're on the third table, by the door.

**3** a) dare   b) toe   c) tin   d) then

   a) dare – tear – there   b) dough – toe – though

c) din – tin – thin   d) den – ten – then

### The sounds /s/ and /z/

1  /s/  /s/  /s/   sad   sell   sorry   system

2  a) sand and sea   b) the second song
   c) Some soap, sir?

3  /z/  /z/  /z/
   zero   zebra   zone   New Zealand

4  a) Brazilian jazz   b) a dozen freezers
   c) Those are crazy sizes!

5  a) Sue   b) zip   c) fuzzy

   a) Sue – zoo   b) sip – zip   c) fussy – fuzzy

# Unit seven

## LANGUAGE FOCUS

1  1  How much are the tickets?
   2  How often do the buses leave?
   3  How long does the journey take?
   4  How far is it from the hotel to the beach?

2  1  well / bad   2  interesting / dramatically
   3  quickly   4  polite   5  careful / dangerously
   6  awful

3  1  punctually   2  quietly   3  slowly   4  clearly
   5  carefully   6  hard   7  well

4  1  Not very often   2  A lot   3  Not long
   4  A long way   5  Not much   6  A long time
   7  Quite often

5  1 c   2 a   3 g   4 f   5 h   6 d   7 i   8 b   9 j   10 e

## SKILLS FOCUS

1  TOM: Hello?
   JAN: Hi, Tom. It's Jan here. Do you want to go and see an exhibition on modern American painting this afternoon?
   T: Er…yes, OK. Where is it on?
   J: At a place called the Smithson Gallery.
   T: Smithson Gallery? Never heard of it.
   J: Well, it's near Oldbury Station.
   T: Oh, OK. I know the station.
   J: Well, what you do is, you come out of the station, and turn left into Friar Street.
   T: Hang on. I'll write it down… left into Friar Street.
   J: Then you go over a roundabout.
   T: Over a roundabout.
   J: And into Broad Street.
   T: Broad Street. Yes?
   J: You go along to the end of Broad Street and cross over Green Road. It's quite a big road.
   T: So, over Green Road.
   J: Yes, and into Stuart Road. Then turn right into Russell Street and then…
   T: Hang on, Stuart Road, then right into Russell Street.
   J: Mm. And the art gallery is on your left. It's opposite a school.
   T: OK. What's that, about a five-minute walk?
   J: Yes, about that.
   T: When shall we meet then?
   J: Oh, um, let's say three o'clock, outside the gallery.
   T: Fine. See you there. Bye.
   J: Bye.

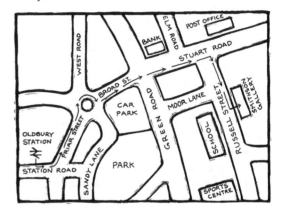

2  Possible answer:
   Dear Nick,
   I know how much you like modern art, so would you like to come to the exhibition of modern American paintings at the Smithson Gallery, on Saturday, at 2 o'clock.
   Let me tell you how to get there. When you arrive at Oldbury Station, come out of the station and turn left. Take the first left into Friar Street, go straight on, over the roundabout, into Stuart Road. Take the first right, into Russell Street, and the Smithson Gallery is on the left.
   Let me know if you can come.
        Love from,

## HELP YOURSELF

### Talking about grammar

1  | Part of speech | Examples |
   |---|---|
   | noun | cassettes   shop   sound |
   | pronoun | we |
   | adjective | new   terrible |
   | article | the |
   | verb | returned   was |
   | adverb | immediately |
   | preposition | to |
   | conjunction | because |

**2** a) 3  b) 1  c) 2

**3** a) 3  b) 1  c) 2  d) 2  e) 3  f) 1

**4** a) can  b) press  c) show  d) turn on

**5**
| | | |
|---|---|---|
| sandwich C | them O | most expensive SA |
| food U | she S | tallest SA |
| apple C | we S | cheaper CA |
| fruit U | me O | more interesting CA |

# Unit eight

## LANGUAGE FOCUS

**1**
1. How much coffee would you like?
2. How many eggs would you like?
3. How much milk would you like?
4. How much mineral water would you like?
5. How much chocolate would you like?
6. How many potatoes would you like?

**2**
1. Can you tell me how much the steak is?
2. Do you know how they serve the fish?
3. Can you tell me if I can pay by credit card?
4. Can you tell me who the manager is?
5. Can you tell me what time the restaurant closes?
6. Can you tell me if there is a no-smoking section?

**3**
1. were a lot  2. wasn't much
3. was a lot  4. Were there many
5. weren't many

**4**
1. cream / butter  2. chocolate
3. peppers / carrots  4. beef / chicken
5. bread / cakes

**5**
1. vegetarian  2. delicious  3. fattening  4. raw
5. frozen  6. unhealthy

**6**
1. A: I'm very keen on Thai food.
   B: Really? I don't like it. But I think Greek food is great.
   A: Yes, I agree. We often go to Greek restaurants.
2. A: I really like the new Kevin Costner film.
   B: Really? I'm not keen on Kevin Costner. But I think the Demi Moore film is excellent.
   A: Yes, that's true. I really enjoyed it.

## SKILLS FOCUS

**1**
1. Morbier  2. Braeburn  3. Skipjack tuna
4. Smoked Scottish salmon  5. Stilton  6. Bramley

**2** Possible answer:
Dear Masterchef,
   Please could you answer my questions on your Cookery Problem Page. Firstly, can you tell me where I can buy traditional German sausages? Secondly, can you tell me what 'guacamole' is? Thirdly, can you tell me how long I should cook bread for?
   Yours sincerely,

## SOUND/SPELLING LINKS

### The sound /eɪ/

**1** /eɪ/ /eɪ/ /eɪ/  take  age  way

**2** a) I'd like this tape, please.
   b) We made some money.
   c) She's a brave woman.

**3** a) He's staying in Japan.
   b) When are you going away?
   c) Did you say something?

**4** a) I ate a lot of cake yesterday.
   b) Shall we play tennis on Thursday or Friday?
   c) What's the name of the place that we came through this morning?

### The sounds /aɪ/ and /aɪə/

**1** /aɪ/ /aɪ/ /aɪ/  five  rise  sight

**2** a) Let's drive to the party.  b) Is that coat mine?
   c) We've been there once or twice.

**3** a) We walked through high mountains.
   b) Is that shirt too tight?  c) The concert's tonight.

**4** /aɪə/ /aɪə/ /aɪə/  wire  fire  admire

**5** a) They had a nice time but now they're tired.
   b) It's the right size, but I don't like the price!
   c) He hired a small plane for a night flight.

# Unit nine

## LANGUAGE FOCUS

**1**
1. you should get more exercise
   you shouldn't eat so much
2. you should study hard today
   you shouldn't stay up late tonight
3. you should move to the country
   you shouldn't stay in the city centre
4. you should join a club
   you shouldn't stay at home every evening

**2**
1. isn't she  2. aren't they  3. hasn't she
4. does she  5. aren't you  6. can you
7. do they  8. is he

**3** Pets
goldfish  dog  cat  hamster  rabbit  guinea pig
budgie

**Farm animals**
duck  lamb  sheep  cow  pig  goat  horse
hen

146

**4**
1. They're washing the dog.
2. He's walking the dog.
3. She's stroking the rabbit
4. She's sweeping out the bird cage.
5. She's playing with the cat.
6. He's riding a horse.

**5**
1 women  2 children  3 mice  4 geese
5 sheep  6 fish  7 shelves  8 knives  9 teeth
10 feet

**6** 2d  3a  4f  5h  6c  7b  8e

1c  2g  3b  4f  5e  6a  7h  8d

## SKILLS FOCUS

**1** PRESENTER: And now, continuing our series on Pet Care, our animal expert, Tim Jackson, is once again in the studio. Today he is going to talk to us about rabbits. Tim…

TJ: Thank you. Yes well, rabbits, like the other pets we've talked about in this series, need more time and care than you think. It's very important that you look after them well if you decide to have one.

Firstly, rabbits don't like the sun, so you should keep them in the shade when it's hot and sunny. But they don't like the cold either, so you should keep them inside when it's cold.

A rabbit needs a big hutch with room for both living and sleeping, and this should be kept clean and tidy – you must change the straw once a week. He should have fresh food and water every day – a mixture of rabbit food, fruit and vegetables is best.

He should have lots of exercise too – you can make a run for him where he can play safely outside. Er, finally, brush his hair often, oh, and you should never pick him up by his ears.

P: Thank you, Tim.

**1**
2. You should keep it inside.
3. You should clean it once a week.
4. You should feed the rabbit every day.
5. You should brush the rabbit's hair often.
6. You should never pick him up by his ears.

**2** Possible answer:
Cleaning the hutch: Please change the straw once a week.
Food: Feed him a mixture of rabbit food, fruit and vegetables every day.
Water: Give him fresh water every day.
Exercise: Put him in his run for 10 minutes every day.
Cleaning Fluffy: Please brush his hair often. By the way, if you want to pick him up, don't pick him up by the ears!

## HELP YOURSELF

**1**  1 K  2 C  3 I  4 F
*Some stuff* refers to something uncountable.
*A thing* refers to something countable.
1. I'd like a thing for putting in the baby's mouth.
2. I'd like a hat to wear in the shower.

**2**  1 E  2 G  3 B  4 H
similar to = like    a type of = a kind of
a) It's a kind of seat for putting the baby in at meal times.
b) It's like a carriage on wheels for putting the baby in.

# Unit ten

## LANGUAGE FOCUS

**1**  1 everywhere  2 everything  3 Everyone
4 someone  5 no one  6 anyone
7 somewhere  8 anywhere  9 nothing

**2**  1 How long  2 How heavy  3 How deep
4 How high

**3**
1 your bag  mine  yours  mine
2 theirs  hers  his
3 your  ours

**4**
1. The brown, leather one with a zip
2. The blue, cotton one with a belt
3. The black, leather one with a hood
4. The cotton one with green and white spots
5. The yellow, silk one with buttons

**5**  Quality: lovely, beautiful, ugly, comfortable
Cost: cheap, expensive
Size: big, small
Age: old, modern, antique, new
Shape: square, rectangular, round, triangular
Colour: red, brown, yellow, black
Material: metal, cotton, plastic

**6**
1. Where did you lose it? What colour is it? What's it made of? How big is it?
2. Where did you lose it? How big is it? Is it heavy? What shape is it?

## SKILLS FOCUS

**1**  1T  2F  3T  4F  5T  6F  7F

**2**  A: Hello. Can I help you?
B: Yes. I posted a parcel two weeks ago and it hasn't arrived yet.
A: OK. What size is the parcel?
B: Er, it's about 30 cms long, and, er, 20 cms wide and about 20 cms high.
A: Uh huh. And when was it posted?
B: On Monday the 12th of June. In Sheffield.

A: Uh huh. And what's the name and address of the sender?
B: Who – Oh me? I'm Paul Castle, that's C-A-S-T-L-E. I live at 77 Sydney Road, that's S-Y-D-N-E-Y Road, um, Sheffield, S8.
A: OK. And who was it addressed to?
B: My mother, Mrs J Castle. She lives at 128, Devon Street, that's D-E-V-O-N Street, Sheffield S3.
A: Good. Now, um, what exactly was in the parcel?
B: Well, it was her birthday last week, and I, um, made her a cake, um, a chocolate one.
A: I see. A chocolate birthday cake. OK, I'll see if we've got it here…

**2** 1 Size of parcel
Length: 30 cm
Width: 20 cm
Height: 20 cm
2 Date posted: Monday 12th June
3 Place posted: Sheffield
4 Name of sender: Paul Castle
5 Address of sender: 77 Sydney Road, Sheffield S8
6 Name of addressee: Mrs J. Castle
7 Address of addressee: 128 Devon Street, Sheffield S3
8 Contents: A chocolate birthday cake

## SOUND CHECK

**The sounds /s/ and /ʃ/**

**1** /s/ /s/ /s/

**2** /ʃ/ /ʃ/ /ʃ/ shape shallow shower

**3** a) a short shirt   b) Shake the shampoo.
c) Should she or shouldn't she?

**4** a) she   b) shoot   c) sip   d) self

a) see – she   b) suit – shoot   c) sip – ship
d) self – shelf

**The sounds /ʃ/ and /tʃ/**

**1** /ʃ/ /ʃ/ /ʃ/

**2** /tʃ/ /tʃ/ /tʃ/ chair child chat

**3** a) Chinese chocolate   b) Change the cheese!
c) Check the children!

**4** a) shoes   b) chop   c) ships   d) cheap

a) shoes – choose   b) shop – chop   c) ships – chips
d) sheep – cheap

**The sounds /tʃ/ and /dʒ/**

**1** /tʃ/ /tʃ/ /tʃ/

**2** /dʒ/ /dʒ/ /dʒ/ jam jeans jacket

**3** a) just a job   b) Japanese journalists
c) Join the jazz club!

**4** a) jeep   b) junk   c) joke   d) chive

a) cheap – jeep   b) chunk – junk   c) choke – joke
d) chive – jive

**The sounds /dʒ/ and /j/**

**1** /dʒ/ /dʒ/ /dʒ/

**2** /j/ /j/ /j/ you yard year

**3** a) your yoghurt   b) I felt young yesterday.
c) Yes, it's yellow.

**4** a) jaw   b) yob   c) yoke   d) jet

a) jaw – your   b) job – yob   c) joke – yoke
d) jet – yet

# Unit eleven

## LANGUAGE FOCUS

**1** 1 Have you made an appointment?
2 Have you said goodbye to Martin?
3 Have you told her about it?
4 Have you listened to it yourself?
5 Have you booked a table?

**2** 1 I've just watered them.   2 I've just listened to it.
3 I've just rung her.   4 I've just found them.
5 I've just packed them.

**3** 1 have you been   2 I've been   3 I've just won
4 I haven't played   5 Have you met
6 haven't introduced   7 have you had
8 we've brought

**4** 1 heart   2 fingers   3 feet   4 arms   5 eyes

**5** 1 I've got stomachache.   2 I've got a headache.
3 My eyes hurt.   4 My back hurts.
5 I've got a cough.

**6** Have you looked in the phone book
Why don't you ask at his college
You should phone quickly

## SKILLS FOCUS

**1** Are you ready? This exercise can help to make your legs and back stronger. First, stand with your feet apart and your arms by your sides. Pull in those stomach muscles. Next, take your head, shoulders and hands down to your left foot, as far as you can. Keep those legs straight – go on, push! Count to eight in this position. Now, staying down, move to the right side and count to eight again. Next, go to the middle, between your legs, and count for another eight. Good! Now relax.

**1** A3   B1   C4   D2

**2** 1 feet  2 arms  3 head  4 shoulders
5 foot  6 side  7 eight  8 middle  9 legs

## SOUND CHECK
### The sounds /m/, /n/ and /ŋ/
1 /m/ /m/ /m/  my  main  mean  move

2 a) more money   b) How much meat?   c) Marry me!

3 /n/ /n/ /n/  not  now  need  near

4 a) nine nights   b) She's a new nurse.
c) Don't you notice the noise?

5 /ŋ/ /ŋ/ /ŋ/  young  hang  wrong  along

6 a) a boring evening   b) two long rings
c) We'll sing a song!

7 a) might   b) rang   c) nice   d) thing

a) might – night   b) ran – rang   c) mice – nice
d) thin – thing

### The sounds /k/, /g/ and /h/
1 /k/ /k/ /k/  car  cat  kid  cold

2 a) The coffee's cold.   b) Keep the key!
c) I'll call a cab!

3 /g/ /g/ /g/  give  game  get  got

4 a) the garden gate   b) a good girl
c) I'll go to the garage.

5 /h/ /h/ /h/  him  have  help  hope

6 a) a huge house   b) happy holidays
c) Here's the hotel.

7 a) came   b) gear   c) heart   d) good   e) hole
f) height

a) came – game   b) gear – hear   c) cart – heart
d) could – good   e) goal – hole   f) kite – height

# Unit twelve

## LANGUAGE FOCUS
**1** 3 has been  4 for  5 hasn't played  6 for
7 has known  8 for  9 have been  10 since
11 has been  12 for  13 hasn't played  14 for

**2** 1 Has Tom ever drunk saki
2 Has your sister ever flown on Concorde
3 Have you ever seen a Chinese film
4 Have Andreas and Maria ever tried skiing
5 Have you ever been to Mexico

**3** 1 Have you ever been to
It's the most wonderful performance I've ever seen.
2 Have you ever seen
It's the most exciting match I've ever watched.
3 Have you ever eaten
It's the most delicious food I've ever eaten.

**4** 1 successful  2 brave  3 honest  4 kind
5 clever  6 unusual

**5** 1 an exam  2 a decision  3 your homework
4 a mistake

**6** a 2  b 5  c 4  d 1  e 3

**7** 1 e  2 c  3 b  4 d  5 a

## SKILLS FOCUS
**1** 1 F  2 T  3 F  4 F  5 F  6 T
**2** Possible answer:
Yulia Makhalina was born in 1969 in St Petersburg. As a child she had a serious illness and couldn't walk well. So she started dance classes to exercise her legs. After a time her teachers realised she was very good and after a year she moved to Vaganova Academy, where many famous dancers trained. At the age of sixteen she joined the Kirov Ballet and in 1989 became lead ballerina. Since then, she has travelled all round the world.

## SOUND/SPELLING LINKS
### The sound /eə/
1 /eə/ /eə/ /eə/  affair  care  aware

2 a) What's her hair like?   b) It's long and very fair.
c) Your sister's downstairs.

3 a) Share those sweets with Tina!
b) Do your parents live here?
c) I'm scared of the dark.

4 a) Be careful of the stairs!   b) Is that a spare chair?
c) I bought a pair of shoes in the market square.

### The sound /ɪə/
1 /ɪə/ /ɪə/ /ɪə/  dear  near  appear

2 a) Did you hear the question?   b) Is it quite clear?
c) In which year were you born?

### The sound /ɔɪ/
1 /ɔɪ/ /ɔɪ/ /ɔɪ/  noise  toy  annoyed

2 a) Don't point at people!   b) Can I join your group?
c) Is there a choice of desserts?

3 a) The boys are very noisy after school.
b) You don't employ a cook to boil eggs.
c) I enjoy hearing her lovely singing voice.

# Unit thirteen

## LANGUAGE FOCUS

**1**  1 woke up  2 didn't have  3 didn't stay
4 didn't drink  5 exercised  6 was  7 had
8 read  9 lived  10 loved  11 didn't like
12 needed

**2**  1 stop  2 eat  3 makes  4 need  5 aren't
6 wear  7 take  8 am  9 am

**3**  1 I asked him what he usually had for breakfast
2 I asked him why he lived in New York
3 I asked him what time he stopped work in the evenings
4 I asked him if he travelled a lot with his job
5 I asked him if he was friendly with any famous people

**4**  1 storm  2 rent  3 proof  4 duty
5 counsellor  6 flood  7 break-in  8 health
9 arrest

**5**  1 e  2 c  3 a  4 b  5 d

## SKILLS FOCUS

**1**  COUNSELLOR: Hello. Come in and sit down.
ANNE: Thank you.
C: Er, can I just check – you're Anne Miles and you're a first year student, is that right?
A: Yes, that's right.
C: And which course are you doing?
A: Well, I'm doing Business Studies with German and Italian.
C: Uh huh. How's it all going?
A: Well, that's why I'm here really. It's not going too well. I mean, I'm not really enjoying the course and, well, I'm not very happy.
C: All right, let's take things slowly. Tell me something about the course.
A: Well, there's just so much work! I thought that to do two languages with Business Studies would be very useful, but I find the Business Course very difficult sometimes, and then to study German and Italian too – it means I'm working all the time and I never have time to relax.
C: What about your accommodation – are you happy with that?
A: Not really. I mean, the other students on my course are living in a student residence so they see each other all the time. I'm living in a rented room in a family house. I eat breakfast and dinner with the family but I get lonely in the evenings and at weekends.
C: So, making friends is a problem too. Do you ever go out with the other students?
A: Well, no, I mean I'm studying all the time. The other students on my course seem to find the classes easy and they are always going out to discos and films. I don't even have time to play any sport any more.
C: OK, well I'm going to make three suggestions.
A: All right.
C: First, which of the two languages you're studying do you enjoy most?
A: German – I find it easier too.
C: So, I'd like you to go and see your Italian tutor and say that you are going to stop attending Italian classes for the moment.
A: OK.
C: Next, I think you should go to each of the four student residences, choose the one you like best and ask if you can move in there. Students are always moving in and out, so there shouldn't be a problem.
A: All right.
C: And finally, what's your favourite sport?
A: Volleyball.
C: Right. I want you to be brave and join the volleyball club before I see you next week. It's always difficult at first to meet new people, but I'm absolutely sure things will get better. Now, when shall we meet again?

**1 Problem:**
1 Too much work.
2 Lonely in the evenings.
3 Difficult to make friends.

**Suggested action:**
1 Stop attending Italian classes.
2 Move into a student residence.
3 Join the volleyball club.

**2** Possible answer:
First of all I'm going to stop attending Italian classes. Then I'm going to move into a student residence. And lastly I'm going to join the volleyball club.

# Unit fourteen

## LANGUAGE FOCUS

**1**  2 Second, Richard Shaw. He's a 19-year-old writer of science fiction books and he has already won the 1992 prize for Best Young Writer. He hasn't written a best-seller yet, but it is his greatest ambition.
3 Third, Lisa Thompson. She's an 18-year-old actress who has already starred in an American TV movie. She hasn't won an Oscar yet, but it is her greatest ambition.

**2** 1 Have you heard the latest song by U2 yet?
   Where did you hear it?
   2 Have you told Chris about our holiday plans yet?
   What did you tell him?
   3 Have you tried the new Indian restaurant yet?
   When did you try it?

**3** 1 an interview   2 abroad   3 a licence
   4 a reception

**4** 1 Dear Mrs Smith
   Yours sincerely
   2 Dear Mum and Dad
   Love
   3 Dear Sir
   Yours faithfully
   4 Dear Lisa
   All the best

**5** 1 d e h j   2 a f   3 b c g i

**6** 1 d   2 e   3 a   4 b   5 f   6 c

## SKILLS FOCUS

**1** 1 No, it was a role-play wedding.
   2 No, it was a formal wedding.
   3 No, only one boy wanted to be the groom.
   4 No, the teacher chose the bride.
   5 No, they are discussing the effects of divorce.

**2** Possible answer:
Dear Everyone,
   We are writing to thank you for all the presents you gave us. They are lovely presents. We will use the camera for taking photos on our honeymoon. The clock will be useful for getting up in the morning and the recipe book will be great for dinner parties!
   We hope you had fun at the wedding. We certainly enjoyed it!
   See you all soon, and thanks again.
      love,
      Lisa and Gavin

## SOUND CHECK

### The sound /s/ + a consonant
**1** /sp/ /sp/ /sp/   spend   space   spoke   spoon

**2** a) I speak Spanish.   b) Can you spell 'special'.
   c) Sport is a spare time activity.

**3** /st/ /st/ /st/   student   still   stand   stairs

**4** a) Stop at the station!   b) She studies in the States.
   c) I'll start the story.

**5** /sk/ /sl/ /sm/ /sn/   skirt   slow   small   snow

**6** a) There's smoke in the sky.
   b) I have a snack after school.
   c) It was a sleepy smile.

### Consonant + the sounds /r/ and /l/
**1** /br/ /dr/ /gr/   break   drink   grass

**2** a) It's a group of Brazilians.   b) What a great drama!
   c) He's a brave driver.

**3** /kr/ /pr/ /tr/   cross   prefer   train

**4** a) Try your credit card.   b) It was a private trip.
   c) She's probably crying.

**5** /bl/ /gl/ /kl/ /pl/   blonde   glad   clever   plan

**6** a) Look! Black clouds.   b) Let's buy blue glasses.
   c) There are places to play.

### The sounds /mp/ and /mb/
**1** /mp/ /mp/ /mb/ /mb/
   compare   complete   November   December

**2** a) It's a company in Cambridge.
   b) Do you remember the example?
   c) These are important numbers.

### The sounds /pʃ/ and /kʃ/
**1** /pʃ/ /pʃ/ /kʃ/ /kʃ/
   option   caption   instruction   fiction

**2** a) It's an Egyptian dictionary.
   b) There's a section for exceptions.
   c) Ask at reception for directions.

# Unit fifteen

## LANGUAGE FOCUS
**1** 1 We'll have it   2 I won't finish
   3 What will you wear   4 She'll buy   5 he won't

**2** 1 Will they win the match?
   2 He won't pass his driving test.
   3 Will you go to Greece this year?
   4 Mark won't be at the party tonight.

**3** 1 Where will it end?
   2 How long will it take?
   3 How will we travel?
   4 How much will it cost?
   5 How many people will there be?

**4** 1 If you stay away for six months, you'll lose your job.
   2 If you have to sleep in a tent, you won't sleep well.
   3 If you're always on horseback, it'll be very uncomfortable.
   4 If you don't visit any towns, you won't be able to call me.

**5 Across**
1 high   4 sunrise   6 equipment   8 heavy
10 as   12 do   13 win   14 average   17 at
18 choose   19 ear   20 dogs   22 My   23 on

**Down**
2 immediately   3 the   4 soup   5 sunshine
7 put   9 year   11 safe   12 decide   16 foggy
21 go

## Functional Language
**6**  1 I hope not.   2 I don't think so.   3 Probably.
4 I think so.   5 Definitely.

## SKILLS FOCUS
**1** Hello there! Welcome to the week which brings you, as a Taurus, through to 31 July. This is a week which will bring you a lot of happiness, but perhaps also some danger – in other words, my advice to you is to enjoy yourself but take care.

You'll probably have to make an important decision, it might be about work, or an important relationship. You'll spend a lot of time thinking about this decision, asking your friends and family for advice, but my advice to you is this: listen to your heart and not to your head. If you stop worrying so much about everything, you'll know what's the best thing to do.

I mentioned happiness and danger before. Your happiness will come from other people. If you spend some time with the people you love, you will feel relaxed and calm again.

The danger will perhaps be related to travel – it's probably better to stay near home if you can, and not to make any long-distance travel plans. But, all in all, you will have a successful week, both at work and at home – so enjoy it.

**1**  1 happiness, danger   2 enjoy, careful
3 important decision   4 ask, advice
5 heart, head   6 worrying

**2**  1 c   2 f   3 e   4 a   5 h   6 g   7 b   8 d

## HELP YOURSELF
**2 Text A**
1 They are detectives.
2 London's most important police station.
3 Facts about difficult cases.

**Text B**
1 The seventeenth century.
2 To go to sea.
3 Unhappy.

**3** a) a special policeman who finds out who has done a crime.
b) a crime that a policeman tries to solve.
c) clever.
d) to ask very seriously.

# Word review

This Word Review appears in the back of the Workbook. Students can use the lists to revise vocabulary at home or in a self-access centre. The words are recorded on the Workbook Cassette so that students can also practise their pronunciation.

## UNIT 1

| | | | | |
|---|---|---|---|---|
| addict (n) | challenge (n) | entertainment (n) | interest (n) | ski lift (n) |
| admission (n) | collector (n) | excitement (n) | interested (adj.) | skier (n) |
| adventure (n) | cost (v) | fair (n) | jump (v) | skiing (n) |
| barbecue (n) | countryside (n) | great (adj.) | leisure (n) | stall (n) |
| baseball (n) | craft (n) | hang (v) | lover (n) | sweep (v) |
| basketball (n) | crazy (adj.) | health (n) | opera (n) | variety(ies) (n) |
| boat (n) | dancing (n) | helicopter (n) | queue (v) | |
| bowling (n) | dislike (v) | hobby(ies) (n) | relationship (n) | |
| bungee jumping (n) | easy (adj.) | housework (n) | research (n) | |

## UNIT 2

| | | | | |
|---|---|---|---|---|
| ability(ies) (n) | career (n) | guidance (n) | intelligent (adj.) | shy (adj.) |
| academic (adj.) | clever (adj.) | happy (adj.) | intention (n) | skill (n) |
| attend (v) | confidence (n) | healthy (adj.) | mind (n) | speciality(ies) (n) |
| automotive (adj.) | cookery (n) | history (n) | practical (adj.) | term (n) |
| bored (adj.) | decision (n) | improve (v) | repair (v) | vocational (adj.) |

## UNIT 3

| | | | | |
|---|---|---|---|---|
| air (n) | convenient (adj.) | loudspeaker (n) | reliable (adj.) | speed (n) |
| bike (n) | delay (n) | luggage (n) | rider (n) | stewardess(es) (n) |
| carriage (n) | distance (n) | miss (v) | safe (adj.) | stop (n) |
| coach (n) | fare (n) | passenger (n) | seat (n) | terminal (n) |
| comfortable (adj.) | fast (adj.) | platform (n) | security (n) | transport (n) |
| confirm (v) | journey (n) | punctual (adj.) | ship (n) | vehicle (n) |

## UNIT 4

| | | | | |
|---|---|---|---|---|
| baggy (adj.) | cotton (n) | glove (n) | sandal (n) | tie (n) |
| blouse (n) | dark (adj.) | length (n) | scarf(ves) (n) | tight (adj.) |
| boot (n) | dull (adj.) | loose (adj.) | size (n) | tights (n) |
| bright (adj.) | earring (n) | medium (adj.) | sleeve (n) | trendy (adj.) |
| cardigan (n) | fashion (n) | model (n) | suit (n/v) | trousers (n pl) |
| clothing (n) | fashionable (adj.) | old-fashioned (adj.) | thick (adj.) | waistcoat (n) |

## UNIT 5

| | | | | |
|---|---|---|---|---|
| announcement (n) | hole (n) | law (n) | officer (n) | tank (n) |
| busy (adj.) | hurt (adj.) | licence (n) | overtake (v) | tyre (n) |
| close (adj.) | illegal (adj.) | lorry(ies) (n) | path (n) | warden (n) |
| cycle (n) | indicator (n) | moped (n) | pedal (n) | wheel (n) |
| cyclist (n) | instructor (n) | motorbike (n) | pedestrian (n) | |
| handlebars (n pl) | junction (n) | motorcyclist (n) | safety (n) | |
| helmet (n) | lane (n) | motorway (n) | save (v) | |

## UNIT 6

| | | | | |
|---|---|---|---|---|
| alarm (n) | effective (adj.) | lever (n) | push (v) | thermostat (n) |
| attach (v) | electric (adj.) | loud (adj.) | stunt (n) | |
| button (n) | heating (n) | object (n) | stuntman(men) (n) | |
| cable (n) | instruction (n) | press (v) | successful (adj.) | |
| calculator (n) | knob (n) | pull (v) | switch(es) (n/v) | |

### UNIT 7

| | | | | |
|---|---|---|---|---|
| attraction (*n*) | director (*n*) | row (*v*) | technology (*n*) | waxwork (*n*) |
| canal (*n*) | employee (*n*) | sculptor (*n*) | teenager (*n*) | zoo (*n*) |
| celebrity(ies) (*n*) | exhibition (*n*) | sights (*n pl*) | tip (*n*) | |
| circus(es) (*n*) | gallery(ies) (*n*) | staff (*n pl*) | tunnel (*n*) | |
| cloakroom (*n*) | human (*adj.*) | statue (*n*) | wax (*n*) | |

### UNIT 8

| | | | | |
|---|---|---|---|---|
| bakery(ies) (*n*) | diet (*n*) | herb (*n*) | natural (*adj.*) | stew (*n*) |
| body(ies) (*n*) | disease (*n*) | hungry (*adj.*) | product (*n*) | supermarket (*n*) |
| burger (*n*) | disgusted (*adj.*) | ice (*n*) | protein (*n*) | vegan (*n*) |
| canned (*adj.*) | fattening (*adj.*) | jam (*n*) | raw (*adj.*) | vegetarian (*n/adj.*) |
| cereal (*n*) | fatty (*adj.*) | junk (*n*) | resist (*v*) | vitamin (*n*) |
| crisps (*n pl*) | fried (*adj.*) | keen (*adj.*) | revolting (*adj.*) | |
| crispy (*adj.*) | frozen (*adj.*) | leek (*n*) | sick (*adj.*) | |
| dairy(ies) (*n*) | goods (*n pl*) | marmalade (*n*) | simmer (*v*) | |

### UNIT 9

| | | | | |
|---|---|---|---|---|
| area (*n*) | east (*n*) | guinea pig (*n*) | pet (*n*) | suburb (*n*) |
| budgerigar (*n*) | farmer (*n*) | hamster (*n*) | protect (*v*) | surroundings (*n pl*) |
| cat (*n*) | field (*n*) | hedge (*n*) | rabbit (*n*) | village (*n*) |
| cow (*n*) | furry (*adj.*) | hen (*n*) | respect (*n*) | west (*n*) |
| crop (*n*) | goat (*n*) | litter (*n*) | season (*n*) | |
| damage (*v*) | goldfish (*n*) | north (*n*) | sheep (sheep) (*n*) | |
| duck (*n*) | goose (geese) (*n*) | pest (*n*) | south (*n*) | |

### UNIT 10

| | | | | |
|---|---|---|---|---|
| baggage (*n*) | denim (*n*) | inch(es) (*n*) | pocket (*n*) | strap (*n*) |
| belt (*n*) | diameter (*n*) | leather (*n*) | portable (*adj.*) | triangular (*adj.*) |
| cashmere (*n*) | dimension (*n*) | material (*n*) | property (*n*) | weigh (*v*) |
| centimetre (*n*) | enquiry(ies) (*n*) | metal (*n*) | purse (*n*) | wool (*n*) |
| claim (*v*) | handbag (*n*) | nylon (*n*) | rectangular (*adj.*) | woollen (*adj.*) |
| collar (*n*) | hood (*n*) | oval (*adj.*) | sale (*n*) | zip (*n*) |

### UNIT 11

| | | | | |
|---|---|---|---|---|
| ache (*n*) | elbow (*n*) | neck (*n*) | runner (*n*) | technical (*adj.*) |
| appearance (*n*) | gesture (*n*) | nose (*n*) | sensitive (*adj.*) | toe (*n*) |
| aspirin (*n*) | headache (*n*) | pale (*adj.*) | shoulder (*n*) | toothache (*n*) |
| ballet (*n*) | hip (*n*) | plaster (*n*) | skin (*n*) | touch (*v*) |
| bend (*v*) | illness(es) (*n*) | prevent (*v*) | smash (*v*) | trust (*v*) |
| bow (*v*) | injury(ies) (*n*) | professional (*adj.*) | soloist (*n*) | tuition (*n*) |
| breathe (*v*) | knee (*n*) | proficiency(ies) (*n*) | stomach (*n*) | waist (*n*) |
| communicate (*v*) | lung (*n*) | quality(ies) (*n*) | suitable (*adj.*) | wrestler (*n*) |
| cut (*v*) | mouth (*n*) | rate (*n*) | swimmer (*n*) | |
| earache (*n*) | muscle (*n*) | rest (*n/v*) | swollen (*adj.*) | |

### UNIT 12

| | | | | |
|---|---|---|---|---|
| abroad (*adv.*) | biography(ies) (*n*) | CV (curriculum vitae) (*n*) | net (*n*) | sudden (*adj.*) |
| achievement (*n*) | brave (*adj.*) | embarrassing (*adj.*) | ordinary (*adj.*) | training (*n*) |
| allow (*v*) | bump (*v*) | ever (*adv.*) | organisation (*n*) | useful (*adj.*) |
| annual (*adj.*) | cannon (*n*) | grade (*n*) | orphanage (*n*) | voluntary (*adj.*) |
| army(ies) (*n*) | cannonball (*n*) | interviewer (*n*) | political (*adj.*) | |
| bacon (*n*) | captain (*n*) | joke (*v*) | prime minister (*n*) | |
| billion (*n*) | create (*v*) | leader (*n*) | status(es) (*n*) | |

### UNIT 13

| | | | | |
|---|---|---|---|---|
| apologise (v) | financial (adj.) | impossible (adj.) | reassure (v) | wallet (n) |
| behaviour (n) | fire brigade (n) | incident (n) | report (n/v) | |
| break-in (n) | firefighter (n) | legal (adj.) | solicitor (n) | |
| counsellor (n) | flood (n) | loneliness (n) | storm (n) | |
| emotional (adj.) | homeless (adj.) | lonely (adj.) | upset (adj.) | |

### UNIT 14

| | | | | |
|---|---|---|---|---|
| achieve (v) | ceremony(ies) (n) | groom (n) | opportunity(ies) (n) | share (v) |
| anniversary(ies) (n) | civil (adj.) | happiness (n) | propose (v) | toast (v) |
| apply (v) | congratulations (n pl) | honeymoon (n) | registrar (n) | wish (v) |
| bride (n) | engagement (n) | independence (n) | registry(ies) (n) | witness(es) (n) |
| celebration (n) | glad (adj.) | marriage (n) | religious (adj.) | |

### UNIT 15

| | | | | |
|---|---|---|---|---|
| accurate (adj.) | crystal ball (n) | horoscope (n) | predict (v) | sunrise (n) |
| amateur (adj.) | data (data) (n) | meteorological (adj.) | prediction (n) | sunset (n) |
| analysis(ses) (n) | depend (v) | meteorologist (n) | satellite (n) | sunshine (n) |
| calculation (n) | fog (n) | method (n) | saying (n) | thunderstorm (n) |
| centigrade (n) | foggy (adj.) | observation (n) | scientific (adj.) | warning (n) |
| cloud (n) | forecast (n) | option (n) | shine (v) | win (v) |
| cloudy (adj.) | forecaster (n) | poll (n) | shower (n) | zero (n) |

# Wordlist

These lists include other key vocabulary from the Students' Book. They also include words from the Workbook Word Review.

## Unit 1

addict (n) /'ædɪkt/
admission (n) /əd'mɪʃən/
admit (v) /əd'mɪt/
adrenalin (n) /ə'drenəlɪn/
adventure (n) /əd'ventʃər/
advertise (v) /'ædvətaɪz/
agency(ies) (n) /'eɪdʒənsi/
ankle (n) /'æŋkəl/
attractive (adj.) /ə'træktɪv/
balloon (n) /bə'luːn/
barbecue (n) /'bɑːbɪkjuː/
barefoot (adj.) /'beəfʊt/
baseball (n) /'beɪsbɔːl/
basketball (n) /'bɑːskɪtbɔːl/
believe (v) /bə'liːv/
blank (adj.) /blæŋk/
boat (n) /bəʊt/
bowling (n) /'bəʊlɪŋ/
bring (v) /brɪŋ/
bungee jumping (n) /ˌbʌndʒi 'dʒʌmpɪŋ/
challenge (n) /'tʃælɪndʒ/
collector (n) /kə'lektər/
cost (v) /kɒst/
countryside (n) /'kʌntrisaɪd/
craft (n) /krɑːft/
crazy (adj.) /'kreɪzi/
dancing (n) /'dɑːnsɪŋ/
dentist (n) /'dentɪst/
design (n) /dɪ'zaɪn/
dislike (v) /dɪs'laɪk/
dog (n) /dɒg/
earth (n) /ɜːθ/
easy (adj.) /'iːzi/
entertainment (n) /ˌentə'teɪnmənt/
excitement (n) /ɪk'saɪtmənt/
fair (n) /feər/
frequency (n) /'friːkwənsi/
fresh (adj.) /freʃ/
gift (n) /gɪft/
great (adj.) /greɪt/
hang (v) /hæŋ/
harness(es) (n) /'hɑːnɪs/
health (n) /helθ/
helicopter (n) /'helɪkɒptər/
hobby (ies) (n) /'hɒbi/
housework (n) /'haʊswɜːk/
interest (n) /'ɪntrest/
interested (adj.) /'ɪntrəstɪd/
jump (v) /dʒʌmp/
kid (n) /kɪd/
leisure (n) /'leʒər/
light (adj.) /laɪt/
limit (n) /'lɪmɪt/
limited (adj.) /'lɪmətɪd/
lover (n) /'lʌvər/
meteorite (n) /'miːtiəraɪt/
moon (n) /muːn/
nearly (adv.) /'nɪəli/
occasionally (adv.) /ə'keɪʒənəli/
opera (n) /'ɒpərə/
produce (v) /prə'djuːs/
queue (v) /kjuː/
rarely (adv.) /'reəli/
relationship (n) /rɪ'leɪʃənʃɪp/
research (n) /rɪ'sɜːtʃ/
rope (n) /rəʊp/
scene (n) /siːn/
ski lift(n) /skiː lɪft/
skier (n) /'skiːər/
skiing (n) /'skiːɪŋ/
stall (n) /stɔːl/
surprise (n) /sə'praɪz/
sweep (v) /swiːp/
value (n) /'væljuː/
variety(ies) (n) /və'raɪəti/
whole (adj.) /həʊl/
wide (adj.) /waɪd/
wild (adj.) /waɪld/
young (adj.) /jʌŋ/

## Unit 2

ability(ies) (n) /ə'bɪləti/
academic (adj.) /ˌækə'demɪk/
accuracy (n) /'ækjʊrəsi/
actually (adv.) /'æktʃʊəli/
attend (v) /ə'tend/
automotive (adj.) /ˌɔːtə'məʊtɪv/
available (adj.) /ə'veɪləbəl/
bad (adj.) /bæd/
better (adj.) /'betər/
bored (adj.) /bɔːd/
career (n) /kə'rɪər/
childcare (n) /'tʃaɪldˌkeər/
clever (adj.) /'klevər/
confidence (n) /'kɒnfɪdəns/
cookery (n) /'kʊkəri/
decision (n) /dɪ'sɪʒən/
dream (v) /driːm/
during (prep.) /'djʊərɪŋ/
feel (v) /fiːl/
fit (adj.) /fɪt/
follow (v) /'fɒləʊ/
foreign (adj.) /'fɒrən/
frightened (adj.) /'fraɪtnd/
garage (n) /'gærɑːʒ/
guidance (n) /'gaɪdəns/
happy (adj.) /'hæpi/
healthy (adj.) /'helθi/
history (n) /'hɪstəri/
immediately (adv.) /ɪ'miːdiətli/
improve (v) /ɪm'pruːv/
insect (n) /'ɪnsekt/
intelligent (adj.) /ɪn'telɪdʒənt/
intention (n) /ɪn'tenʃən/
lend (v) /lend/
lose (v) /luːz/
mind (n) /maɪnd/
normal (adj.) /'nɔːməl/
particular (adj.) /pə'tɪkjʊlər/
percentage (n) /pə'sentɪdʒ/
politics (n) /'pɒlətɪks/
practical (adj.) /'præktɪkəl/
quick (adj.) /kwɪk/
real (adj.) /rɪəl/
repair (v) /rɪ'peər/
salesperson(people) (n) /'seɪlzpɜːsən/
shape (n) /ʃeɪp/
shy (adj.) /ʃaɪ/
skill (n) /skɪl/
speciality(ies) (n) /ˌspeʃu'læti/
strange (adj.) /streɪndʒ/
suitcase (n) /'suːtkeɪs/
taste (v) /teɪst/
term (n) /tɜːm/
tongue (n) /tʌŋ/
toy (n) /tɔɪ/
vocational (adj.) /vəʊ'keɪʃənəl/
water (n) /'wɔːtər/
well (adv.) /wel/

## Unit 3

against (prep.) /ə'genst/
air (n) /eər/
alive (adj.) /ə'laɪv/
announce (v) /ə'naʊns/
arrangement (n) /ə'reɪndʒmənt/
bike (n) /baɪk/
carriage (n) /'kærɪdʒ/
central (adj.) /'sentrəl/
client (n) /'klaɪənt/
coach (n) /kəʊtʃ/
comfortable (adj.) /'kʌmftəbəl/
confirm (v) /kən'fɜːm/
control (v) /kən'trəʊl/
convenient (adj.) /kən'viːniənt/
corner (n) /'kɔːnər/
delay (n) /dɪ'leɪ/
distance (n) /'dɪstəns/
fare (n) /feər/
fast (adj.) /fɑːst/
fear (n) /fɪər/
full (adj.) /fʊl/
hurry (v) /'hʌri/
invitation (n) /ˌɪnvə'teɪʃən/
journey (n) /'dʒɜːni/
loudspeaker (n) /ˌlaʊd'spiːkər/
luggage (n) /'lʌgɪdʒ/
miss (v) /mɪs/
monument (n) /'mɒnjumənt/
passenger (n) /'pæsɪndʒər/
platform (n) /'plætfɔːm/
prefer (v) /prɪ'fɜːr/
promise (n) /'prɒmɪs/
punctual (adj.) /'pʌŋktʃuəl/
race (n) /reɪs/
reach (v) /riːtʃ/
reliable (adj.) /rɪ'laɪəbəl/
rider (n.) /'raɪdər/
safe (adj.) /seɪf/
search (v) /sɜːtʃ/
seat (n) /siːt/
security (n) /sɪ'kjʊərəti/
serve (v) /sɜːv/
ship (n) /ʃɪp/
sightseeing (n) /'saɪtˌsiːɪŋ/
speed (n) /spiːd/
standard (adj.) /'stændəd/
stewardess(es) (n) /'stjuːədes/
stop (n) /stɒp/
suggestion (n) /sə'dʒestʃən/
terminal (n) /'tɜːmɪnəl/
transport (n) /'trænspɔːt/
vehicle (n) /'viːɪkəl/
versus (prep.) /'vɜːsəs/
worse (adj.) /wɜːs/

# WORDLIST

## Unit 4

agreement (n) /əˈgriːmənt/
average (adj.) /ˈævərɪdʒ/
baggy (adj.) /ˈbægi/
blouse (n) /blaʊz/
boot (n) /buːt/
bright (adj.) /braɪt/
cardigan (n) /ˈkɑːdɪgən/
certain (adj.) /ˈsɜːtn/
clothing (n) /ˈkləʊðɪŋ/
continue (v) /kənˈtɪnjuː/
contract (n) /ˈkɒntrækt/
cosmetics (n) /kɒzˈmetɪks/
cotton (n) /ˈkɒtn/
cover (n) /ˈkʌvər/
dark (adj.) /dɑːk/
dull (adj.) /dʌl/
earring (n) /ˈɪəˌrɪŋ/
fashion (n) /ˈfæʃən/
fashionable (adj.) /ˈfæʃənəbəl/
gardener (n) /ˈgɑːdnər/
glove (n) /glʌv/
lead (v) /liːd/
length (n) /leŋθ/
loose (adj.) /luːs/
manage (v) /ˈmænɪdʒ/
medium (adj.) /ˈmiːdiəm/
millionaire (n) /ˌmɪljəˈneər/
model (n) /ˈmɒdl/
old-fashioned (adj.) /əʊld ˈæʃənd/
sandal (n) /ˈsændl/
scarf(ves) (n) /skɑːf/
size (n) /saɪz/
sleeve (n) /sliːv/
success(es) (n) /səkˈses/
suit (n/v) /suːt/
thick (adj.) /θɪk/
tie (n) /taɪ/
tight (adj.) /taɪt/
tights (n pl) /taɪts/
tour (n) /tʊər/
trendy (adj.) /ˈtrendi/
trousers (n.pl.) /ˈtraʊzəz/
uniform (n) /ˈjuːnɪfɔːm/
waistcoat (n) /ˈweɪskəʊt/
worst (adj.) /wɜːst/

## Unit 5

agricultural (adj.) /ˌægrɪˈkʌltʃərəl/
amaze (v) /əˈmeɪz/
announcement (n) /əˈnaʊnsmənt/
announcer (n) /əˈnaʊnsər/
attack (n) /əˈtæk/
busy (adj.) /ˈbɪzi/
calm (adj.) /kɑːm/
carrycot (n) /ˈkærikɒt/
case (n) /keɪs/
clear (adj.) /klɪər/
close (adj.) /kləʊs/
contact (v) /ˈkɒntækt/
cycle (n) /ˈsaɪkəl/
cyclist (n) /ˈsaɪklɪst/
duty(ies) (n) /ˈdjuːti/
handlebars (n) /ˈhændlbɑːz/
headline (n) /ˈhedlaɪn/
heart (n) /hɑːt/
helmet (n) /ˈhelmɪt/
hole (n) /həʊl/
hurt (adj.) /hɜːt/
illegal (adj.) /ɪˈliːgəl/
indicator (n) /ˈɪndɪkeɪtər/
instructor (n) /ɪnˈstrʌktər/
junction (n) /ˈdʒʌŋkʃən/
lane (n) /leɪn/
law (n) /lɔː/
licence (n) /ˈlaɪsəns/
lorry(ies) (n) /ˈlɒri/
moped (n) /ˈməʊped/
motorbike (n) /ˈməʊtəbaɪk/
motorcyclist (n) /ˈməʊtəˌsaɪklɪst/
motorway (n) /ˈməʊtəweɪ/
neighbour (n) /ˈneɪbər/
obligation (n) /ˌɒblɪˈgeɪʃən/
occur (v) /əˈkɜːr/
officer (n) /ˈɒfɪsər/
overtake (v) /ˌəʊvəˈteɪk/
path (n) /pɑːθ/
pedal (n) /ˈpedl/
pedestrian (n) /pəˈdestriən/
pensioner (n) /ˈpenʃənər/
possibility(ies) (n) /ˌpɒsəˈbɪlɪti/
pupil (n) /ˈpjuːpəl/
round (adj.) /raʊnd/
safety (n) /ˈseɪfti/
save (v) /seɪv/
scream (v) /skriːm/
shift (n) /ʃɪft/
suggest (v) /səˈdʒest/
tank (n) /tæŋk/
tyre (n) /taɪər/
varied (adj.) /ˈveərɪd/
warden (n) /ˈwɔːdn/
wheel (n) /wiːl/

## Unit 6

alarm (n) /əˈlɑːm/
arrow (n) /ˈærəʊ/
attach (v) /əˈtætʃ/
button (n) /ˈbʌtn/
cable (n) /ˈkeɪbəl/
calculator (n) /ˈkælkjʊleɪtər/
cattle (n pl) /ˈkætl/
chance (n) /tʃɑːns/
chest (n) /tʃest/
competition (n) /ˌkɒmpəˈtɪʃən/
cowboy (n) /ˈkaʊbɔɪ/
dry (adj.) /draɪ/
effective (adj.) /ɪˈfektɪv/
electric (adj.) /ɪˈlektrɪk/
enemy(ies) (n) /ˈenəmi/
gallop (v) /ˈgæləp/
hard (adv.) /hɑːd/
hat (n) /hæt/
head (n) /hed/
heating (n) /ˈhiːtɪŋ/
horse (n) /hɔːs/
horseman(men) (n) /ˈhɔːsmən/
instruction (n) /ɪnˈstrʌkʃən/
knob (n) /nɒb/
lever (n) /ˈliːvər/
loud (adj.) /laʊd/
mention (v) /ˈmenʃən/
object (n) /ˈɒbdʒekt/
porter (n) /ˈpɔːtər/
press (v) /pres/
pull (v) /pʊl/
push (v) /pʊʃ/
rail (n) /reɪl/
ranch(es) (n) /rɑːntʃ/
specialise (v) /ˈspeʃəlaɪz/
stand (v) /stænd/
star (n) /stɑːr/
stunt (n) /stʌnt/
stuntman(men) (n) /ˈstʌnˌmæn/
successful (adj.) /səkˈsesfəl/
switch (v) /swɪtʃ/
thermostat (n) /ˈθɜːməstæt/
thief(ves) (n) /θiːf/
tricycle (n) /ˈtraɪsɪkəl/
wedding (n) /ˈwedɪŋ/

## Unit 7

antelope (n) /ˈæntələʊp/
attraction (n) /əˈtrækʃən/
bear (n) /beər/
canal (n) /kəˈnæl/
celebrity(ies) (n) /səˈlebrəti/
circus(es) (n) /ˈsɜːkəs/
cloakroom (n) /ˈkləʊkrʊm/
dead (adj.) /ded/
director (n) /dəˈrektər/
elephant (n) /ˈeləfənt/
employee (n) /ɪmˈplɔɪ-iː/
exam (n) /ɪgˈzæm/
exhibition (n) /ˌeksəˈbɪʃən/
gallery(ies) (n) /ˈgæləri/
heavy (adj.) /ˈhevi/
human (adj.) /ˈhjuːmən/
lifelike (adj.) /ˈlaɪflaɪk/
lion (n) /ˈlaɪən/
lock (n) /lɒk/
measurement (n) /ˈmeʒəmənt/
murderer (n) /ˈmɜːdərər/
original (adj.) /əˈrɪdʒɪnəl/
postman (n) /ˈpəʊstmən/
prison (n) /ˈprɪzən/
raise (v) /reɪz/
row (v) /rəʊ/
sculptor (n) /ˈskʌlptər/
sights (n pl) /saɪts/
spokesperson (n) /ˈspəʊksˌpɜːsən/
staff (n pl) /stɑːf/
statue (n) /ˈstætʃuː/
sure (adj.) /ʃʊər/
team (n) /tiːm/
technology (n) /tekˈnɒlədʒi/
teenager (n) /ˈtiːneɪdʒər/
thousand (n) /ˈθaʊzənd/
tiger (n) /ˈtaɪgər/
tip (n) /tɪp/
tower (n) /ˈtaʊər/
tunnel (n) /ˈtʌnl/
wax (n) /wæks/
waxwork (n) /ˈwækswɜːk/
zoo (n) /zuː/

# WORDLIST

## Unit 8

argument (n) /ˈɑːgjʊmənt/
bakery(ies) (n) /ˈbeɪkəri/
body(ies) (n) /ˈbɒdi/
burger (n) /ˈbɜːgəʳ/
canned (adj.) /kænd/
care (v) /keəʳ/
cereal (n) /ˈsɪəriəl/
crisps (n pl) /krɪsps/
crispy (adj.) /krɪspi/
dairy(ies) (n) /ˈdeəri/
diet (n) /ˈdaɪət/
disease (n) /dɪˈziːz/
disgusted (adj.) /dɪsˈgʌstɪd/
fattening (adj.) /ˈfætnɪŋ/
fatty (adj.) /ˈfæti/
fried (adj.) /fraɪd/
frozen (adj.) /ˈfrəʊzən/
goods (n pl) /gʊdz/
habit (n) /ˈhæbɪt/
herb (n) /hɜːb/
household (adj.) /ˈhaʊshəʊld/
hungry (adj.) /ˈhʌŋgri/
ice (n) /aɪs/
jam (n) /dʒæm/
junk (n) /dʒʌŋk/
keen (adj.) /kiːn/
kill (v) /kɪl/
leek (n) /liːk/
marmalade (n) /ˈmɑːməleɪd/
natural (adj.) /ˈnætʃərəl/
owner (n) /ˈəʊnəʳ/
polite (adj.) /pəˈlaɪt/
product (n) /ˈprɒdʌkt/
protein (n) /ˈprəʊtiːn/
raw (adj.) /rɔː/
reservation (n) /ˌrezəˈveɪʃən/
resist (v) /rɪˈzɪst/
revolting (adj.) /rɪˈvəʊltɪŋ/
section (n) /ˈsekʃən/
sick (adj.) /sɪk/
simmer (v) /ˈsɪməʳ/
stew (n) /stjuː/
suffer (v) /ˈsʌfəʳ/
supermarket (n) /ˈsuːpəˌmɑːkɪt/
suppose (v) /səˈpəʊz/
traditional (adj.) /trəˈdɪʃənəl/
trolley (n) /ˈtrɒli/
vegan (n) /ˈviːgən/
vegetarian (n/adj.) /ˌvedʒəˈteəriən/
vitamin (n) /ˈvɪtəmɪn/
voice (n) /vɔɪs/

## Unit 9

advantage (n) /ədˈvɑːntɪdʒ/
amount (n) /əˈmaʊnt/
area (n) /ˈeəriə/
awake (adj.) /əˈweɪk/
behind (prep.) /bɪˈhaɪnd/
blood (n) /blʌd/
box(es) (n) /bɒks/
budgerigar (n) /ˈbʌdʒərɪgɑːʳ/
cat (n) /kæt/
charity(ies) (n) /ˈtʃærəti/
cholesterol (n) /kəˈlestərɒl/
cough (v) /kɒf/
cow (n) /kaʊ/
crop (n) /krɒp/
damage (v) /ˈdæmɪdʒ/
definitely (adv.) /ˈdefɪnətli/
disadvantage (n) /ˌdɪsədˈvɑːntɪdʒ/
drop (v) /drɒp/
duck (n) /dʌk/
east (n) /iːst/
farmer (n) /ˈfɑːməʳ/
field (n) /fiːld/
fire (n) /faɪəʳ/
forever (adv.) /fəˈrevəʳ/
furry (adj.) /ˈfɜːri/
goat (n) /gəʊt/
goldfish (n) /ˈgəʊldˌfɪʃ/
goose (geese) (n) /guːs, giːs/
guinea pig (n) /ˈgɪni ˌpɪg/
hamster (n) /ˈhæmstəʳ/
hedge (n) /hedʒ/
hen (n) /hen/
judge (n) /dʒʌdʒ/
let (v) /let/
level (n) /ˈlevəl/
litter (n) /ˈlɪtəʳ/
low (adj.) /ləʊ/
mad (adj.) /mæd/
north (n) /nɔːθ/
pest (n) /pest/
pet (n) /pet/
physical (adj.) /ˈfɪzɪkəl/
poor (adj.) /pɔːʳ/
pressure (n) /ˈpreʃəʳ/
primary (adj.) /ˈpraɪməri/
protect (v) /prəˈtekt/
rabbit (n) /ˈræbɪt/
recent (adj.) /ˈriːsənt/
respect (n) /rɪˈspekt/
season (n) /ˈsiːzən/
sheep (sheep) (n) /ʃiːp/
should (modal v) /ʃəd, ʃʊd/
south (n) /saʊθ/
stroke (v) /strəʊk/
suburb (n) /ˈsʌbɜːb/
surroundings (n pl) /səˈraʊndɪŋz/
survive (v) /səˈvaɪv/
traveller (n) /ˈtrævləʳ/
unfortunately (adv.) /ʌnˈfɔːtʃənətli/
van (n) /væn/
village (n) /ˈvɪlɪdʒ/
visitor (n) /ˈvɪzɪtəʳ/
west (n) /west/

## Unit 10

anatomy (n) /əˈnætəmi/
baggage (n) /ˈbægɪdʒ/
belt (n) /belt/
cashmere (n) /ˈkæʃmɪəʳ/
centimetre (n) /ˈsentɪˌmiːtəʳ/
charge (n) /tʃɑːdʒ/
claim (v) /kleɪm/
collar (n) /ˈkɒləʳ/
denim (n) /ˈdenəm/
deposit (v) /dɪˈpɒzɪt/
diameter (n) /daɪˈæmɪtəʳ/
dimension (n) /daɪˈmenʃən/
eagle (n) /ˈiːgəl/
employ (v) /ɪmˈplɔɪ/
enquiry(ies) (n) /ɪnˈkwaɪəri/
forgive (v) /fəˈgɪv/
fortunately (adv.) /ˈfɔːtʃənətli/
handbag (n) /ˈhændbæg/
hood (n) /hʊd/
importance (n) /ɪmˈpɔːtəns/
inch(es) (n) /ɪntʃ/
intend (v) /ɪnˈtend/
investigation (n) /ɪnˌvestɪˈgeɪʃən/
leather (n) /ˈleðəʳ/
less (adj.) /les/
male (adj.) /meɪl/
manuscript (n) /ˈmænjʊskrɪpt/
material (n) /məˈtɪəriəl/
medical (adj.) /ˈmedɪkəl/
memory(ies) (n) /ˈmeməri/
mental (adj.) /ˈmentəl/
metal (n) /ˈmetl/
metropolitan (adj.) /ˌmetrəˈpɒlɪtən/
novel (n) /ˈnɒvəl/
nylon (n) /ˈnaɪlɒn/
oval (adj.) /ˈəʊvəl/
pocket (n) /ˈpɒkɪt/
portable (adj.) /ˈpɔːtəbəl/
pram (n) /præm/
property(ies) (n) /ˈprɒpəti/
purse (n) /pɜːs/
railway (n) /ˈreɪlweɪ/
rainy (adj.) /ˈreɪni/
rectangular (adj.) /rekˈtæŋgjʊləʳ/
registration (n) /ˌredʒɪˈstreɪʃən/
remote (adj.) /rɪˈməʊt/
sale (n) /seɪl/
sentimentality(ies) (n) /ˌsentɪmenˈtælɪti/
shame (n) /ʃeɪm/
skeleton (n) /ˈskelətən/
strap (n) /stræp/
sword (n) /sɔːd/
tooth, teeth (n) /tuːθ, tiːθ/
triangular (adj.) /traɪˈæŋgjʊləʳ/
volume (n) /ˈvɒljuːm/
weigh (v) /weɪ/
wool (n) /wʊl/
woollen (adj.) /ˈwʊlən/
zip (n) /zɪp/

# Unit 11

ache (n) /eɪk/
appearance (n) /əˈpɪərəns/
aspirin (n) /ˈæsprɪn/
ballet (n) /ˈbæleɪ/
basic (adj.) /ˈbeɪsɪk/
bend (v) /bend/
bow (v) /baʊ/
boxer (n) /ˈbɒksər/
breathe (v) /briːð/
classical (adj.) /ˈklæsɪkəl/
communicate (v) /kəˈmjuːnɪkeɪt/
contemporary (adj.) /kənˈtempərəri/
cut (v) /kʌt/
dial (v) /daɪəl/
directory(ies) (n) /dəˈektəri/
earache (n) /ˈɪəreɪk/
elbow (n) /ˈelbəʊ/
foreigner (n) /ˈfɒrɪnər/
freezing (adj.) /ˈfriːzɪŋ/
frequently (adv.) /ˈfriːkwəntli/
gesture (n) /ˈdʒestʃər/
headache (n) /ˈhedeɪk/
hip (n) /hɪp/
illness(es) (n) /ˈɪlnəs/
injury(ies) (n) /ˈɪndʒəri/
innocent (adj.) /ˈɪnəsənt/
knee (n) /niː/
knowledge (n) /ˈnɒlɪdʒ/
lung (n) /lʌŋ/
minimum (n) /ˈmɪnɪməm/
monster (n) /ˈmɒnstər/
mouth (n) /maʊð/
muscle (n) /ˈmʌsəl/
neck (n) /nek/
nose (n) /nəʊz/
offensive (adj.) /əˈfensɪv/
operator (n) /ˈɒpəreɪtər/
pale (adj.) /peɪl/
perfect (adj.) /ˈpɜːfɪkt/
pianist (n) /ˈpiːənɪst/
plaster (n) /ˈplɑːstər/
prevent (v) /prɪˈvent/
principal (adj.) /ˈprɪnsɪpəl/
probably (adv.) /ˈprɒbəbli/
professional (adj.) /prəˈfeʃənəl/
proficiency(ies) (n) /prəˈfɪʃənsi/
quality(ies) (n) /ˈkwɒləti/
rate (n) /reɪt/
rest (n/v) /rest/
runner (n) /ˈrʌnər/
sensitive (adj.) /ˈsensətɪv/
shoulder (n) /ˈʃəʊldər/
skin (n) /skɪn/
smash (v) /smæʃ/
soloist (n) /ˈsəʊləʊɪst/
stomach (n) /ˈstʌmək/
suitable (adj.) /ˈsuːtəbəl/
swimmer (n) /ˈswɪmər/
swollen (adj.) /ˈswəʊlən/
technical (adj.) /ˈteknɪkəl/
toe (n) /təʊ/
toothache (n) /ˈtuːθeɪk/
touch (v) /tʌtʃ/
trust (v) /trʌst/
tuition (n) /tjuːˈɪʃən/
waist (n) /weɪst/
wrestler (n) /ˈreslər/

# Unit 12

abroad (adv.) /əˈbrɔːd/
achievement (n) /əˈtʃiːvmənt/
allow (v) /əˈlaʊ/
annual (adj.) /ˈænjuəl/
army(ies) (n) /ˈɑːmi/
bacon (n) /ˈbeɪkən/
billion (n) /ˈbɪljən/
biography(ies) (n) /baɪˈɒgrəfi/
brave (adj.) /breɪv/
bump (v) /bʌmp/
cannon (n) /ˈkænən/
cannonball (n) /ˈkænənbɔːl/
captain (n) /ˈkæptɪn/
create (v) /kriˈeɪt/
CV (curriculum vitae) (n) /ˌsiːˈviː/ /kəˌrɪkjʊləm ˈviːtaɪ/
embarrassing (adj.) /ɪmˈbærəsɪŋ/
ever (adv.) /ˈevər/
grade (n) /greɪd/
interviewer (n) /ˈɪntəvjuːər/
joke (v) /dʒəʊk/
leader (n) /ˈliːdər/
net (n) /net/
ordinary (adj.) /ˈɔːdənri/
organisation (n) /ˌɔːgənaɪˈzeɪʃən/
orphanage (n) /ˈɔːfənɪdʒ/
political (adj.) /pəˈlɪtɪkəl/
prime minister (n) /ˌpraɪ ˈmɪnɪstər/
pyramid (n) /ˈpɪrəmɪd/
reaction (n) /riˈækʃən/
since (prep.) /sɪns/
status(es) (n) /ˈsteɪtəs/
sudden (adj.) /ˈsʌdn/
super (adj.) /ˈsuːpər/
telegram (n) /ˈtelɪgræm/
terribly (adv.) /ˈterəbli/
test-tube (n) /ˈtestuːb/
training (n) /ˈtreɪnɪŋ/
useful (adj.) /ˈjuːsfəl/
voluntary (adj.) /ˈvɒləntri/

# Unit 13

ago (adv.) /əˈgəʊ/
apologise (v) /əˈpɒlədʒaɪz/
behaviour (n) /bɪˈheɪvjər/
break-in (n) /ˈbreɪkɪn/
briefcase (n) /ˈbriːfkeɪs/
connect (v) /kəˈnekt/
counsellor (n) /ˈkaʊnsələr/
direct (adj.) /dəˈrekt/
emotional (adj.) /ɪˈməʊʃənəl/
environment (n) /ɪnˈvaɪrənmənt/
expect (v) /ɪkˈspekt/
financial (adj.) /faɪˈnænʃəl/
fire brigade (n) /ˈfaɪə brɪˌgeɪd/
firefighter (n) /ˈfaɪəˌfaɪtər/
flood (n) /flʌd/
highway (n) /ˈhaɪweɪ/
homeless (adj.) /ˈhəʊmləs/
hydrant (n) /ˈhaɪdrənt/
identification (n) /aɪˌdentɪfɪˈkeɪʃən/
impossible (adj.) /ɪmˈpɒsɪbəl/
incident (n) /ˈɪnsɪdənt/
key (n) /kiː/
ladder (n) /ˈlædər/
legal (adj.) /ˈliːgəl/
loneliness (n) /ˈləʊnlinəs/
lonely (adj.) /ˈləʊnli/
narrow (adj.) /ˈnærəʊ/
reassure (v) /ˌriːəˈʃʊər/
report (n) /rɪˈpɔːt/
solicitor (n) /səˈlɪsɪtər/
staircase (n) /ˈsteəkeɪs/
storm (n) /stɔːm/
upset (adj.) /ʌpˈset/
wallet (n) /ˈwɒlɪt/

# Unit 14

achieve (v) /əˈtʃiːv/
afterwards (adv.) /ˈɑːftəwədz/
anniversary(ies) (n) /ˌænɪˈvɜːsəri/
apply (v) /əˈplaɪ/
bride (n) /braɪd/
celebration (n) /ˌseləˈbreɪʃən/
ceremony(ies) (n) /ˈserəməni/
civil (adj.) /ˈsɪvəl/
congratulations (n pl) /kənˌgrætʃʊˈleɪʃənz/
engagement (n) /ɪnˈgeɪdʒmənt/
glad (adj.) /glæd/
groom (n) /gruːm/
happiness (n) /ˈhæpɪnəs/
honeymoon (n) /ˈhʌnɪmuːn/
horseshoe (n) /ˈhɔːʃuː/
independence (n) /ˌɪndɪˈpendəns/
journalist (n) /ˈdʒɜːnəlɪst/
marriage (n) /ˈmærɪdʒ/
opportunity(ies) (n) /ˌɒpəˈtjuːnəti/
pick (v) /pɪk/
poetry (n) /ˈpəʊətri/
propose (v) /prəˈpəʊz/
recently (adv.) /ˈriːsəntli/
registrar (n) /ˌredʒɪˈstrɑːr/
registry(ies) (n) /ˈredʒɪstri/
religious (adj.) /rɪˈlɪdʒəs/
ring (n) /rɪŋ/
share (v) /ʃeər/
stork (n) /stɔːk/
symbol (n) /ˈsɪmbəl/
toast (v) /təʊst/
wish (v) /wɪʃ/
witness(es) (n) /ˈwɪtnəs/
yet (adv.) /jet/

## Unit 15

accurate (adj.) /ˈækjʊrət/
amateur (adj.) /ˈæmətə(r)/
analysis(ses) (n) /əˈnæləsɪs/
audience (n) /ˈɔːdiəns/
be able to (v) /biːˈeɪbəltə/
calculation (n) /ˌkælkjʊˈleɪʃən/
centigrade (n) /ˈsentɪɡreɪd/
certainty (n) /ˈsɜːtənti/
cloud (n) /klaʊd/
cloudy (adj.) /ˈklaʊdi/
coast (n) /kəʊst/
crystal ball (n) /ˌkrɪstəlˈbɔːl/
data (data) (n) /ˈdeɪtə/
depend (v) /dɪˈpend/
ditch(es) (n) /dɪtʃ/
fog (n) /fɒɡ/
foggy (adj.) /ˈfɒɡi/
forecast (n) /ˈfɔːkɑːst/
forecaster (n) /ˈfɔːkɑːstə(r)/
horoscope (n) /ˈhɒrəskəʊp/
inland (adj.) /ˈɪnlənd/
interval (n) /ˈɪntəvəl/
lazy (adj.) /ˈleɪzi/
meteorological (adj.) /ˌmiːtiərəˈlɒdʒɪkəl/
meteorologist (n) /ˌmiːtiəˈrɒlədʒɪst/
method (n) /ˈmeθəd/
mouse (n) /maʊs/
mystery(ies) (n) /ˈmɪstəri/
northern (adj.) /ˈnɔːðən/
observation (n) /ˌɒbzəˈveɪʃən/
option (n) /ˈɒpʃən/
pile (n) /paɪl/
poll (n) /pəʊl/
predict (v) /prəˈdɪkt/
prediction (n) /prəˈdɪkʃən/
presenter (n) /prɪˈzentə(r)/
profit (n) /ˈprɒfɪt/
radar (n) /ˈreɪdɑː(r)/
rude (adj.) /ruːd/
satellite (n) /ˈsætəlaɪt/
saying (n) /ˈseɪ-ɪŋ/
scientific (adj.) /ˌsaɪənˈtɪfɪk/
script (n) /skrɪpt/
shine (v) /ʃaɪn/
shower (n) /ˈʃaʊə(r)/
spider (n) /ˈspaɪdə(r)/
spin (v) /spɪn/
store (v) /stɔː(r)/
sunrise (n) /ˈsʌnraɪz/
sunset (n) /ˈsʌnset/
sunshine (n) /ˈsʌnʃaɪn/
thunderstorm (n) /ˈθʌndəstɔːm/
viewer (n) /ˈvjuːə(r)/
vote (n) /vəʊt/
warning (n) /ˈwɔːnɪŋ/
web (n) /web/
win (v) /wɪn/
wonder (v) /ˈwʌndə(r)/
zero (n) /ˈzɪərəʊ/